Communication and the Teacher

General Editor

Bob Hodge

Editorial Team

Ian Malcolm

D.C. Courts

Contributing Authors

D.C. Courts

Wilf D'Souza

Bob Hodge

Ian Malcolm

Geoff Peel

Terry Williams

Book I in the Series *Language and Communication for Teachers*

Longman Cheshire

Longman Cheshire Pty Limited
346 St Kilda Road,
Melbourne 3004 Australia

Offices in Sydney, Brisbane, Adelaide and
Perth. Associated companies, branches,
and representatives throughout the world

Printed in Singapore by
Kyodo Shing Loong Printing Industries Pte Ltd.

National Library of Australia
Cataloguing-in-Publication data

Language and communication for teachers.
Book 1.

  Bibliography.
  ISBN 0 582 71465 6.

  1. Communication in education.
  2. Teaching.
  I. Courts, Douglas C.   II. Hodge, Bob.

371.1′022

Contents

General preface

Virtually the entire educational process is mediated through language and yet for years teachers have begun their careers with no understanding of the nature of language structure, its psychological and social functions or the ways in which their own specialization depends on language. Language is at the core of human experience and it is arguable that all teachers in training, whatever their own subject, should be made aware of its nature and its role.

Education 20 July, 1973.

It ought to be obvious that someone who cannot communicate cannot teach. A teacher who cannot understand what students are trying to communicate will not know whether the teaching has been effective or not. If students finish formal education with basic problems in any aspect of communication — literacy is the most prominent area of concern, but there are others — this failure reflects on the education system as a whole. The Bullock Report (1975) focused on this general problem area for Britain. It argued that reading and literacy generally are to be understood in a wider context, and that the child's overall language abilities affected progress in all other aspects of the curriculum. So teachers of all subjects need to understand principles of language and communication as part of their basic pre-service training.

What Bullock says is clearly applicable everywhere, not just in Britain. The basic premise seems unarguable. But what should be done about it? As a group of people concerned with language and communication in institutions that prepare people to be teachers, we asked ourselves what this basic course ought to contain, and what textbooks were available to teach it from. What was needed, we thought, was something which had a solid basis in current theories about language and communication, but which could present this material in a lively and accessible way for students who probably have limited background in this area and no great interest in it to begin with. The theoretical basis ought to be wide-ranging, aware of major issues, impartial, and not entangled in controversy. Above all, it ought to engage directly and visibly with the interests and experience of students in the process of training to be teachers. The best strategy seemed to us to be to confront them with language and situations they were already familiar with but had not fully understood, or with situations they might have to deal with as practising teachers. By moving from practice to theories which illuminate that practice, we hoped that students would see the relevance of the theory and want to explore it further.

We devised the three books in this series on language and communication for teachers with such a course in mind. The first book seeks to bring together theory and practice, starting from concrete examples and working through to a deeper understanding of what is going on in the examples. The aim is a kind of awareness, not particular knowledge. The theory remains implicit or informal: only as much as is needed for the better understanding of particular examples or issues. The second book contains relevant articles representing significant contributions to the understanding of language and communication. The third book offers a range of resources to work on, and materials to enhance students' awareness of how language and communication work as they apply various concepts and methods of analysis to them.

The three books together are meant to form an open-ended introduction to the whole area of language and communication for prospective teachers. The movement between theory and practice, between an interest in communication itself and a concern for the needs of the educational situation, can go on for a long time as individuals improve their grasp of theoretical approaches and the relevance of theory to practice. The package is designed to be flexible and workable at a number of levels, with something of importance for people with rather different backgrounds and degrees of commitment to the study of language. We believe that all institutions concerned with teacher education should have a course of this kind as a core component for all students; but where it fits in will vary from institution to institution. A core course in language and communication will make more sense if connections are made with what students are doing in other core subjects (psychology, sociology and education theory are the most obviously relevant), but these connections are best made by individual lecturers as they arise.

When should students study such a course? When they have just entered training? If so, it needs to draw directly on their experience of just having passed through secondary school, and probably of nearly having forgotten what it was like in the primary classroom. The course should help them to look at their own experience, arbitrary and partial though it may be, with a new perspective, giving them greater self-knowledge as well as preparing them to be better teachers. If the course comes near the end of training, when students have a wider background and are closer to the scent of chalk in their first classroom, it should still function to bring together existing knowledge which they can build on, preparing them in some quite practical ways to be more adequate to the demands of their new profession. For any reader, the test to apply to any part of each of these books is simple and clear: *will a person be a better teacher for having grasped thoroughly what it is saying?*

Introduction

Man has been called the language animal. We have all been communicating fairly effectively for most of our lives. So what can a course on language and communication for teachers hope to offer, especially to a teacher in a particular subject area?

The first step towards an answer is something of a paradox. We need to study communication because our own communication is too familiar to us! We learnt to communicate too early to be able to understand the complex processes involved. This unconscious facility is satisfactory enough if things are proceeding smoothly. However, if there are communication blindspots we were unaware of, we shall never recognise their existence. And we might come into a new situation where our previously satisfactory modes of communication do not work. For most people, teaching provides a formidable variety of such situations. While communication was unproblematic there was no great harm, and there were many advantages, in its being relatively automatic and unconscious. But when it becomes necessary to adapt to a different situation, we shall find it useful to have some consciousness of what we are doing that might have to be changed, together with some general framework which will help us to understand the demands of the new situation and how to meet them.

In any case, we cannot understand communication if we understand only our own communication. Wittgenstein said: 'The limits of my language are the limits of my world'. Even if we communicate perfectly within our own language community we remain bound by it; and since the language provides the language to think about itself, it becomes difficult to conceive of any possible alternative. But there are ways of pushing to the limits of our own language and the assumptions built into it. This is important for everyone's self-development, since knowledge of one's limits is an important component of self-knowledge. It gives a valuable perspective on your own language if you know what it cannot do as well as what it can. And the process of exploring these limits of language is at the same time an exploration of widespread assumptions of one's own culture, and a perspective on them.

Even if students are not particularly interested in this kind of self-knowledge, it has its practical value. Teachers may have to communicate with other people: children and parents from different backgrounds, of different ages, and perhaps from a different nation or race. What happens inside the classroom is affected by what people say and think outside it. Communication across barriers of age or class or race is a primary site of the prejudices that divide a nation. People are apt to see forms of language or communication which are merely different as proofs of stupidity, or worse. Our education system is a concern of the whole community, and teachers have a wider responsibility to the community. Part of that responsibility includes a duty not to perpetuate and reinforce divisive prejudices.

The scope of the field the student needs to become acquainted with is at first sight formidably broad. At the centre is linguistics, the study of language, since language has a privileged place among the forms of communication available to human beings. However, in spite of the importance of language it needs to be seen as part of a larger system. The great Swiss linguist Saussure coined the name **Semiology** for the over-arching discipline concerned with what he called 'the life of signs in society' (1918). The need for such an over-arching discipline is clear. Just as the general principles for understanding how one particular language works come from the discipline concerned with language as a whole, so the general principles for understanding language as one of the natural systems of signification will come from semiology. We can see the need for an integrated approach even in very ordinary and commonplace instances if we consider the words 'What are you doing here?'. Exploded by a purple-faced man waving a gun, the words have a meaning different from when they are said invitingly by a sexy woman at a party to someone she likes.

Over sixty years after Saussure, semiology has still not emerged as a subsuming discipline. The study of human languages has dominated the study of all other modes of communication. Recently the imbalance has begun to be rectified. The systematic study of other sign-systems is now under way and, more important, there is now a recognition that these have to be taken into account in a holistic study of human communication. In this book we have taken this broader approach to the field of study, on the grounds that it is no longer legitimate to study communication through language in isolation from the full set of communication resources available to man.

The formal study of language itself presents many difficulties for a newcomer to the field. Theoretical linguistics as it has evolved has acquired a considerable quantity of technical jargon and specialized methods of enquiry. The insights it has achieved are often locked away from people outside the discipline by impenetrable or off-putting language. The language of linguists is not noticeably a form of mass communication. Some of the specialist terms are nearly indispensable to convey abstruse but important concepts. The importance of the concepts justifies the time spent in grasping the terminology, for people with the time and commitment to persevere with articles and books in the original. Another strength of theoretical linguistics is that its explanations aim to be systematic. They are not just a collection of interesting facts about language; they are an attempt to order those facts logically and to see larger patterns.

There is a second major difficulty with theoretical linguistics, which is liable to be dispiriting to someone beginning to look into the subject. Linguistics is not a stable or homogeneous field of study. There is a range of schools, each with its own orthodoxy and its own set of technical terms. The field has expanded rapidly, especially in the last twenty years, with fiercely competing theories each claiming to have demolished all other contenders. If linguistic theories become obsolete as rapidly as cars, why should a non-specialist make the effort to acquire such transient expertise?

A more basic issue concerns the proper scope of the subject. Should linguistics study only language and its structures, and not take account of the psychological and social processes without which there would be no object for such a linguistics to study? Since there are disciplines concerned with society and the mind, it would be tidier if linguistics could leave social and psychological factors out of account. But the existing boundaries around the disciplines are only political facts about the structures of studies in Western universities. Language, the object of study, ignores these boundaries, and so must anyone who seeks to understand it. It is possible to set up bridge-disciplines in the no-man's land between the main disciplines. So between linguistics and psychology is psycholinguistics. But if language is seen as one of the most revealing properties of the mind, we can argue, as Chomsky has done, that linguistics should be regarded as a branch of psychology.

Language is also a way of making sense, and is vitally concerned with meanings. The study of meanings goes outside language itself, to the individuals and cultures that make meaning. The process of making sense and communicating meanings takes place between human beings interacting in a social context, as the anthropologist Malinowski pointed out half a century ago, and as contemporary linguistics like Hymes and Halliday have continued to argue. Language is used for functions other than to communicate. For instance, it is often used to mystify and obstruct communication. So systematic is this function that many forms have evolved precisely in order *not* to communicate, or to do so ambiguously. Why is this? This question takes us immediately outside language as a self-contained object of study, but it is undoubtedly a question about language. A study that confines itself to the structures of language and ignores the functions and processes at its basis is liable to be dry and unilluminating about things that rightly are of interest to people generally, including prospective teachers.

So, given that this is the state of the field, what should one do to help the inquiring student without giving a misleading account of current opinion in the field? One possibility would be to aim at a simplified account, a consensus view packaged for a fairly low level of consumer: standardised, homogenised linguistics. But what linguists do not agree on includes some of the most exciting and sitmulating areas in the study of language. These are some of the real growth points. And the history of linguistics this century suggests that there is no need to worry too much about premature obsolescence. There are fads in linguistics as in other fields, but the major ideas remain valid even if they sometimes have periods when there is relatively less interest in them. For example, Chomsky drew attention to the work of the 19th century linguist Humbold. Whorf in the 1930s built on the work done by Boas and Sapir early in the century, and his ideas are still influential through the work of people like Bernstein and Halliday. Saussure is still a significant figure, exerting influence through the work of Jakobson and Lévi-Strauss.

Although many linguists now would take issue with some aspects of Chomsky's work, it is safe to predict that his contribution to the understanding of language will be seen to be of permanent value. It is not that linguistics is constantly improving, adding new truths to the old. At times the main stream of the discipline has been diverted, and has either devalued some important ideas from earlier thinkers, or has been unable to use them. But the earlier ideas were not proved wrong. At most, they were just found less interesting and usable in terms of the prevailing concerns of people working in the discipline. They remain as part of the resources available to be made use of by anyone with a particular interest or problem to do with language.

So we decided to take an alternative approach. Why not use the interests and concerns of an educator as the integrating principle, to determine what should be included and how issues should be presented? This is to see linguistics not as a body of knowledge in its own right, but as a set of resources for explaining particular phenomena and clarifying particular problems. With this principle there is no need to attempt a neat synthesis of the field. Our priority remains all the time on what teachers ought to know about language and communication, using that to determine which aspects of which theories should be brought to bear. So we had no strong desire to be comprehensive, or to do full justice to the subtlety of particular theories in their own right. The coherence of our exposition has to come from the connection between the thing to be explained and the concepts and theories that emerge, at first implicitly, in the attempt to explain. It is problem-centred, need-oriented exposition. Any specialist terms had to prove their credentials, to us as to prospective readers, before they were included.

To begin, we did not know exactly what would prove essential by these criteria. The form of exposition in general follows the process of discovery, for the writers as well as potential readers, of what is the relevant theory. The aim was to start with what everyone starts with — a particular situation, experience or event which is either powerfully typical, so that to understand it would be to understand many other examples of the same kind, or challengingly problematic, revealing by the challenge it makes to our previous expectations what is limited or wrong about them. This gives rise to a dialectical movement between practice and theory. Needless to say, the choice of examples was not completely arbitrary. No-one at our stage of life can be totally innocent of theory, and if we had had a different background we might have chosen different kinds of example and written differently about them. Even so, we have tried to be ruthless in our demands on theory, insisting that it must explain, and that it must explain what teachers need to know.

Another reason for this approach is a conviction that *knowledge about* language and communication is useless on its own. It will be inert and will have no effect on teaching competence, except for a few who creatively transform that knowledge into an active grasp of what is happening in the many situations they face as teachers. But these individuals will only be doing, heroically and unrewarded, what the institution ought to be aiming to do itself. The point is to equip them, as teachers, with certain insights and capacities and not with knowledge as such. They will not be teaching language or communication; or if they are they will learn the relevant content in a language arts course. They will *be* communicating, they will be *using* language all the time, every minute of each school day. This is a book for all teachers, in all subjects. They need explanatory frameworks which are simple and powerful enough for them to use. They need approaches, strategies, methods of analysis, things to do to help them think constructively about how they and others are communicating. Hence our emphasis on activities concerned with concrete situations. Knowledge is necessary, but as a means to an end, not an end in itself. The end is, unequivocally, to be a more effective teacher in the widest conception of the role of education and the function of the teacher. Such effectiveness will come from a practical grasp of the networks of communication which constitute the education system, and of the networks in society at large which interact decisively with what happens within the schools themselves.

This book is essentially a collaborative effort. The advisory team discussed at length what should go into the book and into each chapter. The editorial team carried out a general supervisory role. Individual chapters were then written by the respective authors and subjected to general criticism, then revised as necessary. The resulting chapters combine inextricably individual and collective responsibility.

Special thanks are due to Con Coroneos, who subjected every word written to ruthlessly judicious but benign scrutiny, acting as our resident voice of reason and good sense. Others who contributed valuable ideas and impetus at various points in the project include Joy Bignell, Eric Carlin, Mike Jordan, Simon MacPhail, Jill Maling-Keeper and Stan Richards.

Factors in Communication

Chapter 1 Bob Hodge
Models of Communication

Man is pre-eminently an animal who communicates. We have all been communicating from such an early age that we are liable to underestimate how complex a process it is, and how many things can go wrong. We communicate both less and more than we think. Teachers are in the business of communicating, whether they realise it or not. Perfect communication is an unattainable ideal for human beings, but we can all become better at it and more aware of where the problems are likely to arise.

In this chapter we shall look at some models of the communication process, and their implications for teachers and educators. But first, look at this question-answer exchange between an adult and an eight-year-old girl:

What do you think of the education system?
I don't know.
Well what do you think of school?
Good.
Is there anything bad about school?
No.
What does school help you to do?
Sums.
Is that all that school helps you to do?
No.
What else does it help you to do?
Social Studies.
Are they good for you?
Yes.
Why?
Cos it, cos, cos, ... I don't know.
Well does that mean that they're not very good for you?
No.
Well why are they quite good for you?
Cos it helps you learn things.
But why should you want to learn things?
I don't know.

Do you really want to learn things?
Yes.
Why?
Uh – I don't know.
Do you want to stop learning things?
Nope.
Do you enjoy learning things?
Sometimes.
Well what are the things you enjoy learning?
Maths and science.
Why do you enjoy them?
Because science is easy, and I don't have to listen for maths!

How good is the communication in this exchange? What is communicated? Take the first question-answer. The questioner asks about 'the education system'. This is an impossible question to ask of an average eight-year-old. The double abstract is beyond her linguistic range. But she gives an answer, 'I don't know', with a rising intonation. Most of her answers have a rising intonation, which signals uncertainty. Her words are saying 'I don't know (what I think)' but the intonation is saying 'What kind of answer do you want?' Similarly, to the question 'What do you think of school?' she answers 'Good', meaning both 'I think school is good' and 'is "good" what you want?' That is, she is communicating at two levels, through her words and her intonation-pattern. No doubt her expression throughout was reinforcing the sub-message.

The child, then, is communicating a complex message through apparently simple words, mostly monosyllables. One of her messages is about cognitive content. The other is more implicit and is about the nature of the social relationship and the communication process generally. She is asking for feedback. Since she keeps on asking, she is obviously not getting it. So the adult in this exchange is apparently unaware of a whole level of the child's communication and is not providing the necessary messages himself. He fails to realise what the child accurately recognises — that his questions are not innocent; they are powerful and mysterious. He signals that he wants some specific answer, but does not allow the child to find out what it is. Communication breaks down at two points when the girl stutters, pauses, and drags out a painful 'I don't know', which means 'I don't know the answer you want, I don't know what the rules of this game are and I can't cope.' The adult has more power than he realises, or wants to acknowledge, and this power-relationship is part of the very texture of the exchange. Hence he completely misreads the exchange, and mismanages it in a way that is typical of adult authority figures speaking to children.

By the end of the exchange, the girl has picked up enough signals to try a different tack. She realises that a subversive answer is also possible. She enjoys science and maths (acceptable answers) because 'sci-

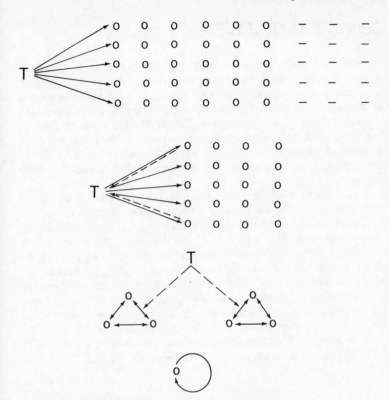

Fig. 1.2 Extremes of Learning-Process Control

ence is easy and I don't have to listen for maths'. This exactly contradicts the first plank in her defence of school, that it helps you to do 'sums'. She accompanied this thrust with a laugh, signalling that it was a joke, and then scanned the face of the listener, to see if jokes were acceptable. We can ask (as the adult did not) what has been communicated by either? The adult still does not really know what the girl thinks of school. The child is more concerned with the specific relationship and the adult's power and ambiguity within it. The adult thought he was simply asking questions; but he was also transmitting unconscious messages about his own power, and more conscious messages — which initially are not believed — that he does not wish to use this power. As communication, what is going on here is mainly under the surface, and is not in the consciousness or control of an adult whose obtuseness is often to be found in non-teaching adults and in teachers in schools throughout our community. The girl really knows a lot about 'the education system' as far as she has experienced it, but the adult does not know how to ask her about it, or how to listen to the answer.

Interaction models

The model we would apply to represent this exchange is the most elementary communication model, a two-person exchange. Teaching in schools usually involves more than two people, so we need to develop a set of models to correspond to the diversity of teaching situations and ideologies of the teaching relationship. Let us take the main versions of teacher-pupil interaction and look at them systematically as models for a communication process, to see how effective each is as a mode of communication as well as where communication failure is most likely to occur.

Ideologies of the teaching relationship range from those in which the teacher, representing the authority of a homogeneous culture, is the sole source of knowledge, and those where each pupil is in control of the learning process, which is a process of self-discovery. We represent the two extremes, with two common intermediate forms, in Figure 1.2. In the first, the teacher is the unchallenged source of all communications. In the second, selected pupils respond but the direction of the exchange is still controlled by the teacher. In the third, pupils communicate in small groups, with the teacher as a resource. In the fourth, the pupils engage largely in self-communication, with the teacher again a resource. To assess how these work as communication, note the more comprehensive model of the communication process as shown in Figure 1.3.

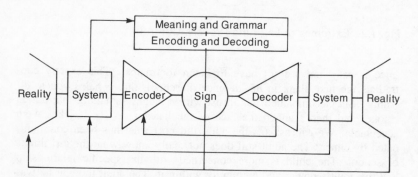

Fig. 1.3 Model of Communication Process

In this model, the two halves of the communication process are separated by a barrier down the middle. The signal that passes between them has two faces. The signal is a *material* sign, which carries meaning. It is important to realise how opaque is the barrier between speaker and hearer, corresponding to this double face of the sign. The speaker is conscious mainly of his meanings, but the hearer receives only physical sounds (or visual impressions, depending on the medium). Meanings are invisible and inaudible, conceived inside one skull and recreated inside another, and no-one knows for sure whether the process has been successfully carried out. Meanings are always guessed at, and communicators can only guess how much has got across. The exchange we looked at showed how tense and fraught with possibilities of error this guessing game is, especially for those who are too complacent about their own communication.

Communication, as Figure 1.3 shows, has a number of stages, each of which is the site for possible communication failure. Reality as perceived by the communicator is made meaningful by a structure of meanings, and these meanings are made available for communication by a structure of rules called the grammar. These structures then have to be encoded, or translated into material forms. Communication has only just begun at this stage. The receiver of the message has to go through the process in reverse, decoding the signals, interpreting them grammatically, understanding the categories, and finally projecting the 'reality' that is the object of communication.

Since every stage of this process involves a potential loss, perfect communication would by-pass the intermediary processes. The ideal is for two people to contemplate the same reality with the same system of meanings, sharing it with a minimum of words. It is worth bearing in mind that that situation is the ideal because many people do not realise how words get in the way of this more comprehensive communication. But words are necessary because people usually do not share an identical reality, or an identical interpretation of it. So the meaning projected by the receiver has to be controlled by a structure which is more or less the same as the transmitter's. This is represented in the model in Figure 1.3 by the box above. Ideally what is wanted is a common encoding system, a common grammar and meaning system, deployed on a common reality. In practice, the encoding system is likely to be sufficiently common if the two speak the same language; but with the grammar and communication between adults and young children, systems of meanings are likely to be different in some respects, and are typically unique. These mismatches are usually deep in the mind of speaker and hearer. How do you know, as teacher, what your words mean to each of the individuals in front of you, separated as they are by age, experience and total system? The problems are even greater if these individuals come from a different culture and language system.

So as well as a common structure guiding the general communication process, redundancy and feedback are also essential. Figure 1.3 shows the possible set of feedback loops. Redundancy is also a kind of feedback, since if the same message is repeated in a slightly different form, the two versions can be checked against each other. It is the same principle as in binocular vision. Two eyes record slightly different versions of a scene, which the brain uses to create a three-dimensional picture. Redundancy and feedback lead to what we can call three-dimensional communication. The adult-child interaction we looked at had no feedback loops, so the child did not know which channels were operating, or which messages were operative. In general, power relationships block feedback loops. Communication about communication can be called metacommunication. Without a channel which is open to both sender and receiver, which allows them to monitor the communication itself, communication is liable to go astray, with no-one aware of how wrong it is or able to do anything to correct it.

Multi-channel models

In the adult-child dialogue we looked at, communication was occurring in at least two channels: the words spoken and the intonation patterns. The child was trying to use intonation patterns for meta-communication, but this was ignored by the adult. In practice, there is a multiplicity of channels of communication. The diagram in Figure 1.4 shows some.

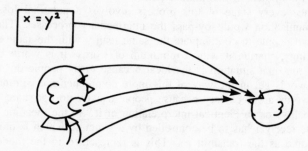

$$x = y^2$$

Fig. 1.4 Some Channels of Communication

Messages are carried by sight and sound, and they can have different proportions of ideational, or cognitive, content (propositions about the world) or interpersonal content (that is, concerned with relationships involving speaker and hearer). (Halliday: see Chapter 6). A more comprehensive repertoire of channels and their typical kind of content is shown in Figure 1.5.

		Cognitive	Interpersonal
Sound	Words	✓	✓
	Intonation		✓
Sight	Writing/diagrams	✓	✓
	Expression		✓
	Movements		✓
	Position		✓
	Clothes		✓

Fig. 1.5 Typical Content of Interpersonal Message

From this list it is evident that there are more channels carrying inter-personal than cognitive messages. Teachers typically are more conscious of the cognitive messages, but they are simultaneously transmitting other messages in clusters — messages which control the conditions of reception of the main message. As well as functioning to control the particular exchange, these channels are carrying implicit, general but powerful messages about social relationships. They are the kind of message that should concern teachers in their role as educators in the widest sense — that nebulous area of a teacher's function that is so hard to define but so important. It is obvious what might go wrong in this area if teachers do not know when they are transmitting such messages, how they transmit them, or even what they are transmitting.

Models and teaching styles

These models are provided to enable you to reflect more productively on the teaching process generally, and to make you better able to analyse any particular communication exchange. So we shall look again at the four models of teaching style in Figure 1.2. (You can do the same thing with other sub-models that represent situations you wish to understand.)

The model in Figure 1.2, the authoritarian one-directional style, departs markedly from the ideal communication form, since there is no feedback loop (except for silence), though in practice, pupils may give some feedback through shuffling and inattention. Its strength is that there can be total control over the form of the message, and the message can be simultaneously conveyed to as many people as can receive it. The model has the strengths and weaknesses of a mass communications system. The analogy is a close one. A teacher teaching in this way ought to try to be as like a good book or a good television programme as possible.

Thinking about a good television programme will help you to see how this kind of teaching can best be done. The producer uses the time at his disposal to prepare a complex message in which both the visual and the verbal components are carefully planned. Visual and verbal channels each contain both interpersonal and cognitive content. The words are scripted, and the intonation patterns are precisely significant. In this way, sound carries both cognitive and interpersonal content. The picture will show people talking, with their expression, distance from the camera, gestures and clothing all carefully monitored, transmitting messages which are controlled by the producer. The picture will also show portions of the 'reality' being talked about. This will be a visual experience. It involves careful selection. It is not total reality experienced by all the senses, but it meets some of the conditions of immediate communication. So although there is no feedback, there is systematic redundancy on both visual and auditory channels. If producer and receiver are linked by a common grammatical and semantic system, this can be good communication.

There are other things teachers in this style can learn from mass communications systems. An important lesson is the content of the interpersonal messages. The reality of mass communication relationships is that they are extremely remote and impersonal, with producers in a position of unchallengeable communicative power over an audience which can affect them only indirectly, through ratings. The messages transmitted about the relationship, however, typically signify intimacy. A good television manner is low-key, subtly expressive, relating directly on a one-to-one basis with each individual viewer. Viewers sitting in their own living room, of course, get a double message, the box with its knobs and cords signifying non-human technology, while the face on the screen seems close and personal, like an instant friend. It is possible for teachers in a mass communication situation to transmit messages which reinforce the objective qualities of that relationship — remoteness, impersonality, alienation of speaker and hearers, inequality of knowledge and power. Their messages, then, will reinforce that relationship, strengthening a sense of weakness and dependence on authority in members of the audience.

But the teacher could equally well transmit opposite messages, dressing and talking in a way that implies intimacy and equality, seeming to defer to the knowledge and authority of the audience, thereby disvaluing the self. To complete the analogy with mass media performances, these signals would have to be framed by signals with the opposite content — clear indications that the teacher is actually remote, expert and powerful. If the first strategy communicates the ideology of power, the second mystifies it. The experience of the mass media suggests that most people in our culture find messages of intimacy and solidarity far more congenial than messages of remoteness and power, even where the solidarity is known to be an illusion. But be warned. Immense technical skill and expenditure of time and resources in setting up the message are required for the seductive intimacy of the mass media message. Teachers using analogous methods have to work very hard if they want to achieve a similar illusion. Should they even want to do so?

To make the discussion more concrete, take this transcript of the opening of a lesson on 'The Agricultural Revolution':

> Now — today's lesson is on the um changes in Agriculture
> which took place at the end of the eighteenth century, and the
> beginning of the nineteenth century. We've talked about the uh
> need for change, the uh fact that uh land was becoming
> enclosed. What was previously uh a strip farming method uh
> was ah changing to what is called uh the enclosed method of
> farming, and uh there were several reasons for uh these
> changes. One was the need to feed the increasing population.

The other was that the landlords, who now owned more land, thought they could make profits if they were able to increase their yield — that is the amount of wheat they could grow or the numbers of sheep they could rear. So um they had an interest to become more efficient and to produce more goods and um which they went ahead doing as best they could um. The Round about this time a number of uh people uh began to uh make developments in agriculture. Some uh research was done and there were four main people, or four main people, who ah took uh part in this research. One was uh a man called Jethro Tull. He invented a drill which planted wheat in straight rows. He had noticed in France that the peasants um hoed around the vines, and he thought it would be a good idea to do this too in the wheat fields, but he also realised that uh if wheat was scattered by hand they could they'd have a hard job hoeing it and so he developed a drill which planted seeds in straight lines and then they were able to hoe it. He also um manured his fields very well and he wrote a book in 1730 called "Horse hoeing Husbandry" in which he outlined his methods.

The communication in this exchange is one way only; $T \rightarrow P \ldots$, where the number of students has no effects on the nature of the communication. This teacher would speak the same text to one as to a hundred, so long as they could all hear her. Looking now at the comprehensive communication model, we can see a number of potential communication problems. The grammar of the teacher is producing long, complex sentences that would be difficult for the children (aged 12 to 13) to process as they hear it. A more important lack is of common reality to refer to. This teacher does not connect her exposition with any experience the children might have. One child, asked what she had got out of the lesson, found it hard to reply, but said 'It could be interesting — if you planted some seeds in lines, and some higgledy piggledy, and seeing if they grow better. It would be more interesting than drawing them'. For this child, more reality would make the lessons more 'interesting'. It would also make it better communication.

While this lesson was being delivered, there was no feedback. Afterwards, children were required to draw a drill and write an essay. So there was delayed feedback; but this is feedback for the teacher, not a constant monitoring of the exchange for students. Nor is there much redundancy. For the teacher, the main point of this lesson was that change can be both good and bad. Most of the detail, therefore, is irrelevant rather than redundant. It can be called 'noise' in relation to the main message intended by the teacher, 'noise' as used here being whatever interferes with the reception of a message. However, students do not know what is in the teacher's mind or lesson plan. They only make guesses on the basis of the signals they receive. In this case the redundant elements concerned notions of improvement (increase, development, invention), with positive evaluations like 'good', 'well', 'more efficient'. The teacher asked the question at the end: 'Were the changes good or bad?' She was disappointed when she got only the answer 'good'. She had thought that the mention of enclosures and the profit motive would set off a balanced judgment, but that was not the message the students received.

The main cognitive message, then, did not get across. What about interpersonal messages coming across via other channels? The intonation patterns are relatively flat, as often happens with carefully prepared material like this. This keeps the text self-contained, not to be broken into by student interjections. The teacher taught from behind a desk, in front of a blackboard, with the class in front of her. (See Figure 1.6.)

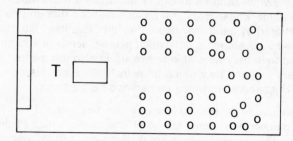

Fig. 1.6 The Teacher-Class Situation

She was neatly dressed, and kept herself remote from the students, at a constant distance from them. She frequently referred to the set book, which the children had in front of them. The message is of remoteness but not power. Authority is an important content, but the teacher's style suggests that authority does not reside in her. The teacher is simply the self-effacing transmitter of the received wisdom, which neither she nor the class is expected to challenge or question.

The teacher using this mass communication style almost merges with a book, and in fact this is a potential strength. Insofar as it is like a kind of voice-over for students reading the text, it has the redundancy which makes for efficient communication. A teacher using this style could hope to have a quiet, passive class, who would be learning more than if they were exposed simply to a continuous monologue, or if they only read the book.

At the other extreme, with the model iv in Figure 1.2, we have teacherless learning. We represented this as a tight reflexive circle: In practice, the process is more complex, and its explanation requires a number of distinct communication models. If the communication is totally reflexive, the self communicating with the self, it would seem impossible that communication could occur. The barrier down the middle seems to be acting like a mirror, sending back a reduced image of what is communicated.

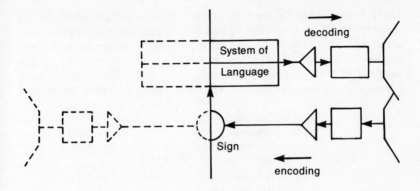

Fig. 1.7 Barrier in Teacherless Learning

Another way of looking at what is happening is to say that the individual is now on both sides of the otherwise impenetrable barrier. The message is not reflected back (the barrier is not a mirror), it has to be projected, and since the individual is on both sides of the barrier, the feedback is perfect. The box in Figure 1.7, containing the regulatory systems linking production to reception, becomes the real content of the communication. The general outcome is enhanced control over this system which is so crucial to production and reception of meaning and messages. The content of the communication act is the system of language itself, rather than any particular content. Examples of this process would include individuals listening to and editing a tape of their own speech, or writing a diary and analysing it carefully.

Reality　Cultural　Theories　Definition　Main　　Tertiary　School　Teacher　Pupil
　　　　Associations　　　　Work　Text　　Ed.　　Text

Fig. 1.8 Transmission of Messages

But many students left to themselves are not studying their own message. The hope is that they will discover general messages for themselves. Consider the model for the transmission of messages in an educational context. A communication chain like this obviously risks reduction or distortion of the message at every point of re-transmission, as in the well-known game of Chinese whispers. Its justification is that at each stage there is a necessary scaling-down of the message content. Students left to the discovery process have had five stages in the transmission process removed. They are expected to by-pass intermediary stages, and perceive and transmit cultural messages directly. They are likely to do so only if the intermediary stages were redundant. In the majority of cases where the intermediary stages have a function, students will not be likely to reproduce the hidden, culturally-determined messages. A more effective way of facilitating this chain is to arrange as many of the stages as possible in parallel rather than linearly, as in Figure 1.9. This creates multiple messages, which can allow the student

Reality
Theories
Seminal Work
Major Text } Child
Courses
School Text
Teacher

Fig. 1.9 Parallel Stages in Chain of Messages

to check version against version and achieve feedback. A more manageable way of achieving the same effect of multiple comparable messages is to have specific duplications available to individual children, as shown in Figure 1.10.

Teacher
A
Teacher } Student
B
Text A
Text B

Fig. 1.10 Duplications in Multiple Messages

If students can understand one text or one teacher, they can understand two texts and two teachers, and use this to achieve a more three-dimensional communication. The role of teacher as an exclusive gateway to transmission of knowledge, which is undesirable on grounds of communication, can be as effectively modified by addition as by removal of teachers. However, with young children, the teacher is more than a gateway. The affective level is also important, and at some stages children may need coherence and someone to relate to, rather than multiple texts and teachers.

A common form of teacherless communication in schools is the use of small group discussion; see model (iii) in Figure 1.2. What is communicated in such discussions? What is the nature of the communication that takes place and how can it be enhanced? Take the following exchange between three eleven-year-old boys, who have been set the task of designing their ideal home. This was part of a curriculum component in social studies concerned with communities, and they had some discussion of local houses available to them in a textbook. They were also given copies of the *West Australian* of Saturday, in which various homes are advertised. The discussion began as follows:

A. And how many dunnies do you want?
B. What did you say?
A. How many dunnies do you want?
B. It's got to be a two storey.
A. O.K. We'll have to do two floors.
B. Two storeys and a basement.
A. O.K. How many dunnies do you want?
C. Um, five.
A. How many do you want?
B. Oh — about three.
A. I'll have about — four. That means we'll have four. Right. Two floors, one basement (spells out). Right.
B. Um. You need an upstairs kitchen.
A. That's right.
C. And a downstairs kitchen.
B. No, no.
C. It's a two storey.
B. The house could be on a hill and it looks over a scenic way, you know?
C. It looks over the river or something.
B. It looks over Kings Park or something.
C. Yeah.
A. Upstairs kitchen.
B. Make it a two-storey house.
   Yeah, it's a two-storey house with a basement.
C. What's a basement?
B. It's a room underground where you keep things.
C. Ah.
B. Like dugites and they attack you and (laughter).
A. Upstairs kitchen, down, vicey versa. That means the other way around. Kitchen downstairs. Brick and tiles? Or asbestos and tile?
C. Ah, asbestos. (laughs)
B. Brick and tile. Brick and tile with some jarrah and (interruption).
A. Brick and tile.
B. And how many bedrooms?
A. We want four bedrooms.
B. No, we want about six.
C. Twelve bedrooms.
B. No, six bedrooms.

A.   Yeah, six bedrooms.
Six bedrooms. (writes)
O.K. We want a twelve-foot verandah.

B.   No, no. Wait a minute.

A.   A 100-metre porch.

C.   We want a study and a huge library.
A huge library.

B.   A study yep.

A.   Automatic doors.

B.   Yep.

C.   And one of those tele, tele —

B.   Telecoms.

C.   Yeah, telecoms.
Um. Um. All patterns on the roof.

B.   No.

C.   A double fireplace.

B.   No, a fireplace in every room.

All. Yeah, yeah, yeah.

The first model we can use for this exchange is the simple interactional one. The diagram we used to represent it is shown in Figure 1.11. In

Fig. 1.11   Model for Interactional Exchange

terms of this model everyone talks and is presumed to listen equally. In the authoritarian model none of these would speak, certainly not at this length, though they would all be presumed to listen. If we analyse the exchange more closely, we find that B speaks 21 times; A, 14, C, 12. C speaks less than the others, and much less than B. We can then ask who the best listener is. One indication of this is that A appointed himself scribe, and copied down the agreed details. Another measure is the number of questions asked: this shows active collection of information. A asks six questions, C one and B one. Acknowledgement that an idea has been heard and approved (affirmation) would be another indication. A has 7 affirmatives; C has 2; B has 2. A emerges as the primary receiver and B the primary communicator, with C rating lowest on both dimensions. B also has the capacity to censor the contribution of others. He uses six negatives, and two rephrasings which annul the previous contribution, (usually C's). We can represent the tendencies of the exchange, then, as in Figure 1.12, and the social power of the participants is clearly as in Figure 1.13.

Fig. 1.12 Tendencies in Question-Answer Exchange

$$B > A > C$$

Fig. 1.13 Social Power in Question-Answer Exchange

Of the three boys, A is regarded by his teacher as academically strong, B is slightly above average, and C has learning problems.

We are now in a position to ask what each seems to have gained from the exchange. A is the most effective communicator. He gets more feedback, and provides more to others. B is the dominant speaker and practises strategies of dominance, but learns less. C alone appears to learn something new from his peers — what 'basement' means, and perhaps what 'vice versa' and 'telecoms' mean. It is not clear that either of the others knows anything more at the end of the exchange; but C also has the experience of being ignored or corrected by a peer, and having a joke treated as a serious but silly suggestion. He is practising disruptive strategies on a minor scale to gain status and attention, but with limited success.

Interpersonal messages, messages about power and solidarity, are more important in this exchange than information or cognitive messages. In these terms, B transmits messages about his power, and C receives and acknowledges messages about his lack of power, both of them within terms of a situation characterised by solidarity. We might compare this exchange with what could happen in an authoritarian classroom. There, even B would be largely repressed. He would have to develop his manipulative skills outside the classroom, which he has obviously been able to do. C, put at a disadvantage in this exchange, would be totally silenced in a large classroom. He has in fact developed the learning problems that would be predicted. It would seem from this exchange that even with his peers the same process of disvaluation occurs as in a classroom, though to a lesser degree. For such a student, a small group discussion does not totally reverse the disadvantages of the dynamics of a large group. It merely presents them in a less extreme form.

The messages in this exchange, such as they are, all have a source outside the small group. If we take boy A as the reference point, some possible communication chains will be as in Figure 1.14. One function of small-group discussion then becomes clear. The community is the common source of messages, which come via a number of channels and sources. Boy A can use the discrepancies and overlap to create a more three-dimensional communication situation, juxtaposing what his parents have said in their kind of language with what his friends say. If the relevant community is a homogeneous one, then this method allows its messages to be transmitted more fully.

In this particular discussion the boys came from a similar social background, and the characteristics of an 'ideal house' were fairly common. But what if one of the boys had come from an entirely different background, and was, for instance, an Aborigine? If he contributed to the discussion, would he be transmitting messages from his own community, or attempting to pick up messages from the dominant European middle-class community? And how would the other two boys interpret his messages? Ideally they would be aware of the different ultimate source of the messages, and treat his input as a radically different and unassimilable message. But if we judge from looking at how they treated the white, middle-class C, it is more likely that they would treat an Aborigine's different messages as inferior and aberrant versions of the dominant community's values, though A would be better able to learn than B.

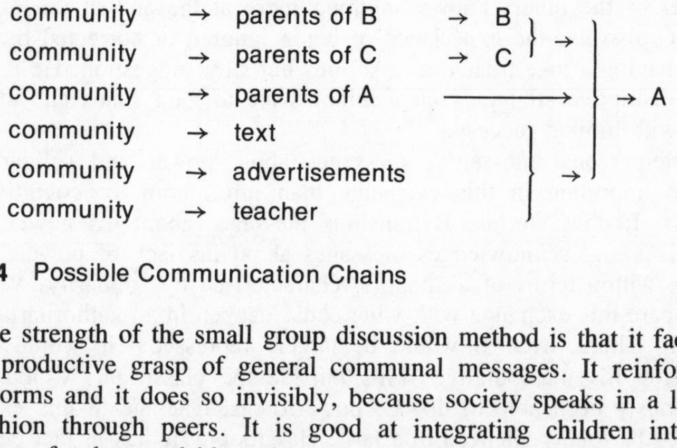

Fig. 1.14 Possible Communication Chains

So the strength of the small group discussion method is that it facilitates a productive grasp of general communal messages. It reinforces social norms and it does so invisibly, because society speaks in a low-key fashion through peers. It is good at integrating children into a shared set of values and ideas, but conversely it is not good at making these available for inspection, unless the group has access to different message-sources. These three boys did not use the written aids provided. These aids might have provided different input, and extended the scope of the communication. As it was, the exchange was largely pseudo-communication which functioned to create solidarity, reinforce social norms, and give training in role negotiations through language: helping the strong to be a little stronger and the weak to realise their weakness better.

Models of language structure

In the general communication model on page 13 we had a box containing the shared knowledge which makes communication possible. This knowledge concerns the structures of language itself. These structures are of two kinds. One is the structure of each message. In linguistic theory, this is called the syntax, or *syntagmatic* structure. The other kind of structure is the way the elements of a language are organised as a system. This is often called the *paradigmatic* structure.

There is a large number of *syntactic* structures in any language (see Chomsky 1957, 1965). The general point that students need to be aware of is that 'these structures exist and profoundly affect the interpretation of an utterance'. Take as a simple example 'I think school is good'. The surface of this has the structure shown in Figure 1.15, if we group

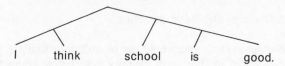

Fig. 1.15   A Syntactic Structure

together the parts that go with each other. This sentence contains five words, but everyone recognises that it is a single idea. It is a single idea because its different components are organised by the common structure. If the words were given in a random order — 'school I good is think' — it would be difficult to say and difficult to remember.

The girl in the exchange we started with used a single-word sentence, 'Good', in answer to the question 'What do you think of school?' Many teachers object to answers which are not complete sentences, but this concern is misguided. Deletion of parts of sentences is natural and functional in normal communication. The child's answer has the structure shown in Figure 1.16, with the underlined part unstated, but understood by the teacher and anyone else who knows the language concerned. So syntactic structures have two important functions. They organise the elements of an utterance into larger wholes, and they are a guide to aspects of the basic structures organising thought and language which may not appear in the words spoken. The context, plus knowledge of

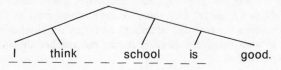

Fig. 1.16   Child's Answer to a Syntactic Structure

English structures, enables us to guess what the child meant. Otherwise, anything could have been 'good'.

Syntactic structures can be more complex, such as that in Figure 1.17, from the teacher-monologue. There are eighteen words in the

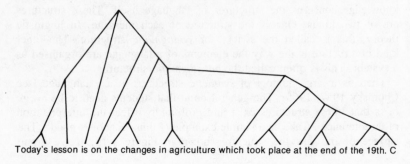

Today's lesson is on the changes in agriculture which took place at the end of the 19th. C

Fig. 1.17   A Complex Syntactic Structure

sentence. Without syntax, you would not be able to assimilate it. What we perceive is stored in short-term memory first, before being transferred to long-term memory. A rule-of-thumb for storage capacity in short-term memory is seven units or chunks, plus or minus two. If these eighteen words were each treated as units, they would overflow short-term memory. In the text as a whole this speaker usually paused or stuttered before she spoke seven words at a stretch. In this sentence, however, there is only one pause, between 'the' and 'changes'; so thirteen words in a row must be organised by syntax into half or less that number of units of meaning. The strain of this sentence on processing equipment is clear. It would not be surprising if the children found this sentence difficult to understand or remember. Listening to this teacher, they have to sort through two kinds of structure — the syntactic structures and the blocks she chops the sentences up into whenever she pauses.

However, the moral of this is not that teachers should use only short, simple sentences. Syntax gives the necessary structure to messages, and a complex message will have to be organised by complex syntax. Teachers should not avoid all complex ideas. What they should do is to be aware of the intrinsic complexity of what they are communicating, and they should try not to give students further problems in processing their language as well as grasping the ideas. They should also realise that students are more likely, therefore, to forget those parts of the lesson which may often be the most important as far as the teacher is concerned, even though the ideas have been, as the teacher thinks, fully and clearly explained.

The other kind of structure is paradigmatic. Syntagmatic structures organise the message. Paradigmatic structures organise the language itself. To illustrate, take the phrase which was incomprehensible to the eight-year-old girl: 'the education system'. Most people would agree that this is too 'abstract' and difficult for an eight-year-old. Why is it difficult? The difficulty in understanding what such a word means is not so much what it refers to, as the way it organises a complex of things. The word refers to buildings, plant, equipment, administration, planners, teachers and children; but this list does not give the meaning of the word. The meaning is a *structure*, a way of organising this diverse material, as well as the content itself. The structure might be such as in Figure 1.18.

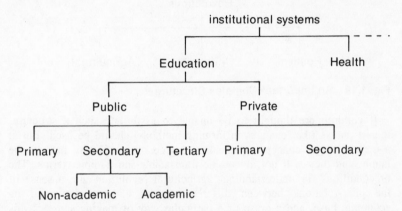

Fig. 1.18 Organisation of Diverse Material

To know the meaning of 'education system' — whatever judgments one might make about it — one needs to be able to grasp a structure of this kind. Less abstract concepts are organised by such structures. The adult asking 'What do you think of school?' of the eight-year-old knows the child will be referring to a particular school, but for him the word also acts to give coherence to a set of people, activities and buildings which are distinguished from 'home'. The adult will be translating out of a complex system, which distinguishes primary from secondary schools and probably makes other distinctions. The child lacks this system. For her, 'school' is not part of a larger system. It organises an important area of her experience, as an over-arching category. If the adult had asked her 'What do you think of primary school?' this also would have puzzled the girl. It would have revealed to her that the word she thought she knew was being used as part of a different, larger structure. She will only be able to grasp the meaning of the word and the question as the adult understood it, when she has grasped the relevant structure.

If this adult thought he was translating his original question into simpler terms, he was wrong: the child simply could not understand or answer the original question. The simplicity of the word 'school' is deceptive, since it hides the vast difference in the conceptual systems it is part of. So if the adult interprets the answer as a simplified response to his original question, he is also wrong. So is a teacher who understands herself to be talking of the 'agricultural revolution' and translates this as 'changes in farming methods'. The translation connects it more directly with language systems and realities that are familiar to the children, but detaches it from the important complex structure shown in Figure 1.19.

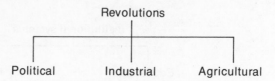

Fig. 1.19 An Important Complex Structure

If children are thought to be unable to assimilate such a structure, then a phrase like 'changes in farming methods' should be used. But at a certain stage, concepts with some degree of complexity have to be taught and they will not always be translatable into simpler terms. The preconditions for understanding 'agricultural revolution' are a sense of the inter-relations between different sectors of a society and its economic base, and a grasp of a particular way of making sense of this complex whole. If a teacher is asked what such a term means, the answer should not be simply what it refers to. Nothing less than the relevant structure and its field of reference will do. Since students will probably not ask, teachers will usually have to feed in the structure and its field of reference.

Conclusion

This chapter is meant to give you models which will enable you to make more sense of your own experience and the experience of others. Models function to allow you to focus on different aspects of a complex whole and to see relationships in a general way. Models present ideas in a form that allows them to be manipulable. Representing experience through these models, you should be able to see where mistakes have been made and how to correct them, or why the communication was so successful.

Suggested activities

1. Analyse a part of a lesson (using a transcript or video tape if possible) in terms of the models in Figure 1.2, looking to see how far the teacher has used the potentialities of the model, and overcome its communication deficiencies.

2. Look at a brief classroom exchange in terms of the model in Figure 1.3, checking on the extent of the feedback and the degree of overlap in the various components of the model. Assess how successful the communication has been and, where appropriate, suggest ways in which the communication might be improved.

3. Look at an exchange where communication seems not to be working well (for example, between an English speaker and a migrant child), and use Figure 1.3 to explain the site of the communication breakdown and what could be done about it.

4. Look at a part of a lesson, testing the messages coming over in each channel (see Figure 1.4). Do they reinforce each other?

5. Plan how you would make discussion by a small group as effective as possible, ensuring a number of sources for the content you wish to be communicated through the discussion (see Figures 1.9 and 1.14).

6. Describe details of presentation for two versions of the same lesson, one carrying authoritarian interpersonal messages, the other expressing equality and intimacy.

7. Have a friend take a school text you have not read, in an unfamiliar subject, and blank out all abstract words from a single page, then try to answer questions on the content. (You will be in the same position as many of the children in an average class.)

8. Plan a lesson in which you analyse the basic concept as part of a structure, and show how you would teach that structure and its field of reference.

Chapter 2 Bob Hodge
Signs of Class and Power

Henry Higgins in Shaw's *Pygmalion* had a remarkable ability to place people by their vowels. He also gambled on his ability to deceive other people whose character judgements were based on style of speech. Eliza Dolittle speaking low-class vocabulary in a low-class accent was despised as an ignorant guttersnipe. The same Eliza, no more intelligent but having mastered upper-class speech forms, was regarded as intelligent, sophisticated, beautiful and of noble birth. Higgins was right about the sweeping nature of judgements we all make about people based on the form of language they use. These judgements usually reinforce social stereotypes. They are a major means of carrying prejudices that divide a society. They give identity to groups within a society, strengthening solidarity and organising relationships between the weak and the powerful. Teachers, as members of the community, are likely to share the common prejudices, and transmit them uncritically unless they understand this whole process.

To see how common processes of judgement work on language met with in everyday life, take the following excerpt from an interview with Smith, an unemployed working-class youth, at present living in a hostel in Perth, Western Australia.

Interviewer:	Do you think it's really important to get legally married — to go off and get the licence and sign it all? Is that what's really important about — getting together and having children?... or not?...
Smith:	I, think (pause) I think...um...ah...y'should actually. (pause ah...This new...living together is better j'. (pause) for a while 'til y'get t'know each other (pause)...'cause it's ah...in a...ah confined space it's...well ah I c'n only talk from my experience...(pause)
Interviewer:	That's what I want you to...
Smith:	Aah... I spent a coupla months with this girl that I thought I was really involved with — oh, I liked her a lot an' she liked me a lot...we —

thought we knew each other...and so we
decided we were going to live in a flat before we
make any real commitments...an'...well
we...um...we moved into the flat...an'...we
found out that we were different than we
thought we were...we still liked each
other...but it was just in a confined space living
there all the time...an' permanent marriage and
the demand it puts on you, it's something
different an'...the relationship is different from
there on...an' I think it's good to live in...with
someone for a period of time before yer really
decide to get married or not...I wouldn't...I
wouldn't suggest ta have a...child before
marriage...that's my personal beliefs.

Compare this with Neil, a middle-class boy from one of the better Perth suburbs who will be taking his university entrance examination at the end of the year.

Interviewer: Do you believe it's absolutely essential to be
officially married? You know, sign the licence in
a registry office or a church before settling
down and having a family?...Purely your
opinion.
Neil: Yea, I think I do; eventually.
Interviewer: You do?
Neil: I think, just to live in our society the way it is
unless you want to live in the middle of the
bush, it's perfectly alright not to get married;
but to get along there just for purely sorta
financial and that; you've got to, I think, get
united eventually. I've got no reason; there's no
harm in it, sort of living together for five, maybe
ten years or until you're twenty-five or thirty or,
you know, but once you're over about thirty, it's
time you should get it all legal, just so you can
get by easier. With everybody else around, you
know, so's they won't sort of look down on you
too much...

(These examples were kindly supplied by Alison Jensen from a project on language and class.)

Many of our character judgments are based on superficial signs. Smith, for instance, was wearing a blue singlet. He had tatoos on both arms, and hair cut short. Neil had an open-necked check shirt and shoulder-length well-groomed hair. What judgments would you make about the social background, level of education, intelligence, and personal reliability of the two? What is your evidence for each, and how reliable is it as evidence? As a tertiary student you have reached a certain level of education and are likely to have certain social assumptions and expectations. Comparing notes with others you will probably find you have come to a common set of judgments on Neil and Smith.

The language itself provides many other cues for judgment. It is difficult to capture the exact differences in pronunciation using conventional spelling. Phonetic script is designed to be more consistent and precise. Using both methods to describe Smith's pronunciation, we can point out a number of fairly consistent differences in his sounds compared with standard English. He pronounces o as in 'go' or 'know' slightly longer, with two vowels run together (as a diphthong). Phonetically the sound shift can be represented as owo → ao. Similarly, a as in 'space' is closer to i in 'spice' (phonetically, e → ay). U as in 'coupla' sounds more like 'carpla' (phonetically ∧ → a), and so on. Conventionally, these are regarded as common characteristics of 'broad' Australian. Smith speaks 'broader' Australian than does Neil or the interviewer. There are further differences between Smith and the interviewer. Smith spoke almost half the number of words per minute, yet he slid over or missed out many consonants. Neil spoke more evenly, at much the same rate as did the interviewer. Smith's voice was quiet, and he often looked down as he spoke. Neil's voice was strong and confident. Again, these qualities will often be used as the basis of character judgments, which especially among educated speakers will be unfavourable to Smith. He will seem less articulate, sloppier in his speech, and possibly shifty and untrustworthy. It is important to point out, however, that all these judgments are the result of guesses, and that the signs the judgments are based on could be ambiguous. One meaning they could have is particular to this situation. Smith may be much uneasier than Neil in this interview, and this may be the main message of his speech forms.

Some words in English have associations with educated speakers in formal situations. We can label such words as 'high'. Other words at the other extreme can be labelled 'low'. In this example both youths mainly employ a middle range of vocabulary, neither high nor low. Most language used in everyday speech in schools is neutral. Neil uses a number of words which could be regarded as tending towards high: 'eventually', 'perfectly alright', 'purely financial', 'united eventually'. He also uses some low forms: 'get by easier', 'look down on you.' Smith says 'confined space' and 'permanent marriage', which could be regarded as high forms. But these phrases are not part of grammatical sentences, as he uses them. So although he uses some high forms, he gives an impression of being unfamiliar with them. This could give rise to a judgment that he does not really understand them, and hence that he is less intelligent than Neil, whereas he may simply be uncomfortable using them. Neil appears to have greater flexibility in vocabulary between high and low forms, but again this may simply indicate greater confidence.

In syntactic forms we find a greater difference between the two. Smith has more sentences which are incomplete or ungrammatical in some way. Neil's sentences also appear more complex. One measure of complexity is the number of clauses per sentence, excluding those linked by 'and'. Smith averages about two clauses per sentence; Neil averages about four. One of Neil's sentences has ten clauses, twice the number of Smith's most complex sentence.

> I think, just to live in our society the way it is, unless you want to live in the middle of the bush, it's perfectly alright to not get married, but to get along here just for purely sort of financial and that, you've got to, I think, get united eventually.

Some of these clauses, such as his two 'I think's, could be regarded as mere mannerisms, although they do signify a self-checking action of the mind. The inserted clause 'unless...' acts to qualify the previous sentence, (as against some ideal alternative) following another qualification 'the way it is'. Together they show Neil's awareness that his statement about 'our society' may not apply to all people or all forms of society. He also contrasts 'just to live' with 'to get along'. Again this sounds like a careful, balanced judgment, seeming to make a fine distinction, though what exactly is at issue is not clear. In general, however, his syntax signifies precision, complexity and self-criticism. All of these are prestigious intellectual qualities. His language does not *prove* he has these qualities. The syntax is just the outward form, a common sign of these qualities of mind.

Smith superficially seems a less complex, self-reflecting thinker, if we go by the same syntactic signs. But take his sentences: 'I spent a couple of months with this girl that I thought I was really involved with. Oh, I liked her a lot and she liked me a lot. We thought we knew each other. And so we decided we were going to live in a flat before we make any real commitments.' This seems to break down into smaller units of thought than Neil's lengthy sentence. It is also less abstract. He is talking only about himself and his own experience. However, his language has its own kind of precision and complexity. Instead of contrasting life 'in our society' with 'getting by', Smith is evaluating the feeling he and the girl had. They 'thought' they knew each other, but events proved them wrong. The contrast works through the past tense: we thought that then, but later we came to realise the reality. Smith's sentences are linked, but there are not so many outward signs of the links. So looking at the language, we can say that Neil has more *signs* of complex thinking than Smith. But Smith does not necessarily think less complex thoughts: it may just be that he has fewer and different signs of complexity (although it may also be the case that on this occasion his thinking is less complex). Similarly, Neil seems more able to consider the issue in general terms, where Smith is much more particular, staying with his own personal experience.

But again, these are only surface indications. Smith may be seeing his individual experience as an illustration of a general truth which he understands but does not state explicitly. By some criteria, Neil's qualities show higher mental abilities than Smith's: powers of abstract thinking are highly regarded by many people in our society. But by other criteria Smith could be regarded as superior. He is talking about what is real for him and he shows honesty and integrity of thought. A harsh critic might say that Neil shows only that he can talk impressively, though somewhat vacuously, about something outside his experience. Which is really the superior?

Many teachers would immediately say: 'Neil'. So would many employers. The interviewer went on to simulate an interview for a job with each of the two. Smith had had some experience, mostly unsuccessful, of such interviews, but he performed unimpressively. His voice became even quieter, his silences longer, his sentences simpler and ungrammatical. Asked why he did not sell himself better, he explained:

> Well...I couldn't you know...ah...I...just...ah...there's not much I can say to him...um...you know? It's always his decision if he'll...wants to hire me or not. There's nothing I can say you know without making myself look like an idiot or something.

Neil, still at school, with his first real job interview years ahead of him, performed with much greater aplomb. His accent, vocabulary and syntax, his whole manner and the way he looked, all combined to send the signal: 'I am confident, I am a winner.' Smith sent out the opposite signals, which become a self-fulfilling prophecy. His last sentence has a bitter truth. Everything he says does make him 'look like an idiot or something', in the eyes of the typical employer, at least.

Our judgments of character typically assume that signs are reliable, and that everyone shares the same value-judgments. A model for this assumption is as follows:

Quality ⟶ *Signal* ⟶ *Value-judgment*
(of mind or   (in language or
character)   behaviour)

But there is a number of important ways in which this simple scheme breaks down. Some people learn the signals but do not have the quality itself. They can sound intellectually sophisticated, for instance, without really being so. Others may possess the quality, but not signal it, or signal it by different means. We can ask: why should a person not want to signal a quality? There is a number of possible answers. Smith, for instance, would not want to speak 'posh' with his mates. They would not value either the quality — abstract thought, for instance — or the conventional signals — for example, complex sentences or abstract terminology. But why does he not try to display these qualities in the interview situations, where they would be more valued? Some obvious answers suggest themselves. He is not practised in the code that signals these qualities. (When he attempts longer, more abstract words he freezes up, because he is less familiar with their use in context.) Partly because of this, he feels the interview situation is loaded against him, with the interviewer a hostile judge who has already decided against him. The effect of this is to inhibit communication generally, making him seem 'like an idiot or something', to use his own words.

All these considerations make judgments on Smith, based on his verbal performance, an uncertain enterprise. What is worse, the hostile judgment makes him perform even less well, which makes the judgment harsher, and so on, in a vicious circle in which youths like Smith are trapped, in classrooms as well as in interviews.

Language and status

Language is always in a state of change. The sound system illustrates the process at its most simple. At any one time, there will be a number of ways of uttering a particular sound which will still be interpreted by other speakers as the same sound. In Australian, for instance, someone saying 'I neffer' would be heard as saying 'I never'. The same person on a different occasion might say 'I never' and would not be conscious that there was any difference. The variation can be called free variation, since any speaker seems free to vary between the two forms. But after a while 'free' variation comes to be more systematic. One group or class of speakers, linked by age, sex, social status, race or region, will use one or other possible form more consistently than other groups do. For a number of reasons, the role of literacy being one, in languages like English the language spoken by the dominant class tends to be more homogeneous. Different regions develop distinct dialects which will be more strongly marked in lower-class speakers. Australian English fits into this pattern.

A classic study of the significance of particular sounds was Labov's work on New York English (1966). Some New Yorkers pronounce words like 'car' with the 'r' sounded, others do not. Sounded-r turned out to correlate with a high social status, and with formality of occasion. It was a prestige form whose significance was recognised by speakers. Other researchers have used Labov's methods with other prestige forms in other speech communities. Some important general propositions seem to be emerging. Labov found, for instance, that speakers are judged consistently on the presence or absence of the prestige form for their suitability for various jobs, varying from television announcer to factory worker. People making a judgment were often not aware of the precise basis for it, but would be quite certain about the judgment itself. This illustrates the unconscious way in which such processes operate, and suggests why they are so dangerous, since they are inaccessible to rational judgment. Labov was studying sound markers. If we include some other signs, such as the forms of syntax and vocabulary that distinguished Smith from Neil in our simulated interview, we see something of the range of signs on which these judgments are based.

Once a form establishes itself as a prestige form, it may seem surprising that everyone does not quickly learn it and create a linguistically egalitarian society. Teachers, we might think, should have a duty to teach the prestige form: a Smith should be taught to speak like Neil. But the stigmatized form seems to acquire a positive value for lower class speakers. Labov showed some of the subjective judgments made on high-versus-low forms by people from different groups (1974). He had them make judgments based on three criteria: job suitability, friendship, and ability in a street fight. The table came out as in Figure 2.1.

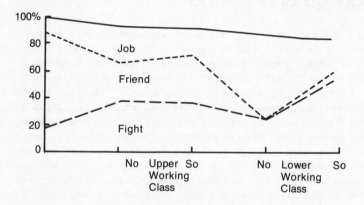

Fig. 2.1 Some Subjective Judgments of Labov

The top line shows all classes accepting the same economic reality. The second line shows a different reaction to possible solidarity. A user of prestige forms is regarded as a likely potential friend by middle-class speakers, but not by lower-working-class speakers. However, the working-class speaker would be better in a street fight, according to all but the lowest group. That is, the low-prestige speech form signifies not only low general status, but also possession of positive qualities that are associated particularly with lower-class speakers. Labov calls them covert prestige forms. It is common to find that males in lower socio-economic categories are more likely to use these non-prestige forms than are females. These forms tend to signify strongly masculine qualities. Australian is typical of this tendency. For working-class males, it is the prestige form which is stigmatised, 'pansy', while the non-prestige form conjures up the image of a beery, hairy, singlet-clad masculine male.

So in a language community like Australia, we have a society stratified in a number of ways — by age, class and sex at least. Various aspects of the language show differentiations corresponding to these social groupings, and these qualities of language come to signify qualities associated with the group itself. Sound, vocabulary and syntax all provide markers. With sound, a number of variant vowels and consonants is regarded as socially significant in this way. 'Broad Australian', which is associated with less educated speakers, has a number of different vowels compared with standard English: for example, day — du (phonetically e — ay) or come — carm (phonetically — a). It is also characterised by frequent dropping of the consonants t, d, th, h, k, and final g, and by failing to distinguish t and d, k and g, f and v. With the vowels that vary, there is a continuum between the two extreme sounds, which merge into one another. With the consonants, there are degrees of omission. With both vowels and consonants, people can use one form at one time, and the other on a different occasion, but still differ significantly from each other in the proportionate use of the two forms.

So any particular marker represents a continuum of possibilities which can be correlated with a society cut up into two, three, four or more categories. However, the basic principle is a division into two: a high form and a low form, with intermediate stages simply sub-categorised by the same principle, such as a low-high, high-low etc. The forms of language are particularly sensitive to two factors: the social status of the speaker, and the nature of the situation. High forms in general correspond to high speaker status, and to formal situations.

Each kind of marker is used as a sign for a whole complex of qualities. Sound-markers are the most arbitrary basis for judgment. A man says 'Goodie mite', and this is used, subconsciously, as grounds for judging him to be of low social status, relatively low education and intelligence, probably employed in an unskilled or semi-skilled job. He will also tend to be regarded as friendly and informal, not a snob. There is nothing about this particular vowel that intrinsically justifies these inferences. However, vocabulary and especially syntax could more plausibly be seen as not signs but proofs of some at least of the inferred qualities. 'High' vocabulary contains terms which are part of large complex paradigmatic sets.

In the previous chapter it was suggested that 'agricultural revolution' was not simply a synonym for 'changes in farming methods', but involved a more complex grasp of a wider range of phenomena. However, is 'children' a more complex concept than 'kids'? It is difficult to see how. The same applies to syntax. A complex, intricate idea will require complex syntax for its expression, but elaborate periphrases like 'I wonder if you'd be so good as to come to our place for dinner' are not self-evidently more complex intellectually than 'Drop in at ours for a bite'. Conversely, the fact that some people do not use a high form might mean that they cannot, or it might simply be a refusal to transmit that social message. Whatever Smith's level of intelligence he would be more reluctant than Neil to use fully elaborated, high forms.

This whole area is a highly controversial one in sociolinguistics and education. Speakers of more prestige forms are likely to accept uncritically that these forms indicate a large number of intellectual virtues. Bernstein has argued that on the whole, the syntactic forms of middle-class language signal higher levels of intellectual capacity, among British speakers at least (1971). Others, including Labov, have strongly denied this, claiming that these forms are equivalent to low-status forms in their essential content, their differences simply being stylistic. We discuss this complex issue further in Chapter 9. It clearly matters a great deal which of the two positions is more right; but whatever final conclusion one comes to, it is certainly the case that many H-forms merely carry prestige, and do not of themselves show or enable a higher level of thought, while L-forms have their own distinctive function, and do not necessarily indicate inability to conceptualise.

Language and situation

Each individual marker is potentially ambiguous on its own, since it could define either the speaker or the occasion. A relatively broad accent or low vocabulary could signify an L-speaker, or an H-speaker in an informal situation. In practice, the fact that there are so many markers means that mistakes will not often be made. However, there is different access to the two basic kinds of language. High-status speakers can use either full H, or a kind of L. Low-status speakers are not expected to function in H-situations, and are effectively silenced by not having a full set of H-forms. The L-forms are felt to be basic, with H-forms added on as an extra resource for specific functions and situations. This has interesting effects on what the two forms signify. H is associated with power and prestige, but it is a language reserved for formal occasions. It is felt to be an inappropriate language for expressing intimate meanings. A high-status lover would not want to have to say to his beloved: 'I wonder if you'd be so good as to engage in osculation with me?' L forms, then, signify both low status, and also intimacy, warmth and directness of relationship. These are general cultural meanings, shared to differing degrees by all speakers in a society. This ambiguity of reference, then, affects the social stereotype signified by the speech form.

The broad Australian accent goes with the image of the real Aussie, and the ideology of mateship, a man who is plain and direct in his dealings, able to express himself forcefully (if over a limited range, and not to women), strongly physical, anti-intellectual, good in a fight, weak at arguing. What seems to be happening is that major polar categories of a culture, such as male-female, mind-body, abstract-concrete, private-public, become the content of a mythology which refers to two primary classes; and the two kinds of language come to signify this full set of categories, becoming rich but contradictory, and out of contact with the social reality of individuals. Labov's study showed that middle-class people more consistently saw L-speakers as good street-fighters. The H-speakers here reflect the stereotype more directly, with its positive as well as its negative qualities. Either way, they are liable to misjudge individuals who use L-forms. Conversely, the stereotype of the H-speaker, especially strong with L-speakers, is that of a pompous, cerebral, alienated individual.

A final problem with judgments about low-class speakers was pointed out by Labov (1969). He strongly criticised the procedures of Bereiter and Engelmann, who had argued that children from ghetto areas were virtually without language at the age of four, on the basis of interviews carried out with a number of such children. Labov showed why this was likely to happen by first showing a typical interview between a large, friendly white interviewer and a young black, who was almost totally inarticulate, used no complete sentences, and was silent longer than he was speaking. Labov then showed a black interviewer with another young boy, who was still semi-articulate, then another interview with the boy's friend there too, plus a bag of chips and an air of informality. The linguistic behaviour changed dramatically. We saw with Smith that his verbal behaviour in what he saw as a hostile situation, the job-interview, gave a poor indication of his capacity to think. The transcript of the general interview shows many signs of the inhibiting effect of the situation. In order to have a better basis for judgment we would need to see him talking with close friends, in a relaxed setting. We must realise that what is apparently the same situation for Neil and Smith — an interview with a middle-class educated interviewer — is probably perceived very differently by them. Labov's point is that this difference can even affect what are regarded as objective test situations.

Markers of sex

In any spoken utterance, there is another marker of great significance: pitch. Again, we have a basic division into two levels, high pitch and low pitch; and again there is ambiguity, because high pitch can signify either a child or a female. These significances of course have their biological foundation, but they have acquired a social significance too. So a person who is biologically female but has a low voice may be perceived as masculine. There are many other markers which serve, like status-markers, not only to label but also to define sexuality. We have seen that female speakers typically use slightly higher forms than do males of the same status level. This might seem to signify ambition, or social aspirations. The language used by women is largely the same as that used by men in our society, but there are typically differences, in degree if not in kind. For instance, female English-speakers generally use raised weak syllables more often than males. Australian English has a characteristic rising tone at the end of sentences which are not questions, signalling uncertainty and inviting confirmation from the hearer. Women probably use this form more often than men. Women's pitch-range is probably greater than men's, signifying that they are more expressive and emotional.

There are also differences in non-verbal communication. Women smile more often than men — a characteristic that one writer has traced back to the submissive behaviour of chimpanzees. They more often tilt their head on one side when talking. Men, however, scratch or rub themselves more often. In vocabulary, there are adjectives used more often by women than men, and vice versa. Typical 'female' adjectives include expressions of positive feeling, like 'adorable', and intensifiers like 'absolutely wonderful'. Taboo words like 'shit' are less taboo for males in masculine company than for females. This is an area where insufficient research has been done, but what there is suggests that there are sets of features that are more strongly associated with either sex, and which not only label them, but also signify qualities of the sexual stereotype. So the qualities signalled by women's language include snobbishness, uncertainty, deference, aimiability and emotionality. A female who avoids giving these signals will seem unfeminine, though she will probably still be sending some signals of femininity, such as high voice pitch, or women's clothing. She will therefore be transmitting contradictory messages, in effect saying 'I am an anomalous female, an unfeminine woman'.

These markers serve to maintain sexist attitudes and roles, because they repeat and endorse sex-role stereotypes continuously and habitually, and they operate as the basis of strong, uncritical judgments on the self and others. Conformity to the sex stereotype is felt as easier and more 'natural', whereas departures from it will be conscious, artificial and 'odd'. A female teacher will be a female as well as a teacher, either confirming sex-role stereotypes through what she says and how she says it, or in some ways invalidating these stereotypes. Since the systems of stereotypes are so numerous and subtle and have been learnt so easily, it is difficult to be conscious of all these signals, or to modify them in a way that feels natural — if the person wants to do so. Sexism in education is a highly controversial issue. In this book we only want to point out how subtle and pervasive sexism is in communication, in schools as in the society outside.

Markers of race

As well as indicating class or status, forms of language signify race or nation. People for whom English is a second language will often speak with a different pronunciation, and use different syntactic forms. These differences are not always as systematic or significant as the differences we have looked at so far. They trigger off stereotypes, but they do not define these stereotypes as systematically as does a class language, for instance. Where speakers mean to speak a more standard English, their performance can be legitimately seen as a departure from the norm. With such speakers it does not create as much social solidarity as the original language does, and as L-forms do.

However, over time, some non-standard varieties of English do acquire the characteristics of a language. They become a language system which is adequate to the needs of the speakers of it, who constitute a full language community. Labov is again a major researcher in this area (1970). He studies Non-standard Negro English (NNE). Some educationists in America had regarded NNE as simply defective English, which ought to be replaced by proper English (White standard/middle-class English) through a language training programme. Labov argued that NNE was systematically different, but not inferior. The language expressed a culture which had its own richness. He saw in it the kinds of quality we have seen typically associated with L-languages: warmth of feeling and directness of speech, and the solidarity of a close oral community.

Non-standard Aboriginal English (NAE) raises similar problems, perhaps in a more acute form. NAE has not stabilised into an autonomous language system like NNE in New York. There is a continuum of varieties merging into standard English (see Malcolm 1979). Many Europeans regard NAE as defective English, and its characteristic forms signify for them stereotypic meanings about Aboriginal life and culture. There is a tendency to see NAE as a crude signifier. The further the forms used are from standard English, the more difficult they will be to comprehend, for typical Europeans. It is temptingly easy to make the judgment that this incomprehensibility is a sign of lack of intelligence, and of 'Aboriginality' generally. So by transference, it becomes a sign of everything the hearer associates with Aborigines. In this way, the linguistic form simply triggers off racial prejudices; and because NAE forms are difficult to understand, and Aborigines often feel ill at ease in talking with Europeans, there may not be much in the verbal performance to challenge these prejudices. This is an area where teachers with classes containing Aboriginal children need to work hard to avoid making simplistic judgments on their pupils.

Language and social interaction

So far, we have looked at linguistic signals of relationships of power and solidarity in society at large. There are also systems of signs which organise exchanges between individuals. One such system is terms of address. [See Brown and Ford (1961), Brown and Gilman (1960).] To show how this system works, let us take just two components; first names, and title plus last name. The two terms are adequate to indicate two primary aspects of the relationship between individuals: power, and solidarity or intimacy. That is, two terms can communicate four possible relationships between two individuals, with one of them either more or less powerful than the other, and their relationship either close or distant. If T1 and T2 are teachers, and S1 and S2 are students, we might have:

T1 → S1   Hello Jill.   S1 → T1   Hello Mr Smith.
T1 → T2   Hello Fred.   T2 → T1   Hello Joe. (informal)
T1 → T2   Good morning Mr Jones.   T2 → T1 Good morning Mr Smith (formal)
S1 → S2   Hello Jill. S2 → S1   Hello Marie.
S1 → T1   Hello Joe.   T1 → S1 (Thinks: That girl is being rather familiar) Watch it, Marie!

From this we can see how the system works. Meaning is carried not only by the choice of first name or title and surname, but also by the sequence. If first names are used by both persons, it indicates a close relationship with an equality of power. If first name is used by one person, and the response is title plus last name, the message is the inequality of power. But when first name is used in response to first name from someone who is meant to be more powerful, this is regarded as a serious transgression. This makes the two kinds of term of address ambiguous on their own. First name either signifies a close, friendly relationship, or interaction with an inferior, or it is offensive. Title plus last name indicates respect for a superior, or a formal relationship between equals, or a coolness between good friends. The full system of terms of address in English has more gradations. At the formal end, there are differences between Mr. Smith and Mr. F. Smith or Sir. At the lower end, there is the possibility of even greater refinement, with various nicknames indicating different relationships of intimacy, with family nicknames near the extreme.

In Australian playgrounds, a common intimate form is monosyllabic surname + ie. So the series for John Watts would be Sir — Mr. Watts — John Watts — John — Wattsie, with the two extremes only usable on occasions of formality or intimacy respectively. With such a series, a progression along it will be interpreted as an advance in intimacy. But the power dimension will remain a covert signal, because the more powerful participant will usually initiate the other's move towards a more intimate form ('Call me Fred'). In a society where power differences are often masked by an egalitarian ideology, such as Australia, we can also have the illusion of reciprocity, whereby an inferior has been given permission to use first name but in conversation uses nothing. In the mind of the superior, intimacy has been established, but the inferior is reluctant to presume on it. This is a common kind of communication failure, since superiors think they are signalling intimacy but are felt to be still communicating power.

As well as terms of address, there are innumerable other ways of signalling power and solidarity, thus helping to control social behaviour. H and L forms of language play a general role here. H forms generally signal formality and social distance, while L forms signal intimacy. Like terms of address, the total meaning of the form is carried by the sequence of the exchange. Take these alternative ways of giving an order:

1. Smith, would you mind opening the door?
2. Joe, go and open the door.
3. Joe, open the bloody door.

In 1, the speaker is maintaining distance, and an appearance of equality with Smith through his syntax. In 2, term of address and language are both L, which expresses greater intimacy. But the social meaning of this is ambiguous. If the expected response is 'Yes sir', then it is non-reciprocal intimacy, which is a mark of power. If a possible response is 'No, you open it yourself', then it is a sign of familiarity. The third version is either non-reciprocal, to a complete inferior, or it is addressed to someone who is on very friendly terms with the speaker, and might reply in a similar tone.

The total set of systems in this area is extremely complex, and their correct use requires a subtle and precise understanding of social relationships. Part of the problem is the systematic ambiguity of the signs. This ambiguity is highly functional, which only makes the problems more acute. The social reason for the ambiguity is that claims about power and solidarity are often risky, and it is useful to be ambiguous about them. Even in a classroom, where relationships are basically well defined, with the teacher relatively remote and powerful, there is a constant need to re-negotiate relationships. Sometimes the teacher will not wish to emphasise the remoteness or relative power so much. There are subtle gradations depending on the formality of the situation, the numbers involved, and the nature of the task. Different teachers develop their own characteristic balance of power and equality, solidarity and remoteness. In a classroom, use of L forms creates cohesion, but if it encourages reciprocation, it is liable to lead to challenges to the teacher's power. People in positions of power are likely not to notice the power dimension in their more friendly interactions with inferiors. Where teachers use first names of students, accompanied with smiles, etc., they are usually more conscious of the message of solidarity. The message of power is only conveyed by the students not using the teacher's first name in reply. The power remains concealed from the surface of the exchange. It is only revealed when a student accidentally or deliberately breaks the rules.

For students, the rules are at their most complex and create most anxiety when they are negotiating a new group. This is so for everyone, since any individual has to have a finely tuned judgment about the stage of relationship and the appropriate language. It is especially true for people from different cultures. The systems in this area are so sensitive to cultural variation that even such similar cultures as American, Australian and English have significant differences. The difficulties for newcomers are especially great, because they will usually be classified as inferior simply because they are different, and the rules governing the development of relationships of solidarity generally require that the superior take the initiative. So newcomers cannot go too quickly to what is interpreted as a familiar form or they will be regarded as 'pushy' — that is, seeming to claim too much power. But if they use remote forms, or retreat into silence, they may remain outside the group.

Successful entry into the full set of groups in which a typical student participates requires a precise knowledge of both linguistic rules and social rules. (See also Chapter 7.) Neither set of rules is ever clearly spelled out, and they both contain inherent contradictions, so that an individual needs intuitive judgment to steer an appropriate course in a variety of situations. None of this is taught in schools, and most individuals develop enough facility to survive, so it might not seem to be a proper concern for a teacher. But students are social animals, and unhappy students do not learn so well. A class with a strong sense of solidarity is a happy class, with a high morale, if everyone understands the rules and can negotiate the prevailing relationship between power and solidarity.

Conclusion

There are many differences, in ways of speaking 'English' and in forms of vocabulary and syntax, which still count as English. Systematic differences can be recognised as distinctive styles of speech or writing. Such styles then carry, over and above the particular content, information about the person's social status, sex and race. They also contain clues about the speech situation. But hearers also make further inferences about qualities of character and mind, which connect features of language with common social stereotypes. So differences of style trigger off stereotype judgments about individuals which can be alienating and inaccurate. Teachers and students are members of society, and will tend to share some of the prevailing social and linguistic prejudices. Teachers will be judged, and they will make judgments, along the grain of such prejudices. Since teachers have a responsibility to educate, not to transmit prejudices, they need to have insight into what these common prejudices are and how they are carried through language.

Qualities of language also organise relationships between individuals as they interact in a group. Teachers need to be able to adjust to the requirements of different situations and relationships, balancing friendliness and authority as appropriate. They need to appreciate the difficulties of the codes and the judgments students have to work with, both in and outside the classroom. They have to cope with students who transgress these complex unwritten rules through ignorance, as well as those whose transgressions are deliberate and cunning manipulations of the common codes.

Suggested activities

1. Listen carefully to tapes of two speakers who are different in speech forms and background (social class, sex, race) and make a list of sounds, vocabulary and syntactic forms that distinguish the two speech types. Or use a stereotype character from a radio or television show, like Paul Hogan.

2. Isolate a significant variable — for example, a particular vowel or consonant pattern, or vocabulary feature — and make two tapes of a text varying the significant form. Then get others to make judgments on the character and intellectual abilities of the two speakers.

3. Present the same essay in two forms, one tidy with correct spelling and punctuation, the other untidy and full of errors, and get it marked with comments by two groups. Note the comments on ideas, and the influence of judgments based on qualities of form.

4. Tape an informal conversation, then try to rewrite it in a more formal language. What is the nature of the changes? Or compare a speaker in both situations (for example, as in the Nixon Watergate tapes, with Nixon's formal speeches). What judgments would you make about the speaker's intelligence and character on the basis of his speech forms in the different situations?

5. Write a dialogue of someone deliberately breaking the rules in a power relationship (for example, a cheeky child to a teacher or parent; or a first year teacher to a principal). What are the rules you have isolated?

The Medium of
Communication

Chapter 3 Wilfred D'Souza
Non-verbal Communication

When people think of language primarily in terms of the words they say or write, they ignore the very significant role played by non-verbal communication. Ray Birdwhistell (1972) estimates that in a normal, two-person conversation the verbal band (that is, the actual words spoken) carries less than 35% of the social meaning of the situation. More than 65% is transmitted via non-verbal bands. These non-verbal bands relate to how people speak, move, gesture, and handle spatial relationships. Thus both *kinesics*, the study of movement and *proxemics*, the study of the ways in which space is handled, are important aspects of non-verbal communication. So are changes in pitch, loudness and length of sound and even such sounds as giggling, laughing, crying, moaning, groaning, whispering and yelling. Many of us are not consciously aware of many of these activities, but they are a necessary part of the communication act.

Intonation

Intonation patterns are the tunes that accompany our speech. These 'tunes' carry important messages about the speaker's attitude to subject and audience. (See Halliday in Kress 1976.) Intonation patterns also help to organise the meaning of sentences. They are part of the grammar of the language. Speakers who speak in a continuous monotone are not only boring, they are failing to communicate on a major channel. Without communication on this channel, the organisation of a sentence is difficult to follow. Intonation is a key to meanings as well as feelings.

Note the following exchange between an interviewer and a 16-year-old pupil, 'Adrian':

LET'S MOVE ON TO THE WHAT WE'VE CALLED THE
PROCEDURES WHEN YOU WRITE DO YOU FIND IT DIFFICULT
TO PUT YOUR IDEAS INTO WORDS? sorta ah yeah keep
thinkin' some'times I think I think ahead of what I'm writing and

I can't write fast enough to write about to write about what I'm
thinking so and sometimes you um think about a subject for a
while and nothing'll come into head but all of a sudden bang
y'know I've got a really good idea and I can get stuck into it but
if if I don't get an idea I's just sortta can't waffle on or start
writing it, so that doesn't work.

Sooby (1979)

Consider the interviewer's first contribution. This is a text which can
be spoken in different ways with very different effects. Intonation, like
other sign systems, works by building up a small number of basic units.
With intonation the main variables are stress (relative emphasis), speed
and continuity (pauses or mergings), and pitch. Between them, these
elements organise the text, reinforce syntax, imply meanings, and
communicate attitudes and feelings. To see what they contribute, first
try reading it out with unvarying stress, continuity and pitch:
Lets-move-on-to-the-what-we've-called-the-procedures. It is difficult to
understand what the simple words are saying.

In analysing the contribution of each of these elements, we shall take
stress first, trying out different stress patterns. In this first sentence, it
would be natural to have a minor stress on *on*, in the first group of
words (up to *the*), and a major stress on *procedures*. The stress
functions to organise the group of words, giving a focus, with a definite
stress on the minor component and a stronger stress on the most
significant group of words. So the stress patterns give a good guide
about priorities in the sentence. Where the stresses are not clear, it is
much more difficult to attend to what really matters in the sentence.

However, other stress patterns are possible. For instance, you could
stress *we've* or *called*. One implication of putting the main stress here is
the same as before. This is the part of the message which is being
brought into prominence. But an emphatic stress of this kind also works
contrastively. If you stress *we've*, you're implying that there are other
people who do not call them this. Similarly, if you stressed *called* you
would be implying a contrast with some other action. Contrastive stress
works as a shorthand for bringing in meanings you have rejected.
Clearly this makes a much more complex message — one which might
be too complicated for a hearer who is not quite sure what the
contrasted term is. So speech which is full of contrastive stresses is
dense, complex and interesting for someone who follows its twists, but
mystifying for someone who does not.

The second element we shall look at is pitch. Since people's voices
have such differences of basic pitch, it is relative pitch which is
significant — movements up or down relative to that person's normal
pitch. The most natural way of reading this first sentence out seems,
like stress, to give a guide to its overall structure. The first sentence
would be

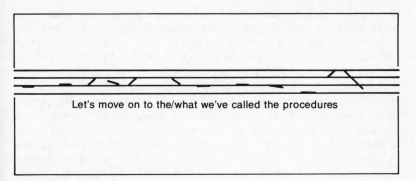

Let's move on to the/what we've called the procedures

Fig. 3.0

The melodic line indicates the shape of the main groups of words, and their relation to each other. In general, a rising pitch indicates a connection forwards with what follows, while a falling pitch indicates a connection backwards, with what has gone before. We can now see these interact with stress by considering two ways of contrastively stressing *we've*. A falling stress pushes the hearer back to an earlier part of the utterance when we shall find the alternative which is being rejected: 'they've called it that: *we've* called it this'. A rising stress points forwards to a following explanation: 'we've called it this, though others call it that'. But in actual conversation these forms are often used without the assumed or promised form occurring. We take it for granted that others know what we mean without our having to say it.

Pitch is a way of organising a complex sentence. Movements of pitch serve the same function as conjunctions like 'although', 'and' and so on. One reason why spoken language transcribed often seems less complex than written language is because pitch movements are usually left out. In this case 'procedures' could be said with a rising intonation, indicating that the idea in that sentence is still incomplete. With written forms, punctuation, for example a colon, ellipsis, dots, etc., has to perform such functions. These are indications of the subtle connection between two sentences/ideas which speakers can manage by tone of voice. The intonation pattern with 'procedures', however, might be a strong falling pitch. That closes off the sentence, and makes it completely separate. Someone who does this at every pause in every sentence will be fragmenting a discourse, thus disturbing the sense of continuity. This habit makes a speech hard to listen to and hard to follow over a long stretch.

A rising pitch at the end of a sentence has the opposite significance, that the sentence/thought is not complete. One common effect of this is to make the sentence a question, though we have noted (see Chapter 2) that in Australian English there is a tendency to use this intonation pattern when there is no question intended. For the standard form of question in English, there would be two signals indicating a question here: intonation, plus 'do you' at the beginning. But sentences with the grammatical form of a question can be said with a falling intonation at the end, indicating a closed field. That is, it is a question which is complete without its answer; a question which is not really a question. Alternatively, the first sentence could have finished with a rising tone on 'procedures', in which case it would indicate tentativeness. The person listening would be likely to say 'O.K.', as though he had been asked it as a question. It is possible to have a rising tone at the end of every sentence, which will seem to be inviting the hearer to complete the thought. At the other extreme, questions can be put which exclude answers. 'Can you get the chalk' is a kind of command, not a real question. Characteristic intonation patterns are an important and sensitive indicator of teachers' attitudes to student response, which are certainly picked up by students. Teachers would do well to listen closely to their own characteristic tones on such occasions.

Breaks and pauses are another signal of the shape of an utterance, but they are sometimes misleading. People indicate the end of a thought by a slight break. But they also pause, often with an 'er' or 'um' when they are trying to find the right word. The boy in this interview is doing this a lot. He also repeats words or phrases for the same reason. 'Sometimes I think I think ahead of what I'm writing and I can't write fast enough to write about to write about what I'm thinking'. The repetition of 'I think' allows the boy time to choose the right word. This serves to draw attention to the word that follows *ahead*, just as heavy emphasis does. What word has been rejected? It is hard to guess, in this instance. Lots of hesitations break up the text, and invite this kind of brief and often unproductive speculation. Hesitations go with careful thinking (see Goldmann — Eisler 1963), but they can also be irritating, since the careful thinking often remains private. So this boy might be judged a thoughtful speaker, or he might be regarded as someone who is difficult to follow.

Relative speed is another signal. People tend to race through phrases they are familiar with, so that the words merge into each other. The result is often difficult to follow for someone who is not so familiar with those phrases. 'Letusmoveontothe' as said by this interviewer might have been incomprehensible to a non-native English speaker, who might not have been able to separate the words out. The blurring together would indicate to such a listener that this is almost to be treated as a single word, and the fact that the component parts were known individually would not be sufficient help. But for someone who is familiar with the phrase as a whole, the merging together is actually helpful, since it indicates, rightly, that the whole phrase is to be taken as a single unit. Someone who separates out every word will be equally hard to follow: 'Lets, move, on, to, the . . .'. In speaking, judgments about the pacing of the utterance, and different parts of it, can be important; yet most people hardly notice their speed of utterance or make efforts to adjust it for different kinds of audience.

Paralanguage

So far we have emphasised the basic contribution of intonation patterns to comprehension, since that is a role that is not generally appreciated. Intonation also has an expressive role, which is built up out of the same basic building blocks, plus a few others. Pitch variations have expressive value. So do differences of speed and loudness. These elements combine to give a large set of messages about attitudes or feelings. Take, for instance, 'Y'know I've got a *really good idea*'. With slow delivery, separating each word, heavy emphasis, low and falling pitch at the end this would express disappointment or perhaps sarcasm. An accelerating delivery with rising pitch expresses enthusiasm, and so on. These decodings are crude and simplified. Try out different ways of saying the same sentence. You will be surprised at how many different shades of feeling you can communicate in this way. Intonation communicates relatively unconsciously. Teachers, however, need to be more conscious of this aspect of speech. Otherwise they may communicate inappropriate attitudes, or by speaking in an unvarying monotone not communicate anything.

It is important to understand how these and other features of the sound of the human voice communicate meanings along with the actual words spoken. An influential figure working in this field was George L. Trager, who gave it the name *paralanguage*, meaning communication alongside language. According to Trager (1958) there are two main classes of paralinguistic sound: voice qualities, and vocalisations. Voice qualities operate as background characteristics of people's voices: their pitch-range, articulation control, tempo and rhythm. Much information can be conveyed, usually without much conscious attention, by the voice qualities. The interviewer we quoted, for instance, had a clear baritone voice and precise articulation, communicating among other things enthusiasm and self-confidence. Adrian, on the other hand, spoke more hesitantly and with less precise articulation. We might ask whether these qualities should be called communication, or whether they are simply signs whose significance is seen by an observer but is not intended by the person concerned. The question raises important issues; but whichever we decide, these aspects of the spoken utterance are certainly worthy of close attention.

Vocalisations, according to Trager's scheme, refer to particular sound effects introduced into the stream of speech. He classified these into three groups: vocal characterisers, vocal qualifiers, and vocal segregates. Vocal characterisers refer to phenomena such as laughing, crying, moaning or groaning. They are generally sounds without words, their effect normally being to communicate attitudes or feelings. If Adrian were quietly sobbing, for instance, while lamenting that he 'can't waffle on', that would be a powerful indication of what he feels about writing problems. If he laughed, his attitude would be more detached and ironic. Vocal segregates are isolated sounds which conventionally carry particular meanings but are not words. Examples include expressions of disapproval like 'poh' or 'brr'. Adrian does not use any in this passage, and they are not normally a large part of anyone's communication. Vocal qualifiers, however, are pervasive. They are the use of features of the sound such as intensity (loud or soft), pitch height (high or low), and extent (drawl or clipping) which we have already looked at. These can modify parts of utterances to indicate quite subtle shifts of attitude. In Chapter 2 we saw how this can happen unconsciously to indicate feelings of uneasiness that the speaker does not particularly wish to communicate.

Proxemics

Some thirty inches from my nose
The frontier of my person goes,
And all the untilled air between
Is private pagus or demense.
Stranger, unless with bedroom eyes
I beckon you to fraternise,
Beware of rudely crossing it.
I have no gun but I can spit.

W.H. Auden *About the House.*

Auden is right. We all act as though there were a boundary line around our body. In fact there is a number of boundary lines, indicating stages of intimacy, with sexual intercourse the most intimate. The significant distances vary slightly for different individuals, situations and cultures. Edward Hall (1959) estimates that it is at about 45–50 centimetres that Americans get anxious with strangers of the same sex.

Hall named this area of communication *Proxemics*. Space or distance is a medium of communication, a set of signs with particular properties, and proxemics is the study of these systems. Individuals can vary the distance between them continuously. This makes distance a very sensitive communicator of proxemic messages. Proxemic language directly codes only one type of message, but that is a crucial one: intimacy and lack of intimacy. It codes this meaning powerfully, because it is a natural sign system, common to men and animals. Because it is felt as natural, it is often felt to be more reliable than words. If you say 'I love you' but hold yourself at a distance, your body is likely to be believed more than your words.

Proxemic codes can be used also to transmit messages of power. The invisible line marks the boundaries of the self's sphere of power. Anyone who crosses that line without permission is felt to be violating private space. Such violations are typically experienced as aggression, pushiness, hostility: the assertion of power. Conversely, anyone who withdraws from closeness is communicating not only rejection of intimacy, but also control over a larger sphere of space around the self: coolness, and also power. The proxemic code works in parallel with other systems communicating power and solidarity examined in Chapter 2. Since there is a number of such systems, they can reinforce each other in a stable system, or contradict one another in a conflict situation.

Auden draws attention to eye contact as another signal of intimacy ('bedroom eyes'). Frequent and extended eye-contact is another signal of intimacy (unless it is unreciprocated, in which case it becomes offensive staring). If an individual invades the body space of another by coming too close, the typical tendency is for eye contact to be greatly reduced. That way, the proxemic meaning (intimacy) is cancelled out, so that the total message is what the invaded individual feels is the true level of intimacy, though the tension of the imposed relationship also would be communicated.

In a classroom, the arrangement of desks and chairs is an important realisation of the proxemic code. This is the institution's (and/or the teacher's) version of the typical relationships in the teaching situation. If the arrangement is fixed, that is a further message, that relationships are non-negotiable. Against the background of this general system, individual proxemic messages gain their meaning. For instance, in a formal classroom setting, a child turning round and establishing eye contact with another child at a distance of one metre has established a forbidden level of intimacy for that situation.

To illustrate how these messages work, take the following description of a classroom:

Classroom setting.

Very decorated room, pictures and mobiles. A light and airy room with a pleasant atmosphere.

Lots of instructions calling the children to order such as 'feet on the floor'. It is important for the chairs to be straight and the room to be orderly.

The room is a bit cramped, desks in groups of six. Teacher sits at one of these and groups of children come to her for work on specific topics. She uses a desk at the front when addressing the whole class.

There are sections at the back of the room put aside for special activities. A carpeted square at the back of the room for news and stories, and another little enclave for silent reading.

Teacher has a pleasant accepting tone, uses a lot of questions.
Deals with one child at a time.

(Example contributed by Anne Davidson)

This class has three spaces, characterised by different kinds of relations.
The main classroom area is obviously fairly formal, with rectangular
structures, though children can move around. The carpeted square
allows children to sit more informally and closer: maximum intimacy
but in a large group. The silent reading area is presumably one where
maximum privacy is possible, an area where no invasions are allowed
(though they may happen, of course).

The observer of this classroom felt that it was 'cramped'. Teachers
are often not in control of how many children they have to teach in a
given space. So what happens to proxemic messages in this typical situation? To some degree for many people, proxemic messages are simply
cancelled out or not attended to. To do this, however, requires an effort
of will. It takes the same kind of energy as blotting out any other message or stimulus. So adults can stand packed together in a lift or a football crowd and not react to proximity as meaningful. But even so there
is often a sense of claustrophobia or panic, even if that is not conscious,
and there will be a sense of relief when the boundary can be restored.

The strategies for coping with proxemic messages of excessive
intimacy are compensatory actions to remove the sense of closeness.
Lack of eye contact, and aversion generally, are common strategies.
This classroom arranges children in groups of six. (See Figure 3.1.)

Fig. 3.1 Pupil Arrangement in Classroom

Take child E. If the chairs are straight, as this teacher requires, the relationship with D and F is not felt as threateningly close, because eye
contact can be avoided. A and C are potentially more threatening but
they can be avoided too. B, however, can be avoided only by E having
her eyes downwards, staring at the table in front. The best way of neu-
tralising proxemic messages is clearly to have all persons facing the
same way, as in a classroom where all desks face the front in rows.
This form of organisation respects private space to the maximum for a
given size of room. At the same time, of course, it prevents intimacy
between any individuals. It assumes that children should not interact
with each other. The only permitted relationship is every child's relationship with the teacher.

While the teacher is at the front, the proxemic message is remoteness, formality. The teacher has a large space in front of her, which signals power. She is able to move around, walking between desks as close as she likes, but children are not allowed to approach her. Without any other modifying signals, this arrangement would communicate the teacher's power, and students' lack of power. This teacher, however, allows children to approach her and presumably they will get as close as they feel comfortable though the teacher is still able to indicate subtly how close students are allowed to get. She also interacts in a friendly fashion with individual children. As so often in the teaching situation, the messages about relationships involved are complex and various, containing a personal balance of contradictory components.

A different style of teaching and proxemics comes across in this description of another class in the same school:

A fairly large room, enough space to move easily between groups of desks.

A placid, happy atmosphere.
Children in uniform, nun in habit. Teacher puts her arm around the shoulders of an inquiring child. Children come up to speak to teacher individually. Steady eye contact while explaining.

Desks in clusters of about four, the teacher's desk at the back. She does not use this to sit at and is usually moving around the room.

The size of the room here clearly allows a more interactive arrangement. The desks are in clusters, with only four at most. The arrangements allow much more interaction between children, flexibly controlled by them; also more invasion of intimate space, which might be felt as threatening by children who are shy. This teacher invades body space by touching children, which is either high intimacy or extreme invasion. She does not remain in a fixed, distant position in front. She has a desk at the back, but does not use it. This asserts relationships of intimacy between teacher and students, as well as between students. The first teacher valued weaker bonds of both kinds, but seemed to encourage the individual student-teacher relationship more strongly than relationships between the children. The second teacher's classroom is characterised by intimacy, or invasions of the self. To some, it will seem to have a 'relaxed, happy atmosphere'. To others, classrooms with this kind of prevailing organisation might seem too noisy, interfering with individuals' ability to work on their own. There is no separate area for private reading; but in this example as in the other, some of the messages modify others. The teacher, a nun, is in a habit, the children in uniforms, indicating that formal, distant relationships are the norm. Individual teachers do not always have total freedom about the messages they transmit, in proxemic or other channels; nor do children. As educators, however, teachers should be aware of the full set of messages transmitted in a particular situation whether or not they are in control of them, because that is what the children will receive.

Kinesics

Kinesics is another useful term to describe a kind of non-verbal communication. It refers to the use of movements of the face and body to communicate. The main researcher in this area is Ray Birdwhistell (1973). Birdwhistell analyses the kinds of movement which are significant for American speakers. Examples include raising or lowering the eyebrows, nodding the head etc. He sees meanings of this kind as built up from a few basic building blocks. A typical gesture, such as eyebrow movement, is like the stem of a word. The complete 'word' is made up of a stem (for example, moving eyebrows) with a further addition (for example downwards movement). In this example, the 'word' means strong concentration. If combined with narrowed eyes it can mean anger. Accompanied by scratching of the head, it can indicate puzzlement.

There is no need to be too technical in analysing the meaning of gestures and facial expressions. One main difficulty for the analyst is the speed and subtlety of gestures and facial expressions. This means that they often act unconsciously for everyone concerned.

'He that has eyes to see and ears to hear may convince himself that no mortal can keep a secret. If his lips are silent, he chatters with his finger tips, betrayal oozes out of him at every pore.' So wrote Freud in 1905.

But the eyes and ears required to see this kind of message often have to be helped by technology: videotapes played over and over, or high-speed photographs. But children in classrooms have an alternative to technology. They see the same gestures repeated again and again, and finally some children can mimic the teacher's typical gestural messages, which everyone recognises with instant delight — everyone, perhaps, except the teacher.

As an example, look at the photograph of a teacher teaching some Vietnamese children (Figure 3.2). Note the eyes and eyebrows first. The central girl is looking upwards, not at the teacher: meaning 'I can't do it'. Neither the boy on the left nor the girl on the right is looking at either teacher or central girl. What does that say? The teacher's eyebrows are raised (inquiring) and she is looking at the central girl (you answer). Look at the mouths. The central girl has an open-mouthed smile. Its meaning for an Australian, combined with the eye movement, would be something like 'I can't do this and I am ridiculous'. But this girl is Vietnamese. The meaning of a smile for Vietnamese is very different. They smile on occasions which would be inappropriate in white Australians: when they are being reprimanded and corrected (as here), for instance, or when they feel confused, shy, or even disappointed or angry (Doung Thanh Binh 1975).

Fig. 3.2 Some Teacher-Pupil Attitudes

The Vietnamese smile can be used also as a polite screen to hide fear or contrition. White Australian teachers have been irritated and frustrated when Vietnamese students smile in what appear to be the wrong time and place. They cannot understand how the students can smile when reprimanded, when not understanding the lessons explained, and especially when they should have given an answer to the question instead of sitting still and smiling quietly. The Vietnamese people smile about almost everything and anything. This enigmatic smile in all circumstances, unhappy as well as happy, is puzzling to white Australian teachers. The boy, however, is not smiling, and the girl on the right covers her mouth. The teacher does not smile. A wide smile would carry the message 'I find you or your problems ridiculous'. So the non-smile means 'I am sympathetic to your problems'. Finally, look at the postures. The central girl hugs her arms, another gesture of helplessness. The teacher leans (sympathetic) with elbows close to the body (slightly tense) and body not turned towards the girl but parallel and leaning slightly away (keeping her distance). From this example we can see some of the problems of kinesic communication across cultural barriers.

Some of the communication we have looked at transcends barriers of language and race, since movements of eyes, mouths, arms have a similar meaning for these Asian children and their European teacher; but the smile carries different meanings for the two cultures. The difference is particularly likely to create misunderstandings. With verbal communication, at least we know that we cannot understand a foreign language. With non-verbal language we may think we recognise familiar codes, but we may be seriously wrong.

Non-verbal communication and culture

Non-verbal language can differ subtly from culture to culture, and carries important messages for members of a particular culture. Here is an anecdote to illustrate how important such messages can be for a teacher. Julius Fast (1970) tells us the story of Livia, a fifteen-year-old Puerto Rican girl at high school in New York who was caught in the washroom with a group of girls suspected of smoking. Most of the group were known trouble-makers; and while Livia had no record, the principal after a brief interview was convinced of her guilt and decided to suspend her with the others because 'There was something sly and suspicious about her. She wouldn't meet my eye. She wouldn't look at me'. He blamed her attitude and not what she said. Livia's mother insisted that she was a good girl, and Puerto Rican parents demonstrated the next morning at the school. There were ugly stirrings of a threatened riot.

In this instance, John Flores, the Spanish teacher, lived only a few doors from Livia and her family. He understood the cultural background to Livia's behaviour. Summoning his own courage, he asked for an interview with the principal.

'I know Livia and her parents', he told the principal, 'and she's a good girl. I am sure there has been some mistake in this whole matter.'

'If there was a mistake,' the principal said uneasily, 'I'll be glad to rectify it. There are thirty mothers outside yelling for my blood. But I questioned the child myself, and if ever I saw guilt written on a face . . . she wouldn't even meet my eyes!'

'In Puerto Rico a nice girl, a good girl', John explained, 'does not meet the eyes of an adult. Refusing to do so is a sign of respect and obedience. It would be as difficult for Livia to look you in the eye as it would be for her to misbehave, or for her mother to come to you with a complaint. In our culture, this is just not accepted behaviour for a respectable family.'

Fortunately the principal was a man who knew how to admit that he was wrong. He called Livia and her parents and the most vocal neighbours in and once again discussed the problem. In the light of John Flores' explanation it became obvious to him that Livia was not avoiding his eyes out of defiance but out of basic demureness. Her 'slyness' he now saw was shyness. Julius Fast adds that the outcome of the entire incident was a deeper, more meaningful relationship between school and community.

Teachers need to realise the barriers that exist when teaching children from different cultures. These children are not only trying to learn lessons unfamiliar to them; they also have to adjust to a new and strange environment. Teachers will want to achieve rapport with their students, but the rules governing non-verbal communication may be different for the child. For example, a teacher when praising a Vietnamese boy must never pat his head. In Vietnamese culture the boy's head is considered sacred, the temple of his wisdom. A pat will be interpreted as desecration, not encouragement.

Communication with the Australian Aboriginal child is often difficult until one becomes aware of the customs and laws of that particular area. In the Warburton Ranges area, although the children are alike in appearance, by tribal law they are divided into *skin groups*. An interesting diagram was devised by Douglas (1964) explaining this grouping which has implications for the teacher, who should be aware of Kinship and Avoidance systems in that tribal society. According to de Hoog and Sherwood (1979) and Jacobs and Berndt (1979), teachers should make sure that children who are related to one another in terms of avoidance and constraint do not find themselves sitting, playing or mixing together. For instance, if you are setting up a discussion group, children who call each other by terms that can be translated as 'mother-in-law' and 'son-in-law' should not be put together. They should not be told to ask the other a question nor should there be any form of discussion with the other. In some areas this applies to sibling relationships. Teachers should be careful when asking these children for other people's names, especially those names of people who have died, or for the name of someone a child cannot speak freely to or about (for example, a mother-in-law). Traditionally it was not polite to address someone directly by his or her personal name. (See also Chapter 7.)

Some teachers of Aboriginal children feel that the children often encroach upon their personal space. Webber (1978) notes that there is a great deal of physical contact which accompanies verbal interaction in Aboriginal society. An implication of this which he notes for teachers is that those who rely on physical isolation, rebuke and other methods of increasing social distance in order to maintain dominance, will not be accepted by Aboriginal children.

As the preference for particular physical arrangements and interpersonal spacing is culturally determined, it would be advantageous for teachers wanting to maximise successful classroom interaction in multicultural settings to be alert to the various preferences children in their class may have. To recognise and capitalise on such choices may give opportunities to children to learn in situations which, for them, are the most comfortable. Ian Malcolm (1979) states that Aboriginal children are most likely to communicate freely when in an outdoor setting and when they are within touching distance of close friends.

Non-verbal communication and large groups

The possibilities for communication change with the size of the group. Non-verbal channels are affected, along with verbal channels. In an authoritarian teaching style, where the teacher is the main source of messages, non-verbal signs ought to reinforce the main message. Ideally, in this style the teacher dominates in all channels except writing, where students produce more than the teacher does. Only one student speaks at a time, and most non-verbal communication from students is noise — that is, alternative messages which disrupt the teacher's message.

What happens in a large classroom with an 'open' style of teaching? W. D'Souza worked with a situation of this kind in Uganda in 1965. For 200 students and six teachers, English was studied in a single room formed out of four classrooms, with other rooms available for special activities. This was a multiracial school, with European, African and Asian students — a greater mix than is usually to be found in Australian schools. Ugandan education is normally traditionally organised, so the effect of the experiment on attitudes was even more dramatic than it would be in Australia. Arrangement of furniture was a particularly powerful code in this situation. Elizabeth Richardson (1967) has written about 'the ritualistic use of chairs'. She claims that the traditional arrangement of desks symbolises the remoteness and infallibility of the teacher, and the submissiveness and helplessness of the students. She argues that just as the ritualistic use of furniture reinforces authoritarian structures, so changes in furniture can bring about innovations of attitudes and behaviour. There are subtle messages possible in this area which are dependent on general cultural attitudes. In Uganda, for instance, tables are a rare commodity, so the tables (instead of desks) scattered throughout the block carried a message of rarity or value, as well as spontaneity. In Australian schools, students are sensitive to the messages transmitted by furniture, whether it is old or new, in good or poor condition, comfortable or not, rigid or free-standing, 'adult', or associated with school and children.

The noise-level in the large room was high by traditional standards. The total quantity of communication would be greater than in traditional classrooms, because students would be communicating simultaneously. As a result the communication of teachers would be interfered with by the noise. Students also are distracted by noise, so there had to be provision for special activities protected from interference by competing messages. Drama, for instance, where communication works through all channels, verbal and non-verbal, was done in a separate area. From the point of view of a communicator, anyone else's message, whether verbal or non-verbal, is 'noise'. If we take into account non-verbal messages as well as verbal, the 'noise' potential of an open classroom situation is even greater than people usually realise. There are a lot more messages flying round; communication is richer; but a smaller proportion reach a target. There is a balance to be struck here, which will vary for different subjects, purposes and ages.

One compensation for this situation is where communication of this kind becomes part of the content of the subject. Here is a poem written by one of the students in the Block:

3A At intensive writing

Sit and watch
Stare
At every person
Stare at minds
Through a glass wall
Thoughts stealing into the mind
Fingers sliding on paper
A thought brushed away
Eyes
All glassy and silky
Jaws hanging
Concentrating
Lips twitching
To a crooked smile
To an ugly face
But work has to be done.

Susan Chacko (age 15)

It is interesting that the content of this poem is non-verbal communication, but the poem itself is effective verbal communication, done by a silent observer in an intensive *writing* class. Different forms of communication can benefit each other.

Non-verbal channels: a check list

Different writers dispute what should be included under the category of non-verbal communication. Here is a list compiled by John C. Condon and Fathi Yousef (1975), which is a useful summary of what you might include. Try to group them under general headings (for example, fixed/variable; conscious/unconscious; visual/auditory/other senses). Or explore the relevance of each for a teacher's understanding of communication and the school.

1. Hand gestures, both intended and self-directed (artistic), such as the nervous rubbing of hands.

2. Facial expressions — such as smiles, frowns, yawns.
3. Posture and stance.
4. Clothing and hair styles (hair being more like clothes than like skin, both subject to the fashion of the day).
5. Walking behaviour.
6. Interpersonal distance (proxemics).
7. Touching.
8. Eye contact and direction of gaze, particularly in 'listening behaviour'.
9. Architecture and interior design.
10. 'Artifacts' and non-verbal symbols, such as lapel pins, walking sticks, jewellery.
11. Graphic symbols, such as pictures to indicate 'men's room' or 'handle with care'.
12. Art and rhetorical forms, including wedding dances and political parades.
13. Somatypes of bodies; ectomorphs, endomorphs, mesomorphs.
14. Smell (olfaction), including body odors, perfumes, incense.
15. Paralanguage.
16. Colour symbolism.
17. Synchronisation of speech and movement.
18. Taste, including symbolism of food and the communication function of chatting over coffee or tea, oral gratification — such as smoking or gum-chewing.
19. Thermal influences, such as influences of temperature or communication, sensitivity to body heat.
20. Cosmetics: temporary — powder, lipstick; permanent — tatoos.
21. Drum signals, smoke signals, factory whistles, police sirens.
22. Time symbolism: what is too late or too early to telephone or too short to make a speech or stay for dinner.
23. Timing and pauses within verbal behaviour.
24. Silence.

Practising non-verbal skills

Microteaching methods are a valuable way of practising non-verbal skills. In the microteaching situation, prospective teachers can try out a variety of skills with feedback and evaluation. Each student should prepare a brief 5–10 minute lesson concentrating on one set or cluster of skills with a class of about four other students who can give their comments. A video-tape is also invalubale for study of non-verbal language. Some exercises that can be tried out are the following:

1. Intonation

In this exercise the teacher practises reading a list of commonly used phrases to convey different meanings, concentrating on voice inflections, pitch, tone, pauses and hesitation. An audio tape will show whether the desired effect was achieved. For example, the question 'what did you say?' might convey a threat, enthusiasm, or uncertainty, depending on the way it is said. The teacher will be made aware of these paralinguistic features.

2. Kinesics

The teacher tries to exercise particular meanings through the use of gestures, facial expressions and body movements. For example, teachers may convey enthusiasm by snapping the fingers, or clapping hands, or smiling and nodding.

3. Stimulus variation

Teachers must vary the stimuli they present to their students. If they stand still and talk in a monotone, students may get bored and 'tune them out'. Never let a lesson degenerate into a dreary monologue. Five kinds of attention-producing behaviour are practised in this exercise:

a. Gestures . . . hand, head and body movement.
b. Focussing . . . controlling the direction of students' attention by gestures and verbal statements (for example, the teacher says, 'look at this diagram' as he or she points to the board).
c. Pauses — using silence effectively.
d. Shifting sensory channels . . . shifting from one means of communication to another (such as from speech to gestures). The shift demanded of students (from ears to eyes) increases their attention.
e. Movement — simply moving around the room to vary visual and aural stimuli.

4. Non-verbal reinforcement

The teacher nods, smiles, writes the students' response on the board, or indicates disapproval non-verbally.

5. Recognising attending behaviour

The teacher should be alert to cues that reveal how much attention students are paying to the lesson. By observing students' facial expressions, body postures and other behaviour, the teacher can decide whether to continue the activity (such as lecturing), change the pace (perhaps by asking questions), or use a different means of communication (such as diagrams).

6. Silence

Usually, it is the students who use silence (consciously or not) to control the teacher. Teachers will change their tactics when they get no response from a class. The teacher may use silence to stimulate students to think, or to indicate the importance of a statement.

Chapter 4   Geoff Peel
Reading

There is a large amount of research into the theory and teaching of reading, and yet there is still no definitive account of the reading process. To understand what happens when we read is part of a wider effort to discover how the mind processes language — a search that extends from linguistics into psychology and neurology. Some awareness of the process of reading and its relation to language processing in general is necessary if we are to chart any course through the range of current approaches and methods. (Perhaps these terms are, in fact, synonymous.)

The teaching of reading is usually associated with the primary grades of school, and certainly the basic reading skills are established before the normal child moves to the secondary level. But reading is a continuously developing skill which requires specific attention through the secondary school and even into the tertiary level of education. Children must *learn* to read more efficiently. They must be able to vary their reading speed according to purpose and material; they must be able to read critically and with understanding; they must be able to apply their reading skills to a range of purposes and functions. These skills of the efficient reader are developed through their application in all curriculum areas. Reading is the concern of *all* teachers at *all* levels.

If we try to examine what we do as efficient adult readers we find that the very process of trying to analyse what is normally a subconscious process distorts that process. It is only when we encounter some degree of difficulty in our reading that we become aware of the component skills we normally employ subconsciously. Read the following short passages and consider the difficulties you experienced and how you tried to overcome, or by-pass, the problems:

1. The attacks by the Panzer divisions in the initial stages of the Blitzkrieg achieved spectacular results. Przemysl fell in the first day's fighting as the Wehrmacht pushed north from recently annexed Czechoslovakia while in the west Lodz and Bydgoszez were soon captured in the drive towards Warsaw.

2. A contingent relationship in the full sense, however, is a sequential relationship of intelligent individual occurrences where what comes after is recognized to be conditional upon what went before, not merely because before and after cannot here be reversed, nor (of course) because what went before is recognized as a causal condition or because they are recognized to be functionally related, but because they 'touch' and in touching identify themselves as belonging together and as composing an intelligible continuity of conditionally dependent occurrences.

— M. Oakeshott: *On Human Conduct*

3. As the sample size increases, the coefficient of skewness of the Fisher's transformation $z = \tanh^{-1} r$, of the correlation coefficient decreases much more rapidly than the excess of its kurtosis. Hence, the distribution of standardized z can be approximated more accurately in terms of the t distribution with matching kurtosis than by the unit normal distribution. This t distribution can, in turn be subjected to Wallace's approximation resulting in a new normal approximation for the Fisher's z transform. This approximation, which can be used to estimate the probabilities, as well as the percentiles, compares favourably in both accuracy and simplicity, with the two best earlier approximations, namely, those due to Ruben (1966) and Kraemer (1974).

Fisher (1921) suggested approximating distribution of the variance stabilizing transform $z = (1/2) \log ((1 + r)/(1 - r))$ of the correlation coefficient r by the normal distribution with mean $= (1/2) \log ((1 + p)/(1 - p))$ and variance $= 1/(n - 3)$. This approximation is generally recognized as being remarkably accurate when $|p|$ is moderate but not so accurate when $|p|$ is large, even when n is not small (David (1938)). Among various alternatives to Fisher's approximation, the normalizing transformation due to Ruben (1966) and a t approximation due to Kraemer (1973), are interesting on the grounds of novelty, accuracy and/or aesthetics. If $r = r/\sqrt{(1 - r^2)}$ and $\tilde{\rho} = \rho/\sqrt{(1 - \rho^2)}$, then Ruben (1966) showed that

$$(1) \qquad g_n(r, \rho) = \frac{\{(2n - 5)/2\}^{1/2}\tilde{r} - \{(2n - 3)/2\}^{1/2}\tilde{\rho}}{\{1 + (1/2)(\tilde{r}^2 + \tilde{\rho}^2)\}^{1/2}}$$

is approximately unit normal. Kraemer (1973) suggests approximating

$$(2) \qquad t_n(r, \rho) = \frac{(r - \rho')\sqrt{(n - 2)}}{\sqrt{(1 - r^2)}\sqrt{(1 - \rho^2)}}$$

by a Student's t variable with $(n - 2)$ degrees of freedom, where after considering various valid choices for ρ' she recommends taking $\rho' = \rho^*$, the median of r given n and ρ.

— Australian Journal of Statistics 20—3, November 1978.

4. Riverrun, past Eve and Adam's, from swerve of shore to bend of bay, brings us by a commodius vicus of recirculation back to Howth Castle and Environs.

Sir Tristram, violer d'amores, fr'over the short sea, had passencore rearrived from North Armorica on this side the scraggy isthmus of Europe Minor to wielderfight his penisolate war: nor had topsawyer's rocks by the stream Oconee exaggerated themselve to Laurens County's gorgios while they went doublin their mumper all the time: nor avoice from afire bellowsed mishe mishe to tauftauf thuartpeatrick: not yet, though venissoon after, had a kidscad buttended a bland old isaac: not yet, though all's fair in vanessy, were sosie sesthers wroth with twone nathandjoe. Rot a peck of pa's malt had Jhem or Shen brewed by arclight and rory end to the regginbrow was to be seen ringsome on the aquaface.

— James Joyce, *Finnegan's Wake*

Are there different problems when the passages are read aloud?

In the first passage the difficulties come from the German words and the Polish place names. When we encounter words from other languages that employ different spelling patterns from those in English, we are conscious of our decoding or word-attack skills in operation, skills which we have developed to deal with the spelling system of English. This, of course, is why in English we anglicise foreign place names to accord with our own pronunciation and spelling systems: København becomes Copenhagen; Nürnberg becomes Nuremberg; and Moskva, Moscow. In reading silently we may, in fact, by-pass this particular problem but in reading aloud it cannot be avoided.

The second extract poses very different problems. The vocabulary is abstract throughout, but probably the chief problem is the complex sentence construction which, although it contains sequence markers and conjunctions such as 'however', 'not merely', 'nor', 'because', is not easily predictable. We are not able to forecast or anticipate what is likely to come next. This is a good example of a sentence structure to be found almost solely in writing, hardly ever in speech. Try to examine why this is so and then think how, in conversational speech, we string together ideas which qualify, expand, and progress into a reasonably coherent argument.

The third passage is written by and for statisticians and clearly no concessions are made for the non-specialist. The technical vocabulary enables precise reference to be made while the use of mathematical symbols and formula introduces what is virtually a separate language.

The mathematical expressions could be translated into normal language only with the greatest difficulty, and inevitably the expression of the relationships would lose precision and become lengthy and unwieldy. This is a type of language use that exists only in the written mode, readable only by the specialists for whom it is written. It is a classic example of an efficient but restricted use of language.

The fourth passage strains all our reading resources, and our language resources too, by seeming to violate all our expectations about word structure, sentence patterns, and meaningfulness. Our normal processing strategies fail and we have to consider a wholly new approach if we are to realise the 'meaning' of the passage.

Basically the reading process involves the re-creation in the reader's mind of the ideas, the information, and even the emotions intended by the author. Rarely, however, are we consciously aware of the writer behind what we are reading. We tend to regard the text as autonomous, as an end in itself. This may be a source of difficulty for children. They have been used to stories told or read to them by a person to whom they can relate, who is communicating also in non-verbal ways as they talk or read, and of whom they can ask questions and who, above all, interprets the written word as expressive speech. When the child begins to read on his own he is faced with a new impersonal communication situation. Reading as a communication act is perhaps made less strange for children if they are introduced concurrently to the process of writing; they come to realise that the two activities are related as are listening and speaking.

There are probably two basic components in the reading process — decoding and prediction — and they may involve simultaneous activity at different levels of language. Figure 4.1 attempts to relate these processes to the textual features involved and also to the context in which the process takes place.

Efficient readers may use a different range of skills from beginning readers, and respond to different textual cues. They are likely to place more emphasis on prediction than word attack skills and will 'chunk' the text into larger units, both through fewer eye fixations per line and through the ability to process larger syntactic and semantic (meaning) units.

The various component skills in reading that one finds referred to in practically every book on reading can be matched with the various linguistic levels of a text. Once the reader begins to process the text at word level and above, the semantic or meaning level of language is involved. Without the apprehension of meaning, reading as a significant language activity does not occur. It is, of course, possible to read a text fluently without understanding it, perhaps because it deals with a topic outside one's experience; but it is debatable whether this is reading in the full sense, though clearly it is a response to the phonological and syntactic aspects of language structure and does involve some of the skills of efficient reading.

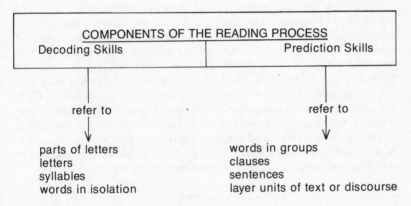

CONTEXT OF READING
1. Reader's knowledge of Language.
2. Reader's knowledge of subject about which he is reading.
3. Reader's purpose in reading.
4. Reader's perception of the function of the text.

COMPONENTS OF THE READING PROCESS

Decoding Skills	Prediction Skills

refer to — refer to

parts of letters
letters
syllables
words in isolation

words in groups
clauses
sentences
layer units of text or discourse

Fig. 4.1 Language and Reading.

Discussions of the reading process and of the teaching of reading assign different importance to the various aspects of reading. Some focus on the decoding stage. Others argue that the apprehension of meaning does not demand progression through a sound-symbol correspondence stage but rather that it is possible to proceed directly from print to meaning. To focus on these 'skills' of reading in our subsequent discussion enables us to see most clearly the links between language and reading, and especially the teaching of reading.

The model of the reading process that accords with the mature expert reader does not apply, in every aspect, to the beginning reader. The extent to which decoding, prediction and comprehension skills are employed, and the balance between them, vary according to the subject, the degree of complexity of the material being read, and the reader's ability. Obviously these component skills overlap and interact; and, although it may be necessary to focus reading instruction on one of them at a particular stage in reading development, in the *mature* reader they fuse into a total reading strategy. To see them as separate components is perhaps necessary for the teacher, but is less justifiable from a linguistic or psychological viewpoint.

Linguistics and reading

Over the last quarter of a century, linguistics has moved from a pre-occupation with structures of language, often accompanied by a total lack of interest in meaning, through a concern for the relation of grammar to meaning, to the present keen interest in semantics and the social context of language. The focus in reading has also shifted, perhaps less dramatically, from what now seems an over-concern with the relations between writing and sound to the study of psychological and even social factors.

Underlying any discussion of the reading process must be some notion of the language. This does not require an elaborate phonological or grammatical model, nor even a powerful and coherent theory of meaning, but rather an awareness of the relation between the different levels of language — between the sound and writing systems, the grammar, and the semantic level. In the foreword to the American edition of the *Breakthrough to Literacy* Teacher's Manual, Halliday (1963) suggests a simple representation of this (see Figure 4.2), or using more technical terminology, as in Figure 4.3. He says: 'Language is a system of meanings: an open-ended range of semantic choice that relate closely to the social contexts in which language is used. Meaning is encoded as wording; and wording, in turn, as speaking or writing.'

Fig. 4.2 Halliday's Suggested Semantic Levels

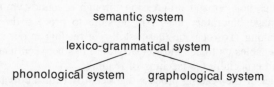

Fig. 4.3 Technical Terminology in Semantic Levels

Much of the current debate about reading and the assumptions that underlie teaching methods in reading can be related to Halliday's diagram. The psycholinguists who argue that meaning is derived directly from the written text without recourse to 'sounding' see the process as represented in Figure 4.4. The 'traditionalists' argue that, at least for some considerable time in the process of learning to read, what happens

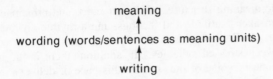

Fig. 4.4   A Psycholinguist Version

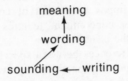

Fig. 4.5   A Traditionalist Version

is as shown in Figure 4.5. However, most would accept that as the reader becomes more efficient the 'writing — sounding-wording' path gives way to a direct 'writing-wording' one. Both views agree that meaning is primary and that the aim of efficient reading is to grasp meanings.

The relationship between speech and writing has implications for the problems involved in teaching reading (and writing) skills. Some of the difficulties that children experience can be traced back to the inherent differences between these two methods for the transmission of language. Speech, unless recorded, is transitory and is perceived as a sequence of sound, whereas writing is permanent. If we want to check on what we have heard we can, at least in a face-to-face situation, ask speakers to repeat what they have said. They may be able to do this; but it is more likely that, if they feel we have not clearly understood them, they will re-phrase their thoughts for us. In writing, readers can back-track to clarify their perception. They can re-read at leisure, but cannot ask the author to express his thoughts in a different way.

Speech is normally part of a person-to-person communication act that enables the speaker to monitor the effect on his audience of what he is saying and, if necessary, modify what he says according to their reaction. Both speaker and listener are simultaneously involved in the communication process. With writing, this type of feedback is impossible.

In the act of writing, the writer is alone and is in sole control of the first stage of the communication process. In the second stage the reader is in control and the onus is on him to interpret and understand the text; he cannot normally contact the writer to help him. Speaking and listening are concurrent; writing and reading are disjunct.

The actual words and sentences used are only part of the act of communication in speech. They are accompanied by the prosodic features of word and sentence stress; intonation; the pattern of pitch variation related to the meaning structures of the utterance and principally indicative of the speaker's attitude and feelings; and a rhythm characteristic of the language. (In English, this is based on an approximately equal time interval between stressed syllables.) In addition, there is the individual accent and tone of voice of the speaker, his pace of delivery, his use of pauses, and all the non-verbal aspects of communication such as facial expression, gesture and position. With all these, the young child is familiar; they are the context in which language is apprehended. By contrast, reading is an impoverished act of communication. It is the absence of this range of concomitant features that makes the reader forget the writer behind the printed text.

One result of these differences between speech and writing is that the written language has to be self-contained in a way that speech need not be. Writers must be explicit so that the reader can grasp the meaning accurately. This accounts, in part, for the carefully structured sentence patterns characteristic of the written language. It is possible to talk of a standard written language across the English-speaking world, whereas the extent of regional and social variation in spoken English often makes us less aware of the language patterns that are common to all spoken utterances.

In writing, each letter is recognisable as an entity and each word is separated from the next by a space, while punctuation provides a visual clue to demarcate grammatical and semantic units. In speech, the boundaries between these structural and meaning units are signalled by combinations of stress, intonation and brief pauses; but word boundaries are not necessarily explicit — we segment the continuous flow of sound into words because we know the language — and we are practically never conscious of sound elements corresponding to the letter in writing. One has only to listen to a foreign language to realise that, without knowledge of that language, word boundaries are virtually impossible to determine.

By having stories read to them, children are helped to come to terms with the written language. Through a speech activity they understand and enjoy, they come to associate the printed word with meaning and also become aware of the characteristic structures of the written language. Beyond the beginning stages, writing is not 'talk written down'. The child has to learn to respond to the characteristic features of the written language in reading, and then produce them in writing.

The context of reading

The importance of a 'rich language background' as a preparation for beginning reading is generally acknowledged. The value of mother-child conversation is often emphasised as the crucial factor in developing the child's ability to categorise experience and develop a range of language uses. Bernstein and others have indicated that the language ability of the child is related in complex ways to his social background. The importance attached to reading and to books in the home is likely to determine the child's attitude to learning to read. But whatever the background, the normal child will have acquired a considerable vocabulary and have mastered the majority of the grammatical structures by the time he begins school. Very often, the teacher who claims to be enriching the child's language in the pre-reading stage is, in fact, providing a range of experiences for the child to talk about rather than providing additional language 'resources', although, of course, new vocabulary will be acquired. This type of 'language experience' should be seen as extending and consolidating the child's ability to categorise experience through language use, and developing his functional use of language in a range of situations and for a variety of purposes.

Halliday has suggested that reading readiness might be interpreted in social and functional terms; but whatever criteria are used, the overriding factor is the desire of the child to learn to read, and this derives from a realisation of the function and purpose of reading. It is unfortunate that the term 'language experience' has been appropriated for a specific approach to reading. The language experience of the child is the *context* of reading, in which learning to read takes place. 'Language-experience' approaches aim to provide a range of experiences, to associate these with relevant talk and so provide a base for initial reading and writing. Typically the words and phrases that emerge from teacher-child talk are written down and used as initial reading material or stimulus.

The *Mount Gravatt* reading materials are based on a project in which the language used by a group of children of different ages was recorded and the frequency of occurrence of words and word groups was computed (1977). The frequently used word groups — groups such as 'I've got a —' and 'I'm going to —' — were then used as the basis of early reading materials; so that after structured oral work with the teacher, the children encounter written language using the syntactic patterns they are familiar with in their oral language.

Breakthrough to Literacy, developed by the Schools Council Programme in Linguistics and English Teaching, also uses the child's own language, but in this case the child is able to compose his own sentences using word cards that he can put into a frame (1970). A basic vocabulary is supplied but this can easily be supplemented if required. This enables the child to compose his own sentences, bypassing the problem of the slow acquisition of the motor coordination required for writing. Using the 'sentence maker' makes the child familiar with the left-to-right directionality of writing, word spaces, word order, the use of grammatical suffixes, simple punctuation and the appearance of units such as the phrase and the sentence. The scheme also makes provision for work with word structures and spelling patterns.

It is interesting to compare the approach of the *Mount Gravatt* and

Breakthrough to Literacy materials with that common to many basal reader series. Nearly all such readers employ a controlled and graded vocabulary and sentence structure, though often the basis for this control is uncertain. It is easy to criticise basal reading series, especially the early books in a series, for the unreality of their language (see Chapter 8); but one must remember that in the beginning stage children need to concentrate on word recognition, and this slows their rate of 'reading' so much that they cannot process any significant length of text as a whole in order to realise the meaning. In addition, the books may be concerned with repetition of spelling/sound patterns rather than providing a cohesive text. Clearly though, if one can develop the early skills of reading with the use of language meaningful to children, as their own language must be, then reading is seen as a real and relevant activity.

Decoding: sound and symbol

Emphasis on the decoding or word-attack skills has for long been the dominant feature of many approaches in reading. Underlying this concern is the assumption that there is, at least in the learning-to-read stage and possibly beyond, a need to transform the written symbol into its sound equivalent before there can be any recognition. This view has been challenged recently by Frank Smith (1978) in particular who, from his psycholinguistic standpoint, argues that in normal reading we cannot possibly decode into sound because our reading speed does not allow time for even sub-vocal articulation. By responding to a selective range of textual cues ranging from the critical features of letters to whole phrases and above, and by using our acquired expectations of likely sentence structures and vocabulary items in a given context, we are able to process text rapidly and derive meaning from it without recourse to an intermediate stage of saying each word to ourselves.

The contentious issue, however, is not whether Smith's account of the process as it occurs with a mature reader is correct — it is whether children in learning to read need to progress through a stage of sound realisation. Traditionally it has been assumed that they do, and it is certain that many backward readers require a specific focus on decoding skills if they are to progress. Phonics approaches have concentrated on developing sound-symbol correspondences, while look-and-say emphases have usually acknowledged the need at some stage to develop decoding skills.

Unfortunately the area of 'decoding' is beset with terminological confusion and misapprehensions about the nature of the relationship that exists between written symbol and speech sound. Both Bloomfield and Fries in their work in reading tried to clarify the terminology used, but their strictures on the looseness of much thinking in this area have been little heeded.

The three vital terms are:

Phonetics : the study of speech *sound*: the mechanisms of articulation and, in acoustic phonetics, the physics of sound.

Phonology : the study of the systems of speech sounds that are significant for speakers in each language.

Phonics : a system of teaching reading concentrating on decoding written symbols into their sound equivalents.

If these terms were generally understood we should avoid the embarrassment of statements like 'English is not a phonetic language', or 'English spelling is inefficient'. Such sentiments reveal serious misconceptions about the real nature of sound-symbol correspondence in English and seem to be shared by those who periodically call for the reform of English spelling. A close one-to-one relationship between written symbol and speech sound is rare in the world's languages, Finnish perhaps being nearest to this illusory ideal. There are other more powerful relationships possible between sound and writing systems. Furthermore, unless inevitable changes in pronunciation are matched over the years by recurrent spelling reforms with all the disruption they cause, the degree of correspondence will in time become less close.

What, then, is the relationship in English between sound and symbol? In order to answer this, two further terms need to be explained — *phoneme* and *grapheme*.

The concept of a *phoneme* has been a fundamental one in linguistics in general and phonology in particular. There is no absolute definition of the phoneme, though the following is of use, at least as a base for further explanation: 'A phoneme is the smallest unit of sound by which a change of meaning can be effected in any one language'. A list of the phonemes, or 'recurrent distinctive units', of a language is usually established by a commutation procedure in which the contrastive sound units can be established in a series of trial frames. The word 'pin' contains three sounds: if we keep the second and third sounds constant as our frame and then list the sounds that can fit into the first position, we shall build up a list of words which exhibit a series of the contrastive sounds which, because they signal differences of meaning, are *phonemically* distinctive. For example:

-in
bin
din
fin
kin...

Other frames could be substituted for *-in* so that eventually all 45 English consonant and vowel phonemes would be isolated; in other words, there are 45 contrastive sound units in the language.

The matter, however, is more complex than this. If we listen to several people's pronunciation of any particular phoneme we shall find considerable variation; for example, /r/ can be a tongue tip trill, a frictionless continuant, a tap, a uvular roll, etc. These are clearly different sounds yet all are still realisations of the /r/ phoneme. In English they do not serve to distinguish meaning differences between words. These variants are called *allophones*. They may be conditioned by the context; clear and dark [1] sounds as in *like/full*, or they may be in free variation as with the different varieties of /r/.

Different languages have their own phoneme inventory: in Japanese, for instance, the sounds [1] and [r] are one phoneme so that the allophones of these two English phonemes are allophones of the same phoneme in Japanese. Just as the English speaker finds it difficult to distinguish the allophones of the /k/ phoneme in 'kingcup', which are phonemically different in Polish, so the Japanese finds it difficult to distinguish the [1] and [r] sounds. We hear what we need in order to determine phonemic differences, and are not generally aware of non-phonemic distinctions except with respect to vowel qualities which are largely responsible for dialect variations.

The phoneme is the basic unit in the phonological system and is, in fact, an abstraction from the phonetic data. (The definition of the term given above can now be seen to be not strictly accurate.) The phoneme is a *phonological* unit, not a *phonetic* one: the phonemes are, as it were, mapped out on to the sound data, so that the allophone is the realisation in phonetic substance of the phonemic form. Note that whereas the symbols for actual sounds are given in square brackets, the phoneme symbol, which may in some cases be identical with the phonetic symbol, is enclosed in slant lines: /e/, /p/, /s/.

A *grapheme* corresponds in writing to the phoneme to speech. Like the phoneme, the grapheme is strictly an abstraction underlying the actual letters used in the writing system. The grapheme can be represented in letters which may take various forms, such as A a *a* or B b *b* etc., or by a group of letters, such as th, qu, ck, or even a discontinuous sequence o — e, which functions as a unit in the spelling system. The grapheme may be indicated by < > and the letters realising it may be underlined.

The relation between sound and symbol can then be shown as in Figure 4.6.

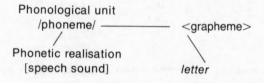

or in a simpler form:

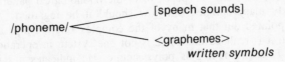

Fig. 4.6 Relation between Sound and Symbol

The important feature of this relationship is that there is *not* a direct correspondence between speech sound and letter(s) but rather that both are *translations* of the phonological unit, one into sound, the other via the abstract grapheme into letters.

One problem in discussing these relationships is the use of the same letters as symbols at different levels. For example, k is a letter of the alphabet k; a grapheme symbol, <k>; a symbol in the inventory of phonemes /k/ and a symbol in the phonetic alphabet [k]. The bracketing is essential!

The complexity of relationship can be seen in the examples in Figure 4.7.

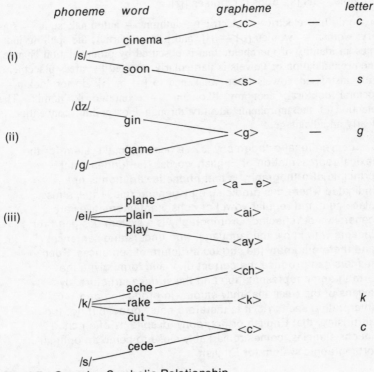

Fig. 4.7 Complex Symbolic Relationship

To view English spelling as a very inadequate representation of the phonetic structure of speech or of the phonological pattern of English is clearly inappropriate. But how should it be regarded? Albrow (1972) has pointed out that many of the complex relationships are explainable when it is realised that there is not one system in operation but several, that English spelling is polysystemic. He indicates a system operating for grammatical words (function words) distinct from that for lexical words and a system operating in monosyllabic words different from that in polysyllabic words. There are sub-systems for the spelling of surnames and for words borrowed from other languages, and so on. Albrow's work is tentative but it shows clearly that the system as a whole, though complex, is far from arbitrary or irrational.

Venezky (1976) has argued that the English spelling system is a representation of the phonological or, more strictly, morphophonological structure of the language. It retains a continuity in spelling for a given morpheme (unit of meaning) even though, because of the operation of pronunciation constraints or because of the stress alternations, the actual pronunciation changes. For instance, the letter *s* indicates the plural when suffixed to nouns even though it is realised as [*s*], [*z*] or [*iz*] in speech.

Example: cats [s], dogs [z], horses [iz]

In words like electric — electricity; autumn — autumnal; sign — signify; woman — women [ʊ] — [i], and part — partial, the spelling indicates an identity of morpheme that is obscured by pronunciation change. The pronunciation of vowels is particularly affected by stress placement, with unstressed vowels often weakened to [ə] or [i]: doctor 'doktə — doctoral dəktorəl; economy i'konəmi — economic ikə'nomik. The retention of the morpheme identity through the spelling convention is clearly an advantage.

.... conventional orthography is...a near optimal system for the lexical representation of English words. The fundamental principle of orthography is that phonetic variation is not indicated where it is predictable by general rule. Thus, stress placement and regular vowel or consonant alternatives are generally not reflected. Orothography is a system designed for readers who know the language, who understand sentences and therefore know the surface structure of sentences. Such readers can produce the correct phonetic form, given the orthographic representation and the surface structure, by means of the rules that they employ in producing and interpreting speech...It is therefore noteworthy, but not too surprising, that English orthography, despite its often cited inconsistencies, comes remarkably close to being an optimal orthographic system for English.

— N. Chomsky and M. Halle (1968)

Some approaches to reading have focused specifically on this sound-symbol relation. Pitman, for instance, introduced an amended and expanded alphabet, the *initial teaching alphabet* (ita), for beginning reading in order to regularise the sound-symbol correspondences, while in *Words in Colour* (Gattegno, 1962) the different spellings associated with particular phonemes are shown grouped together on reference charts using different colours for each phoneme set. Other schemes have employed colour coding and diacritical marking systems to supplement the normal alphabet. Some of these approaches, however justified and however successful on educational grounds, ignore the essential quality of the English spelling system.

Traditional phonics has attempted to teach the speech sound correspondences in a sequential order of assumed difficulty (see, for instance, the order suggested in Zintz, 1976) with, in some materials and books, heavy emphasis on pattern repetition irrespective of meaning. In others, as in the *Royal Road Readers*, phonic correspondences are developed within words occurring in a meaningful story text. In all cases it is recognised that many common words are irregular and cannot be introduced early in a graded phonics scheme, and these are dealt with as sight words.

Fairly typical of phonics materials is the *S.R.A. Reading Program*. (D. Rasmussen and L. Goldberg):

> Nan can fan
> Can Nan fan the pan
> Can Nan fan the van
> Can Nan fan the man
> Nan CAN fan the man

(Level A p.11)

> Ted had a pet pup
> The pup was sad
> Not a bit of ham was in his pan!
> The pup has to get fed but
> Ted was in his bed,
> The pup ran to Ted's bed.

(Level B p.40)

The emphasis here is on the recognition of phonic regularities with repetition of a limited number of sound symbol correspondences at one time. It is easy to criticise the banality of content; but firstly, the scheme is primarily concerned with developing pattern recognition skills which it believes are essential to the reading process, and secondly, it enables many children to establish confidence in their reading abilities as they master each step of the graded material. The layout of the readers, with each line equating with a simple syntactic unit, enables the child to concentrate on decoding print to sound.

It is interesting in passing to compare current approaches with that exemplified in a late 19th century primer which assumed that words of two letters were easier to read than those of three letters, and so on. Restriction on word length, like restrictions on sound-symbol correspondences, immediately poses problems in devising a meaningful text:

Am I by an ox? No.
Jo is by it. So he is.
 He is by me so.
Am I to go by an ox?
My ox is to go by it.
 Is my ox in? No.
Go to my ox. So I go.

Whether to emphasise phonics, which approach to employ, and how to relate it to the other components of reading skill, is a pedagogic decision, but the linguistic correlates are important and should be considered. It is worth noting that Chall (1967: p. 307) stated convincingly that coded methods are superior for many children. Up to the age of eight, children do not have an adequate conception of the spoken word unit, much less a recognition of a speech sound (phoneme). In a phonics approach the child faces a double recognition problem: that of identifying the spelling units (graphemes) and also the sound units that he has never experienced before in isolation. Some phonemes, the plosives /p, b, t, d, k, g/, cannot be pronounced without a following vowel element. The notorious '[k' æ t'] says cat' is patently a distortion of phonetic reality. Even when a child has decoded into sound he has no means of knowing whether his pronunciation is correct unless he recognises the word as one in his active or passive vocabulary. The child has to become aware of the abstract phonemic structure of the language, an implicit awareness that parallels the internalisation of grammatical rules abstracted from speech during the language-acquisition stage.

It is likely that for most children specific reference to letter-sound correspondences is a necessary factor in learning to read, but it is also certain that as reading proficiency increases, such reference becomes less significant, to be used only as a reinforcement and check on the accuracy of other word and phrase recognition techniques. Even for beginning readers, whole-word recognition and prediction skills are involved. It has been noted that where a child substitutes one word for another in reading, the substitute relates in visual form up to about the age of 7, but that by the age of 9 when reading is firmly established, the substitute approximates rather in meaning.

Prediction

If the speed of reading is restricted by a word-by-word decoding strategy, then apprehension of the meaning of a continuous text is inhibited, even though the meaning of the individual words is realised. For the brain effectively to process the text so that meaning can be apprehended, a minimum speed of reading is required. The adult reader, with a reading speed of about 250–350 words per minute, must be using processing techniques different in nature from those involved in decoding.

To read efficiently requires the deployment of a range of prediction skills that correlate with the lexical, syntactic and semantic levels of language structure. At its simplest, such prediction can be illustrated in the children's 'hangman' game, where each letter of the word or sentence to be guessed is represented by a dash. If one plays this letter-by-letter from the beginning of the message, it soon becomes apparent that often only one or two letters need to be established before the word can be completed, and the first words will often predict the remainder in a short text.

In the following example:

ALL CHILDREN HAVE TO GO TO SCHOOL

most people will suggest T as the initial letter of the first word on the basis that 'the' frequently begins sentences. However, once they guess the A they tend quickly to reach ALL, perhaps *en route* suggesting ARE as a possibility. Several attempts will be likely before the first two letters of 'children' are established; but having established these, many people, particularly teachers, will be able to guess the rest of the word — clearly influenced by their constant use of the word. 'All children' is then recognised as a noun phrase in what is almost certainly a subject position. The expectation that a subject is, at least in a short sentence, most likely to be followed by the verb phrase, helps to predict 'have'; and the frequency of 'have to' + verb as a unit, together with the rarity of two-letter verbs, usually triggers the rest of the sentence — 'go to school'. This is clearly influenced by the syntactic predictability of 'to' after 'go' and the contextual and semantic certainty of 'school' in such a sentence. This process of informed prediction is used in the cloze technique where every nth word in a passage is omitted and the student is required to insert the missing word. Such a technique is widely used in testing, but it can be used effectively as a teaching tool.

At the lexical level, prediction involves the recognition of characteristic word patterns and word lengths; the collocational probabilities — the likelihood of certain words occurring in the context of other words such as *dark* with *night, pretty* rather than *handsome* with *women*; and the recognition of the function of particular words in the given grammatical context, as with *go* above. At the syntactic level, prediction is based on the likelihood of a particular structure in a given context and the known frequency of different phrase and sentence patterns. Subject + verb + complement or object is a common pattern; so that having recognised, subconsciously, a nominal and verbal group in sequence, it is easy to predict that an object or complement will be most likely to follow. The more complex the sentence pattern, as in the passages quoted on pages 61–63, the more difficult it is to predict on this basis and consequently the harder it is to read. As the readers make predictions they scan ahead in order to check their prediction and, as they realise the prediction is correct, begin the next cycle of the process.

Most poetry and much literary prose utilise complex and often difficult-to-predict patterning and therefore make greater demands on the reader. In poetry, the unpredictability at the lexical and syntactic level and the use of original imagery are perhaps counteracted by the predictability of the underlying metrical pattern.

At the semantic or meaning level, prediction relies on a recognition of the meaning of words, phrases and sentences, and of the 'argument' of the whole text. Clearly this is linked with syntactic prediction on the one hand and with comprehension on the other. For the beginning reader, prediction at this meaning level is aided by the use of pictures which substitute for the textual meaning acquired by the mature reader, and enable the child to contextualise the text within a perceived frame of reference.

Goodman (1969) has argued, in his work on miscue analysis, that our predictions or expectation patterns are conditioned by our past experiences of both language and the content of what we are reading. They are based on awareness of sound-grapheme relations, the semantic system, and grammatical structure. The reader uses the cues inherent in the text selectively, shunting from level to level of linguistic structure. This is possible because of the high level of redundancy in language, both written and spoken. Goodman sees the process as a cycle of selection of cues, prediction and confirmation. Where a misreading occurs, there has been a *miscue*, and Goodman sees these as productive — evidence that the prediction process is operative. By analysis of miscues it is possible to devise appropriate instructional strategies to make the prediction process more sensitive, and so raise the level of reading efficiency. Goodman's conception of reading embraces the processing of textual cues at all levels of language, and recognises the continual interaction between levels that characterises the efficient reader.

Comprehension

Prediction is, in some ways, part of the comprehension level of reading. To define comprehension is perhaps more a matter for psychology and learning theory than for linguistics; but, acknowledging this, there is a language factor involved. Whether comprehension is a unified process or whether it is divisible into literal, implied and critical components, it is dependent on the reader's purpose in reading and his recognition of the function of the text being read.

Language activity is purposeful: one speaks to express an idea or emotion, to convey information, to find out, to further a relationship, and so on. This is another way of saying that language serves various functions. Purpose and function are inherent in the use of language. In reading it is essential to have a purpose in mind — to discover, to explore an idea or, perhaps, to enjoy oneself. To do this efficiently one needs to become aware of the writer's aims and purpose. Function and purpose are part of the context of the whole reading process and also of the current perspective on language as a functional communicative act.

There is a strong tendency to think that when children have attained a basic competence in reading — they can read aloud with adequate expression, can answer simple questions on what they have read, and are capable of reasonably sustained silent reading — then a specific focus on reading in the curriculum is no longer necessary. At the secondary stage the children's reading ability is taken for granted by most subject teachers; and even in English, where there is always an emphasis in writing skills, the only attention usually given to reading development is in the ubiquitous comprehension exercise, often employed more as a testing than as a teaching activity. Both reading and writing skills need to be developed throughout the secondary stage to help the child cope with increasing educational and social demands. As the curriculum develops, so children have to process language expressing more complex ideas and more involved information; and increasingly this is mediated through written language.

Each subject develops its own specific vocabulary, and in some cases there are also recognisable syntactic features — for example, the use of past tense forms in listening and the passive in some scientific writing. In addition, in many areas the use of diagrams, graphs and tables extends the scope of the written language.

Special problems, of course, emerge in literary prose and in poetry especially, where to some extent the style of expression is part of the content of what is presented. Special reading skills have to be developed involving a conscious attention to the language in which literature is written. The length of text which the reader must deal with extends considerably, so that the prediction and comprehension skills must embrace units of text such as the paragraph, the chapter and, of course, the book itself. Although all these features widen the range of reading abilities required, they are secondary to the essential ability that must be developed at this stage. The ability to think, however defined, is paramount. In reading it is usually referred to as critical comprehension, but that is too narrow a definition of a process which must include the ability to read a text with full realisation of the facts and ideas expressed; the ability to relate this new information with ideas already held; and the ability to think beyond developing a new synthesis of facts and ideas.

Conclusion

As the Bullock Report emphasised, an understanding of the role of language in the reading process is essential for the teacher of reading: the four component factors in the teaching of reading — language, the child, teaching strategies and reading materials — interact in one of the most challenging and crucial areas of teaching.

Suggested activities

1. Using the examples on page 75 as a basis, try to discover further examples to illustrate the complexities of sound-symbol relationships in English. Remember that you are looking for cases where one phoneme is realised by several graphemes or where one grapheme is a realisation of more than one phoneme.

2. Using IPA symbols, try to work out the restrictions that apply in English on the grouping of consonant *sounds* at the beginning of syllables. You will find that there are quite severe constraints on the permitted clusters. These constraints are part of the *phonotactic* rules of English. When you have done this, compare these with the range of *spelling* patterns available in the same position.

3. The Cloze procedure involves deleting words from a text at regular intervals. Prepare passages using deletions ranging from every tenth word down to every fifth, and assess the results when they are used on members of your group. Try to determine the basis on which the readers make predictions of the omitted words. Among the factors are: the reading level of the reader; the readability level of the text; and the knowledge of the subject which the reader brings to the text. Consider also the balance between syntactical and semantic predictions.

4. Select a page in a book, and before you start to read, cover the first and last third of each line of text leaving visible only the centre section of the page. Now read down the page and see if you can follow the general drift of the text. What conclusions do you draw from this experiment? Repeat the experiment with different types of material ranging from fiction to College texts. Consider the implications for the understanding of what we read and for the speed at which we read.

Chapter 5   Doug Courts
Writing

I catch my meaning in a web of ink and pin it to the paper.

What is 'writing'?

Communication in human society is often considered primarily as an oral activity, writing being regarded as merely a means of recording what has been said. This is not strictly true. A good deal of communication exists quite effectively, independently of the spoken or written word. Road signs, for example, can communicate information or warning without either spoken or written language being necessarily used: we take extra care automatically when we see the symbol marking the proximity of a school, even though we do not consciously say 'Ah, yes, there is a school here', and the word SCHOOL no longer appears on the sign. The message itself has no specific precise form either: it could just as well be rendered by 'Take care, there are children about.'

These signs, of course, represent only one way of recording communication; and Goody and Watt (1963) and McLuhan (1962) suggest that there are really four periods distinguishable in the development of recording language: an early period when there was no written record; a second period when writing was done only by hand; a third when printing made mass literacy possible; and a fourth period recently begun when the ability to record language includes the use of tape-recorders and video-recorders which can reproduce the actual spoken sounds and facial expressions used.

We are concerned here, however, with writing itself: with the actual process of recording language by means of visual symbols. Try to make a list of the wide variety of uses we still have today for writing. Try also to think through the act of writing — what is actually involved?

Consider the example of writing by a boy in grade 6: Figure 5.1. The characters or letters are, of course, identifiable and the division into words is clear, marked by very definite spacing. The use of a margin, heading and date tells us that this is formal writing from school, and consideration of the text shows some of the difficulties experienced in

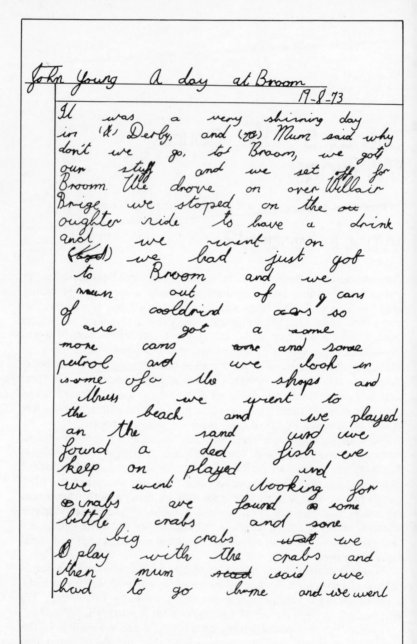

Fig. 5.1 Handwriting of a Grade-6 Boy

writing it. Erasures, false starts, the increasing lack of conventional punctuation and the frequent use of 'and' suggest something of the struggle to put the story down on paper. How much easier it would be to tell! The unevenness of the handwriting suggests that the sheer motor activity of the hand in forming the letters is still hard work, and some of the spelling suggests that the sound of the words is still very much predominant in the mind. This pinpoints some of the differences between spoken and written English. The story told is spontaneous and rapid: writing is a labour (but with writing, revision and careful attention to detail are possible). The spoken language is a face-to-face communication: the written may evoke response only after some time has elapsed (and many written forms are not designed to be answered).

Look at the examples of writing in Figure 5.2. They represent very different ways of recording language. Do they have anything in common? You may notice that each consists of a series of graphemes, but you probably cannot tell what the graphemes represent nor how the language is divided into grammatical units. Some graphemes are clearly more complex than others, while some are almost indistinguishable to the unaccustomed eye. Yet each also represents an attempted solution to the problem of recording language.

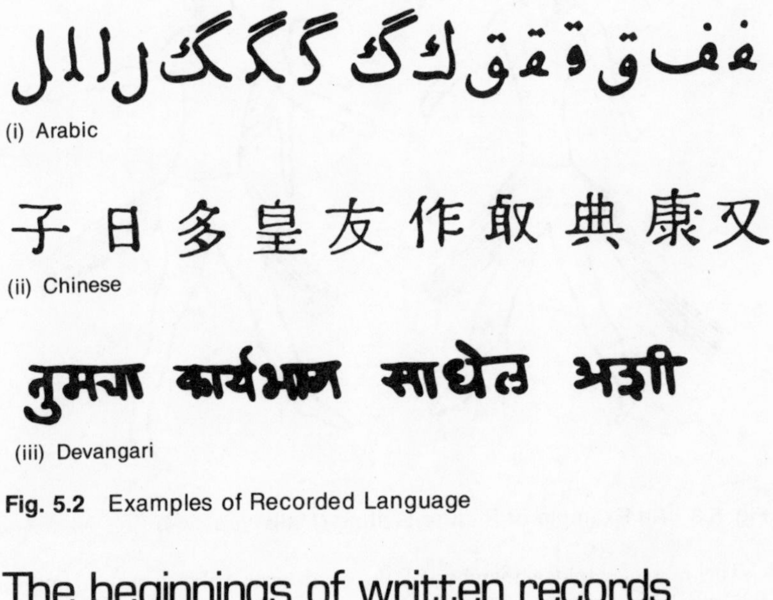

(i) Arabic

(ii) Chinese

(iii) Devangari

Fig. 5.2 Examples of Recorded Language

The beginnings of written records

How have they been developed? What techniques are needed to turn the fleeting sound into permanent written record? Early attempts seem to concentrate on the message to be conveyed and are largely pictorial in form. Unfortunately, the vagueness of the pictorial record makes it inefficient as a means of written record. What do you make of the message in Figure 5.3, a letter actually sent to a Cheyenne Indian? Can you interpret it successfully without a knowledge of the conventions in use? Is the message really self-evident?

(from Mallery, *Picture Writing*,
p. 364)

Fig. 5.3 An Example of Picture-Writing (Mallery, p. 364)

The message told a member of the mud-turtle tribe to return home, for which purpose 53 dollars had been sent via the trading-post. The recipient duly turned up to collect the money and understood that he must return home, as had been made clear in the covering letter to the agent.

This message attempts to represent objects or ideas directly. It lacks the linguistic detail of a spoken utterance. Perhaps an approach to a written form based on the words which make up the message would be more precise. This does imply, of course, that we can divide the stream of sound which constitutes an utterance into units which we recognise as 'words'. We are so familiar with this process, which we usually associate with the appearance of words on the printed page, that our inability to distinguish words in rapid speech in an unfamiliar dialect or language is often quite a shock to us.

Concrete ideas such as 'a sheep' or 'a house' are quite easy to distinguish and represent, and early scripts show many traces of this. The major difficulties come in representing abstract ideas — 'thought' or 'interest' — or the words which show grammatical relationships.

Writing based on the word as the unit is called *ideographic*, and Chinese could be cited as an example of this approach. There are many Chinese dialects — some could be regarded as language themselves, as they are mutually unintelligible — but the basic idea of picture-and-word relationship is common to all, and each dialect therefore has its own sound corresponding to each character. It is therefore possible for two Chinese to communicate with each other through the written characters, even though they may not be able to understand each other's dialect of the language.

To appreciate the strengths and weaknesses of an ideographic method of writing, we might compare Chinese and mathematics, the latter of which is also an ideographic form. One strength of these forms is their independence of the way sounds are spoken in any particular language. Just as the Chinese can understand each other's writing even when their spoken Chinese is different, so a Russian mathematician can understand a French mathematician's proof, in spite of the language barrier between them. Mathematics also shows the capacity of an ideographic language to handle abstract concepts and complex relationships. These kinds of writing are compressed, compared with the alphabetical writing system as used for English. This makes them useful instruments of thought. Teachers of writing in English-speaking schools do not usually teach ideographic methods of recording ideas as such, and mathematics teachers do not usually realise that they are teaching *a form of writing*. Students would benefit if teachers in these subject areas combined to help them realise that writing is a very flexible instrument and takes many forms.

The major disadvantage of ideographic form is that it cannot keep up with the variations of the spoken form. To build up a vocabulary of 5 000 distinct characters is a considerable feat; and although most Chinese characters have more than one meaning and can be combined to produce more complex concepts, the written vocabulary is smaller than any individual's spoken vocabulary. Mathematics makes do with a smaller number of symbols and calls on the normal spoken language, but it would prove difficult to describe the beauties of spring, or your feelings towards another person, using mathematical symbols alone!

Sound and writing systems

So instead of trying to represent meanings or whole words in some way, most writing systems represent the sounds of the language. Some systems, such as Japanese, try to represent each syllable by a separate symbol. A syllable is easier to recognise than an individual sound, and is clearly an interchangeable unit within the word. There are fewer syllables than words, so that fewer characters are needed. The Japanese syllable is a regular combination of a consonant and a vowel, as can be seen by considering English renderings of Japanese words: to-yo-to, Fu-ji-ha-ma, Su-zu-ko, Da-tsu(n), (in which our 'n' represents a nasalisation). The Japanese simplified the Chinese character writing to suit their syllabic approach: see Figure 5.4.

Katakana

ア	カ	サ	タ	ナ	ハ	マ	ヤ	ラ	ワ		ガ	ザ	ダ	バ	パ
a	ka	sa	ta	na	ha	ma	ya	ra	wa		ga	za	da	ba	pa
イ	キ	シ	チ	ニ	ヒ	ミ		リ	ヰ		ギ	ジ	ヂ	ビ	ピ
i	ki	si	ti(tsi)	ni	hi	mi		ri	wi(i)		gi	zi	di	bi	pi
ウ	ク	ス	ツ	ヌ	フ	ム	ユ	ル			グ	ズ	ヅ	ブ	プ
u	ku	su	tu(tsu)	nu	hu	mu	yu	ru			gu	zu	du	bu	pu
ヱ	ケ	セ	テ	子	ヘ	メ	エ	✓	ヱ		ゲ	ゼ	デ	ベ	ペ
e	ke	se	te	ne	be	me	ye	re	we (e)		ge	ze	de	be	pe
オ	コ	ソ	ト	ノ	ホ	モ	ヨ	ロ	ヲ		ゴ	ゾ	ド	ボ	ポ
o	ko	so	to	no	ho	mo	yo	ro	wo		go	zo	do	bo	po
ン (n)															

Fig. 5.4 Japanese Simplification of Chinese Writing (Gelb, p. 161)

A much more economic system is the alphabetic script, based on the smallest units of sound, the phonemes. Most languages function with about forty or fifty phonemes or less, and in an alphabetic script the aim is to represent each phoneme by its own written symbol. Few actually achieve this, but their imperfections are often the scars left by the accidents of historical development.

These scripts can be traced back to Egyptian and Phoenecian attempts to construct a writing system. They had as a language base a system of word roots in which two or three letters remain constant and variations of meaning and grammatical relationships are represented by varied patterns of vowels interwoven with these consonants: k-t-b is the general root for 'writing'; kitabun means a writing (a book); katibun: a writer; katbun: the act of writing; yaktuba: he will write; kutiba: it has been written; and so on. This system highlights the individual sound, and it is interesting to note that the variable element, the vowel, is the one not indicated in the scripts developed. The Egyptians developed a cumbrous system for indicating the words based on pictures, in which the consonants were confirmed by the use of additional signs, and signs were also added to indicate the general areas of meaning. In the group the throne also represents the sounds 'st'; the half-circular loaf of bread reinforces the 't'; the egg shows that we are dealing with a female entity; and the seated figure represents a god. The four symbols together represent a goddess whose name contains the consonants s-t: Aset (whom we usually call Isis in English). (From Time-Life books: *The Birth of Writing*, p. 44). An Egyptian text is therefore a mixture of signs, some having individual phonetic value and some having semantic or marker content.

Fig. 5.4(a) Egyptian Word (from Time — Life, Birth of Writing)

The Phoenecians improved on this by omitting everything except the symbols which were phonetic. Each of these was established as a representation of some object, the word for which began with the sound to be recorded, and the representations were simplified to form a usable phonetic alphabet of twenty-two letters. No vowels were included. When this tremendously simplified alphabet was adopted by the Greeks, they added letters to represent the vowels which they needed, since in Greek as in English the word structure requires the representation of vowels. For this purpose they made use of symbols representing Egyptian or Phoenecian sounds not needed for Greek. Aleph, for instance, a consonant in Phoenecian absent from Greek, was adopted to represent the vowel 'A' — alpha — for the Greek alphabet. With some modification of content and design, this was adopted by the Romans and has become the basis of most European scripts today. (See Figure 5.5.)

The main problem for us with this alphabet which we have inherited is the loss of the one-to-one correspondence between sound and letter. We use two letters for some sounds: ch, ck and th, for example, whilst frequently one letter may represent a variety of sounds according to context, mostly as a result of historical accident (for example, the 'a' in *name, father, man, about*). We also retain some letters which have outlived their phonetic function, for example, 'k' in *knight*, 'g' in *gnome*,

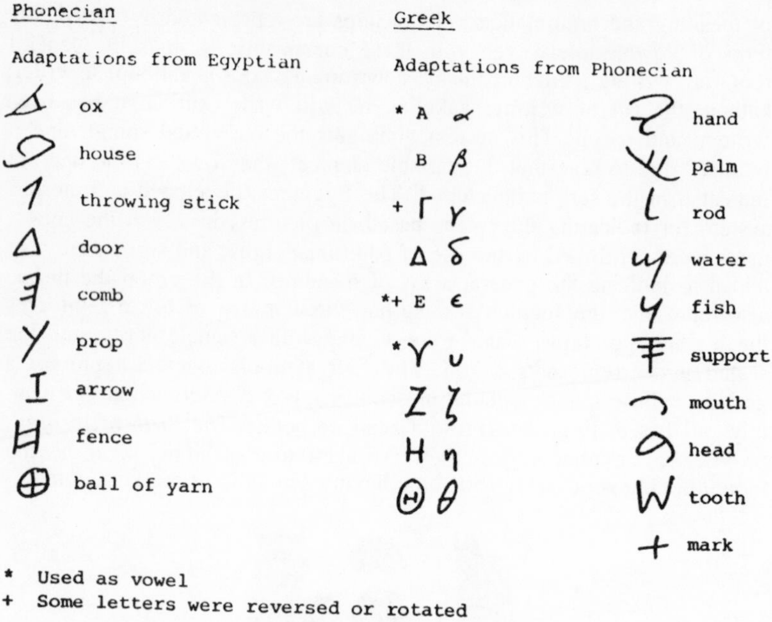

Phonecian

Greek

Adaptations from Egyptian

Adaptations from Phonecian

⊿	ox	* A	α		₹	hand
૭	house	B	β		⩛	palm
1	throwing stick	+ Γ	γ		L	rod
△	door	Δ	δ		ɯ	water
∃	comb	*+ E	ε		Ψ	fish
Ϋ	prop	*Υ	υ		∓	support
Ⅰ	arrow	Z	ζ		⌒	mouth
Ⲏ	fence	H	η		⌂	head
⊕	ball of yarn	⊖	θ		W	tooth
					+	mark

*   Used as vowel
+   Some letters were reversed or rotated

Fig. 5.5   Phoenecian/Greek Alphabets (Based on Diringer, *The Alphabet*, Hutchinson, London, 1978.)

and others which serve only to indicate the pronunciation; for example, the 'e' of *name* or the second 'p' in *hopping*. Nor has the pronunciation itself remained as it was first recorded. A major change in the pronunciation of vowels and the development of some of these into diphthongs took place at the end of the fourteenth century and is not reflected in the orthography. Nevertheless, English writing is still largely regular in its correspondence between phoneme(s) and letters(s). Most of the discrepancies occur in the commoner and older parts of the vocabulary.

The development of handwriting

The orientation of the script, left to right, was settled firmly in the later Greek period, although some earlier texts are known written right to left in the Semitic tradition and some in which the lines reverse alternately, a style known as 'boustrephedon' (as the ox ploughs).

All the letters in the early scripts were what we now call majuscules or capitals. (See Figure 5.6.)

The development of a minuscule script came from a Latin script called 'half-uncial', in which the ends of certain letters were prolonged

THEORIENTATIONOFTHESCRIPTLEFTTORIGHTW
ASSETTLEDFIRMLYINTHELATERGREEKPERIODAL
THOUGHSOMEEARLIERTEXTSAREKNOWNWRITT
ENRIGHTTOLEFTINTHESEMITICTRADITIONANDS

Fig. 5.6 Ancient Majuscules (Capitals)

outside the general line to form ascenders and descenders. Large letters were still retained in this script for the beginning of sentences, hence our present use of initial capital letters. Subsequent changes in the form of the letters to allow the script to be written more easily and without the need to lift the pen from the writing surface produced the cursive styles which underlie today's handwriting. These fall into two main groups: the roundhand styles based on the old manuscript hands of the middle ages, and the Italic script based on calligraphic developments largely in Italy at the time of the Renaissance. The roundhand script is formed on a square module, the Italic on an oblong one: this is also characterised by the use of a broad-nibbed pen which produces characteristic thick and thin strokes. It can be written faster than roundhand and retains its legibility longer under pressure. (Refer to Figure 5.7.) Originally the text was written continuously, but the inconvenience of this led to the use of space to indicate word boundaries and to the development of punctuation.

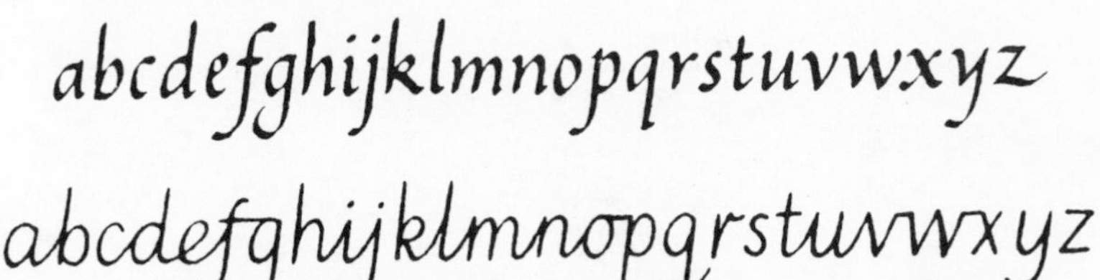

abcdefghijklmnopqrstuvwxyz

abcdefghijklmnopqrstuvwxyz

Fig. 5.7 Roundhand and Italic Script (Fairbank, *A Handwriting Manual*, Faber, London, 1975; Inglis & Gibson, *Handwriting Workbook No. 3*, Nelson.)

The chief function of punctuation marks is to give some indication to the reader as to the natural divisions of the text for reading, especially for reading aloud, and to make complex syntactic constructions clearer. Punctuation began with the major stops which are used with some regularity. Minor stops developed later and show considerable variation in intention and frequency. The inherent difficulties in transforming spoken into written language, and vice-versa, make this a very difficult area, and the wide variety of practice between authors and in the house-styles of various printers is evidence of this.

The major problem of capturing the sound-sequences and committing them to paper is not just a matter of securing an efficient sound-symbol relationship, and other devices besides punctuation are used in an attempt to record meaningful utterances adequately. One of these is the use of space. This is most evident in the contrast between verse and prose, in which the attention is concentrated on the measured lengths of the lines of verse by their isolation and positioning on the page. Some poets go beyond the conventional patterns and design their lines to create or fill a particular shape, adding to their meaning. The poem 'Fury said to the mouse' in Carroll's *Alice in Wonderland*, (Chapter III) is a well-known example of this:

FURY AND THE MOUSE

```
        FURY said to a
        mouse, That he
        met in the
        house,
      " Let us
    both go
      to law :
      I will
          prosecute
            you.  Come, I'll
              take no denial ;
              We must
              have a trial :
              For really
              this morning
              I've nothing
          to do."
        Said the
        mouse to the
        cur, " Such a
          trial,
            dear Sir,
                With no
              jury or
            judge,
          would be
        wasting
        our breath."
      " I'll be judge,
    I'll be jury,"
        Said
          cunning
            old Fury :
              " I'll
                try the
              whole
            cause,
          and
        condemn
        you
          to
            death."
```

Fig. 5.8

The isolation of the line in verse-writing helps to point the pattern of the stanza as a whole and the metrical pattern within the line. Rhyme and alliteration are also devices used to enchance the meaning more particularly in verse than in prose. They help to mark the pattern and point up the intonation and stress and other unwritten features of the utterance. Space is also used meaningfully in the layout of magazines and books, in advertising and in display. When arranging our correspondence and addressing an envelope we use space to give clarity and shape to our writing. Look around and see how many instances you can find of the effective use of space. An extensive range of type faces and typographical devices is also available, and students should be encouraged to notice and take pleasure in the aesthetic possibilities of writing, especially in those which increase its expressive possibilities.

Conventions of the written language

Another problem which has become more pressing is that posed by the wider acceptance of varieties of language which at one time would not have been regarded as suitable or proper for recording. The written language recorded only such language as approached the grammatical norm of the formal or frozen styles of writing, and more recent attempts to record more exactly the spoken forms, such as the casual and intimate forms (see Joos, 1962) have only served to highlight the inadequacies of the written medium for performing such a task. Experiments have been made with variant sizes and styles of type face — heavy type; *italic* or decorative faces; underlining; multiple exclamation marks (!!!) to add weight or emphasis; multiple periods to indicate hesitations, pauses, innuendoes, implications. . . . All of these add to the vividness of a written message, particularly in the novel, but give rise to many problems in the classroom where the casualness of much that children see about them and find in reading books clashes sharply with the more traditional techniques still taught as formal written skills.

Spelling is probably the most noticeable of these written skills. Spelling was first regularised in England by the tenth-century scribes of Wessex under the guidance of King Alfred, a scholar king greatly interested in books and learning; but dialectal variations elsewhere were strong and many words show the persistence of such variants: 'old' is a form from central England, while the Kentish 'eld' is found in 'elder' and the northern 'ald' in 'alderman'. The Scot retains the form 'auld' in 'Auld lang syne'; the West Saxon scribes preferred 'eald'. After the Norman Conquest in 1066 the influence of continental-trained scribes with a Latin-based education gave rise to many anomalies apparent in modern English; for example, 'qu' was introduced for the 'cw' forms. Some Old English letters were replaced or acquired new values, for example, ʒ became gh as in night, and has now been lost as a speech-sound in that word. Written English of the twelfth-fourteenth centuries has a variety of permissible spellings which reflect dialectal differences, but is still fairly phonetic and seems to reflect the spoken language as

ˈfautagraːf
photograph

faˈtografa
photographer

ˌfautaˈgræfik
photographic

faˈtogrefiˊ
photography

Fig. 5.9

far as we can reconstruct it. At the close of this century, however, occurred the phenomenon known as the Great Vowel Shift which changed the major vowel sounds: the long /a/, /i/, /o/, and /u/ became diphthongs and long /e/ was raised to /i/. Since this was not reflected in changes in the spelling, it may be that the development was not generally realised, although it has created a good deal of confusion for subsequent learners of our spelling system, both native and foreign. Probably the spelling patterns had already become fairly conservative. Chaucer certainly used variant spellings to indicate dialectal features, which suggests that his usual forms were accepted as regular.

The implication would seem to be that English spelling was already morpho-phonemic; that is, it was based on the word-structure rather than on a faithful representation of the sounds. For example, in such a group as photograph, photographer, photographic, photography the vowel sounds are changed by the influence of the stress pattern occasioned by the varying number of syllables — but this is not reflected in the spelling.

('fəutəgraːf fə'togrəfə ˌfəutə'græfik fə'togrefiˈ')

The present rigidity became the regular practice in the eighteenth century, reinforced by early dictionaries. The spellings used, some showing the personal idiosyncrasies of the compilers, were seized upon by zealous schoolmasters and established as authoritarian. Noah Webster in the United States effected a partial reform backed up by legal process and the United States Congress, which accepted most of the spellings suggested for use in his dictionary; but even he was unable to establish a completely efficient or logically based system.

Another facet of this problem is the sheer variety of the forms of spoken English: what would be accurately phonetic for one area is not phonetically acceptable in another. The present system, anomalous though it may be, does enable speakers of English to have a standard representation of the words used, irrespective of the dialect spoken. This development and acceptance of a standard form was at one time also fairly true of the written language itself, as was noticed on page 92; but whilst the spelling system proved resistant to change, the experiments with the writing system have continued in the effort to reflect the various forms which the language used — such as are found in display advertising.

Before the advent of printing, manuscripts copied by hand could be adjusted by the careful copier to accommodate unfamiliar spellings, words or expressions. Indeed, the provenance and wanderings of some early texts are revealed by an investigation of such changes. But when Caxton introduced printing into England in 1476 the text became fixed and universally available, and the form used by the printer became the standard. Caxton's preface shows his awareness of the problem, and he discusses the difficulty he felt in choosing words which may not be intelligible to all his readers. A lively example of the kind of difficulty he expects is illustrated by his story of the group of merchants sailing down the Thames who landed near a farmhouse in Kent and asked the farmer's wife for eggs. They met with an uncomprehending refusal until one of them remembered that the local word was 'eyren'. His choices of word, therefore, based on the English of the Court, have had a good deal of bearing on the development of a standard form of writing which does not reflect dialectal differences but represents a form mutually intelligible to all educated men however they may speak in their own home districts.

This establishment of the practices and forms of the English spoken by the educated men from the Universities and the Court produced a standard which was particularly noticeable in the written form and which influenced English writing until developments in drama and the novel produced attempts to represent the variety of forms of speech of the characters. These are shown specifically as variants from the standard forms used in the basic narration and by the educated characters.

These educated men had been brought up to use Latin as the prestige language, and for centuries Latin, as the language of the Church and the scholar, was regarded as language *par excellence*, the use of other tongues such as English, French, Spanish being 'vulgar' and of much lower status. Latin vocabulary, rhetorical devices, figures of speech, grammatical terms and expressions were introduced freely into English and provided a range of choices of expressions between those characteristic of the native Germanic stock of the language and the more scholarly and learned borrowings from Latin. In common speech, I 'get off' the bus: the formal notice requests (not asks) me not to 'alight' until the bus stops. A policeman never 'goes' anywhere: in his written report, traditionally, he 'proceeds' — although this usage has begun to be regarded as pompous and amusing. Some expressions have, indeed, gone: (or should I say, 'succumbed'?). 'No spitting' is probably commoner than 'Expectoration is forbidden', but we constantly find traces of the preference for a 'scholarly' Latin-based expression whenever we feel that formal language is called for, especially in written forms.

Form and style

Chapter six considers a variety of taxonomies which attempt to categorise language according to the functions it performs. These functions are also reflected in the forms which language takes in writing, whether in the manner of presentation or the 'style' which characterises literary forms.

Some variations are absolutely fixed, representing the frozen level (see Joos, 1962): set forms of address; invitations and replies on formal occasions; religious formulae. Others show a modicum of variation, moving through the styles of oratory and report; formal documentation; academic writings, towards the variety and looseness of expression found in the novel and other forms of fictional writing. Generally speaking, non-fiction uses a formal style, fiction a consultative or casual style, moving at present in many cases towards an attempted representation of the intimate. The rigidity of expression in some formal or 'frozen' documentation becomes a social convention and thereby facilitates mutual understanding; the flexibility in other writing enables a more personal communication to be expressed.

Writing generally acts as a conservative influence on language. The business of the school has been largely regarded as teaching such acceptable language, and producing people capable of writing a formal business letter or an academic paper. In the nineteenth century, accuracy in spelling and the niceties of formal, 'correct' grammar was expected and the conventions of punctuation were therefore perfectly adequate. The existence of the standard was not only accepted but also socially expected. Education was restricted in range and availability, and much time was spent in securing this adherence to the accepted written standard. Novels still maintained the formal standard, on the whole, although some novelists were beginning to experiment with word forms and sentence patterns.

With more attention given to the spoken word and a widening of the availability and range of education, there has been an increased demand for more varied forms of written record, and a lessened demand for the traditional forms. The language of persuasion in advertising; the popularisation of the newspaper and the development of the magazine; the increasing influence of overseas varieties of English (chiefly the

American dialects through the medium of the film), all created fresh pressures on the traditional techniques which proved neither adequate nor suited to the new forms of expression.

This will be much clearer if you can find and study an example of a piece of information treated in a variety of ways — for instance, a piece of Parliamentary reporting. Compare the entry in Hansard with its treatment by a selection of newspapers, both in the news columns and in the editorial comment. Or take an item of news and compare the treatment given in newspapers and magazines. It will be clear how writing takes into account not only the message itself but also the context in which it is to be recorded — the audience for which it is intended; the medium in which it is to appear; the effect which the writer wishes to produce. No writing can exist without consideration of these points — not even the notes which I make for my own personal use. Do they need to be full, or brief? Will a point-by-point outline be clearer, or would it be easier to write in continuous prose? Would a diagram, flow chart or explosion chart record the matter more clearly? Are the notes to be filed or written up in a notebook? How are they to be made quickly and simply accessible? How much contraction and simplification of language can they stand without becoming obscure later?

Different people will have different answers to these questions, possibly different answers within their own writing, for it is very clear that we do not all react in the same way to the written word. An understanding and appreciation of our individual approach and variety is also essential. Writing must be done for a purpose. The old concept of 'composition' was often language rendered down into the production of formless continuous strings of words which could be applied in any situation: the new approach must regain a sense of purpose and fitness for the specific task the writing has to serve. This does include attention to the courtesies of acceptable spelling, thoughtfulness about structure and order, and an awareness of one's audience.

This is shown also in the choice of appropriate syntax and vocabulary. Language provides a wide range of choice, enabling the selection of a simpler or a more complex term for a great number of occasions so that the language may be varied to reflect the purpose and the level. We are also able to choose from the varieties of syntactical organisation to construct sentences of varying complexity. It is part of the business of a writer to choose, from the variety of sentence patterns that are available, those patterns which match his thought patterns and enhance readability and clarity of the work.

Writing is therefore more than just the recording of words, syllables or sounds: we must consider sentences and their place in the whole communication. Our means and methods of writing arise from the demands of the past: modern demands and situations have produced language which is not bound to the old concept of the sentence — forms, advertising material, newspaper styles — and these will affect the future development of language. Change is always a mark of a living language. We may well devise acceptable means of recording the part-sentences and other fragments of the spoken language. Certainly we must be aware of the effect of these demands and examples on the children who try to write for us in school.

This chapter has mainly focused on the form of writing. Writing cannot, however, be considered apart from the total resources of language and the varied functions it serves. Writing and reading are obviously interdependent. Readers create a need for particular forms of writing, just as writing allows more satisfaction for the reader. This relationship holds good for individuals as well as for cultures. Fluent readers and writers constitute a special class within even a literate community. The vocabulary and syntax of the written language become increasingly specialised and distinctive, as we saw in Chapter 2. Because of its association with high-status speakers and messages, it is constantly in danger of losing contact with the vitality of speech and the capacity to deal with nuances of feeling and complexities of social interaction. Britton has argued (1970) that schools should pay more attention to expressive writing, because this important function of language is in danger of atrophying, especially in the upper reaches of the school system (see Chapter 6). Britton may be overstating his case (Williams, 1977); but the point remains a valid one of which all teachers in all subjects should be aware. Nor should the teacher neglect to identify the qualities of the other kinds of writing which he wishes the student to produce and be prepared to teach the techniques which will enable the student to write well. The channels between speech and writing ought to remain as open as possible for thinking to remain a satisfying social process, and the tendency for written communication to become depersonalised must sometimes at least be resisted if the thinking of students is to remain individual, as it surely must.

Conclusion

The invention of writing lies at the foundation of civilised culture, and writing remains an essential skill for all citizens in contemporary society. Different kinds of writing systems have existed, with different strengths and weaknesses. In Western societies an alphabetic script has to be mastered, but other writing systems have their own distinctive functions and value. Teachers and students should learn to appreciate the full flexibility of writing and the variety of its forms. The major difficulty of an alphabetic script such as English comes from the lack of a perfect match between units of sound (phonemes) and units of writing (graphemes). This has arisen partly as a result of the rigidity of a writing system which has not found it easy to evolve over time to accommodate itself to the changes in the sounds of the spoken language, and partly because it has also to correspond to dialectal variations within the same language community. Writing offers a further difficulty, in that it evolves distinctive forms of vocabulary and syntax and specific rules and conventions prescribing their use. Full mastery of the written language involves control over both forms and functions of the medium.

Suggested activities

1. Compare characters from different writing systems, looking specifically at the implement used and the surface upon which the character appears: what are the strengths and limitations of each as a means of communication or as an aid to thought? Is the aesthetic value, perhaps, paramount?

2. Take a transcript of a conversation and write it as a passage of acceptable written English, noting the kinds of change that you need to make.

3. Give an account of some incident which has happened to you recently or that you have seen (a) in a dialogue with a close friend; (b) in a letter to a close friend; (c) in a letter to an older relative; (d) in a formal account — for example, in testimony in court; (e) as if reported on by some bystander; (f) as reported in the Press. What changes of approach, stress, or accuracy do you make from one account to another? What linguistic features convey these changes? Is it merely syntax and vocabulary?

4. Discuss the differences between styles of invitation to a party, and draw conclusions as to the social implications as well as to the linguistic variations. How far would this apply to wedding invitations?

5. Monitor all the uses you make of written language in a week, and make an attempt to categorise them. Ask others of your acquaintance to do the same, and compare the kinds of language activity peculiar to various occupations or life styles. Take samples of the various forms used and estimate how far each affects the kind of language in use.

6. Make tape recordings of dialogue from television or radio productions. Transcribe them and note what difficulties you encounter. How do they differ? Compare them with published scripts and possibly the original books if they are adaptations.

The Context of
Communication

Chapter 6 Terry Williams
The Functions of Language

'Language is not a lifeless tool, but an act of coping'
— Paul Goodman, *Speaking and Language: Defence of Poetry*

Introduction to language function

The following parent-child dialogue is so typical that it would hardly
draw the notice of grammarians, but it leads to powerful insights about
our abilities to use language. A father, intent on reading the evening
newspaper, is interrupted by his four-and-a-half-year-old son, eager to
tell his father of an exciting day at school:

Son: Dad, dad. Do y'know what? Dad, Dad.
Father: Colin, I'm *trying* to read!
Son: But Dad, I wasn't talking to you, I was just talking to
myself.

If we look closely at this exchange, a puzzling fact emerges: neither
speaker seems to attend to what the other says. The father, obviously
disturbed by his son's interruptions, does not actually command his son
to be quiet. He does not use one of the normal forms for commanding
or requesting his son to stop talking (for example, 'Shut up!' 'Be quiet!'
'Would you stop talking please?' etc.). His sentence seems to be a
statement of fact. Yet the four-and-a-half-year-old boy correctly understands the apparent statement *as a command-request*. (Father: 'Look,
I'm trying to read my newspaper. Stop interrupting me with your talking so I can continue reading it.') The son's answer is, interestingly
enough, as oblique as the father's message. (Son: 'I couldn't have been
disturbing your newspaper reading, since it was myself I was talking to,
not you.') Perhaps the son's oblique answer — a 'white lie' in more
common terms — is an attempt to save face. In the exchange that followed, the father signalled his understanding and acceptance of this
most reasonable answer with a smile and a nod of the head.

Until recently, a linguist analysing this conversation would have looked only at the formal properties of the language used — the structure and organisation of its various elements.

This approach to the analysis of language has prevailed in the academic world, including the primary and secondary classroom, for the past hundred years. From this standpoint, speaker and hearer can communicate because they know and share the structures into which their ideas and experiences are encoded. In the past twenty years, Noam Chomsky and his students have looked at the acquisition of such structures by children. Chomsky has argued that a child is born with the in-built means for generalising the language heard around him into a set of formal 'rules' which the child applies in the creation of his own language. Thus, a child can speak and understand the language of his society, because he knows the structural make-up of that language.

However, this approach to language does not explain the ability of the four-and-a-half-year-old boy in the extract above to translate what is structurally a statement of fact into what is functionally a command-request. Nor does it explain the child's ability to make an oblique answer. It is evident that this child is sensitive to past experiences with his father, the 'tone' of his father's voice, and the expectations his father has of him; but structural analyses do not and cannot (given their goals and objectives) take these factors into account.

In other words, there is more to a speaker's knowledge of his language than a knowledge of the structure of the code. A speaker must be able to know how to use his language — how to exploit the resources of his language so that he can make it work for him. In short, the speaker must 'know' (in an abstract, unconscious sense) the *functions* of his language. This perspective assumes a more profound yet general view of what it means to learn and know a language. The demands we place on language, the use we put it to — the functions, in other words — lie at the heart of man's behaviour and are a determining influence on the structure of language.

The communication between father and son in the extract above is successful, not so much because both speakers are able to pattern and structure discrete language elements into meaningful wholes, but also because they 'know' that language serves their needs and allows them to achieve goals that would be impossible without it. This perspective reverses the traditional approach to language analysis. Rather than focusing on the language code with incidental illustrations of what speakers can do with language, functionalists emphasise the way in which functions of language actually shape and influence the code itself. In other words, the internal organisation of language — its grammar and structure — is determined by the functions it serves. This assumption about how language is organised runs contrary to how generations of school-children have been taught to regard language. Parsing sentences and labelling parts of speech were thought to lead to a better 'sense' of grammar and structure, which in turn was to have led to better writing and speech. Little attention was paid to the purposes for which children used language or the demands they placed upon it, even though such a study would have been relevant to their educational needs. In particular, the view that function determines the language code would have been a liberating one for teachers struggling to make work on grammar more practical and relevant.

Illustration of language functions

To illustrate the functions that appear in the language of children and to investigate these functions more closely, we shall make use of an extended extract of language. The speakers in this extract, which was selected from a four-hour tape recording, are two sisters and a brother of Macedonian parentage: John, aged six years; Rosemarie, aged eight; and Margaret, aged ten.

(The children have arrived home from school and are making paper-cup hats. The television is playing in the background.)

1 *John*: Here...here.
2 *Margaret*: What?
3 *John*: Here. String.
4 *Margaret*: That's not string
5 *John* (laughing): Here.
6 *Margaret*: Let's see John.
7 *John*: Open up. (Searching through drawer for strings. Affecting a Macedonian accent.) Take some colour photo. What's happened to dis? Is it det?
8 *Margaret*: Here, if I...give me some string.
9 *John*: What?
10 *Margaret* (measuring John's head with string): Yeah, I've got to see how long your head will be first for the string. Just put this through there.
11 *John*: There? Put it through that then.
12 *Margaret*: Yeah, it's too little...right. Right, nearly got it. (Sounds of struggle fitting string into hat) Doesn't fit...what are you doing Rosie?
13 *John*: (Nonsense sounds in Macedonian)
14 *Margaret:* John, did you take this out?
15 *John*: No.
16 *Margaret*: Then, who did?

(long pause)
17 *John*: I don't know.

(Children watch television and work for one minute)
18 *Margaret*: There, I got it in...Now.

19   *John*: Hurry up! This is my hacks (hat).

20   *Margaret* (fitting up string): There.

21   *John*: Thank you very ⌈ much.

22   *Margaret*:   ⌊ What did you do?

23   *John*: It stuck over there.

24   *Margaret*: Now we've to take it out again.

25   *John*: Ah — that's this. (pulls string out of hat)

26   *Margaret* (exasperated): Don't! Look what you did! Now I have to start all over again!

27   *John*: Ooh! You put it that with that (?) (unintelligible)

28   *Margaret*: You have to wait again, because I have to start again.

(Children finish with hat making and fitting)

29   *Margaret*: Let's go and play t(unintelligible). Wanna go outside, John?

30   *Rosemarie*: Do you want to stay (?) here?

31   *John*: Wanna colour in something?

32   *Margaret*: What? I want that book, Rosie, to colour in.

33   *John*: Which book?

(The children go into John's room)

34   *Rosemarie*: I've got a book to colour in and I'm gonna colour it in.

35   *Margaret*: I know, let's write letters.

36   *John*: No, no. I'm not. Who said you could take mine? (referring to paper?)

37   *Rosemarie*: These aren't all yours.

38   *John*: Yeah. They're mine. They're all mine.

39   *Margaret*: What about these? (sounds of physical struggle) Ooh, these are mine.

40   *John*: These're Rosie's?

41   *Margaret*: They're mine.

42   *John*: These are yours.

43   *Margaret*: I done mine in order. Rosie's is that one.

(Children whisper until Margaret speaks)

44   *Margaret*: Pretend — ah — why not we write letters to each other?

45   *John*: No...no.

46   *Margaret*: I'll (?) writing a letter to Johnnie.

47   *John*: I don't wanna.

48   *Margaret*: I'm gonna write a letter to Rosie then.

49   *Rosemarie*: I don't wanna.

50   *John*: Get out my room! What are y'staying here for? This your fing? (?)

51   *Rosemarie*: John.

52   *John*: Yeah?

53 *Rosemarie*: Do you wanna write a letter?

54 *John*: Okay. (Goes into lounge room with a cigar which he pretends to smoke and sings, partly in Macedonian) Smoke cigara.

(Rosemarie calls out to John who is in the lounge)

55 *John*: What?

56 *Rosemarie*: I'm gonna get some paper.

57 *John*: What?... what? Oh thanks (?), I could have your Easter egg.

58 *Rosemarie*: Oh, don't! Give me my Easter egg back!

(After returning to his own room, where he gets pencil and paper, John goes into the kitchen and joins his sisters)

59 *Margaret*: I'm going to write it down.

60 *John* (wanting something from Margaret's writing materials): Give me one. Can you give me one?

61 *Margaret*: No, you go and get one of yours, because I've run out.

62 *John*: I'm going to get a nicer one than yours. (referring to letter?) Nah!... (unintelligible)... Mine's a more nicer one than yours. Who put this here? (referring to paper Rosemarie has left on chair)

63 *Rosemarie*: I did (?)

64 *John*: I was here. (Sings in Macedonian)

(Children now seated at kitchen table, writing letters)

65 *Margaret*: Whadja take?

66 *Rosemarie*: (haughtily, in mock superior tone): They are mine if you would like to know.

In this lengthy extract, we can 'see' and 'hear' John, Rosemarie and Margaret doing and saying what children throughout the world do and say. They argue, fight, command, control, submit, pretend, tease and make sense out of one another's meanings and points of view. Yet most people, when asked what language is used for, recognise only the communicative or referential function: Speaker A, in referring to object C, transmits information about C to speaker B. It is true that language serves to inform — any parent who listens to the eagerly-told experiences of a child can testify to this — but language has other functions as well. What John, Rosemarie and Margaret do with their language extends far beyond any simple transfer of information. They use language to effect changes in their surroundings and in the behaviour of others, and to construct a 'picture' of themselves and their environment. Children use language in sophisticated and complex ways: to establish and maintain social relationships, to create a concept of 'self' and 'other', and to interpret their world for themselves and for others. Yet teachers have traditionally regarded language solely as a communicative tool. This narrow perspective has resulted in classroom language work that typically consists only of essay and 'creative' writing, written projects and occasional oral recitations — all with the teacher as audience.

As we examine the language of the extract from a functional point of view, we are led to pose several questions. What are the kinds of functions which reveal themselves in the speech of the children? What sorts of functions do not appear in their speech (for example, because there are no adults present for the children to interact with), but which they might use on other occasions?

The Jakobson model of language functions

Roman Jakobson (1960), in an important article on linguistics and poetics, based a classification of functions on a model of the communication process in which a speaker and hearer in a speech event (for example, a conversation, lecture, discussion, etc.) exchange messages that are shaped by a number of attendant factors:

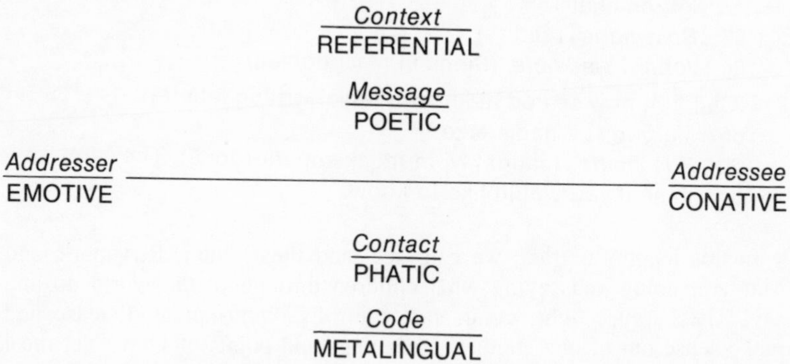

Context
REFERENTIAL

Message
POETIC

Addresser　　　　　　　　　　　　　　　　　　　　　　　*Addressee*
EMOTIVE　　　　　　　　　　　　　　　　　　　　　　　　CONATIVE

Contact
PHATIC

Code
METALINGUAL

Fig. 6.1 The Jacobson Model

In Figure 6.1, the *Addresser* imparts a *Message* or content to the *Addressee*. To be operative, the message requires a *Context*, which can be grasped by the Addressee; a *Code* or ordering system (into which the Message is encoded), at least partially common to the Addresser and Addressee; and a *Contact*, a physical channel (for example, writing, gestures, speech, drums, smoke signals, the telegraph, etc.) and 'psychological connection', which enable the Addresser and Addressee to be in rapport and engage in communication. For Jakobson, language functions (appearing in block capitals in Figure 6.1) arise and are defined according to the focus on one or another 'factors' (italicised) in the speech event. Jakobson's list of language functions includes the following:

1 The *expressive* or *emotive* function highlights the addresser's feelings. This function is revealed in John's and Margaret's 'Ooh!' in the extract (27, 39).

2 The *conative* or *directive* function focusses on the person(s) addressed. This function is expressed grammatically as the 'vocative' (calling the attention of the person spoken to) and the imperative (requesting or requiring the addressee to perform some action), as when Margaret says to John (58), 'Give me my Easter egg back!' or when John says to Margaret (19), 'Hurry up!'

3 The *referential* function, a predominant function of language, is oriented toward the context of the speech event. The referential function relates to the ability of language to impart ideas about something. Significantly, few 'pure' examples of this function occur in our extract, since in speech events involving only children, the speech is oriented toward the children themselves, rather than the context. A possible illustration of the referential function is to be found at (43): 'Rosie's is that one.'

4 The *poetic* function centres on the message itself, for its own sake. It relates to the verbal art and the aesthetics of language. At (7), John seems to put on a Macedonian accent (almost in an absent-minded sort of way): 'What's happened to dis? Is it det?' At (54), John deliberately joins a Macedonian-inflected English verb *smoka* and the Macedonian noun *cigara*, using the poetic device of assonance, and at (13), he alliterates and assonates Macedonian nonsense sounds. Although we can only guess why John plays with these sounds, we can see the pleasure it gives him to twist and distort Macedonian, the language he speaks for part of the day, occasionally mixing it with his first language, English. In the created world of rhymes, alliteration, assonance, sounds and rhythms, little content is communicated; but the delight taken in creating language out of language points to a very basic language function in the child's world.

5 The *phatic* function (the term 'phatic communion' was coined by anthropologist Bronislaw Malinowski) indicates that the addresser is well-disposed and favourably inclined toward the addressee. For example, the seemingly empty greetings, 'G'day!' 'How are you?' and 'Hot, ain't it?' convey little, if any, actual information; yet they serve to open the channel to the speech event and 'say' to the addressee, 'I am a human, just as

you are; I am aware of your presence and I am friendly.' Such expressions as 'small talk', 'cocktail party talk', 'idle chatter', 'chin wagging', 'gab' and 'kaffeeklatsch' tell us of the existence of the phatic function of language. You can test whether an addresser really intends you to answer a phatic question by replying to a 'G'day-how's-it-goin' greeting with 'Well, I've been laid up for a week with a bad back, the wife's in hospital with jaundice, and....' Not unexpectedly, we find no examples of the phatic function in the extract; the channel has already been opened before the events of the extract occur.

6   The *metalinguistic* function focusses on the linguistic code. John's awareness of this function occurs (64) when he sings in Macedonian, breaking with the language code used throughout the rest of the extract. The metalinguistic function is important in the classroom, since it figures prominently in the process of learning and the development of language. We also learn to employ linguistic and grammatical terminology which, by allowing us to talk about the language code, has a metalinguistic function: *noun, verb, function, phoneme, sentence, relative clause*, etc. That the metalinguistic function is basic to human language is shown by the fact that humans can talk about talking, but parrots cannot 'parrot' about 'parroting'.

We have listed a number of functions and the language serving them in order to illustrate one particular model of language functions. We can add more functions to this list by determining what use is being made of various kinds of language. Following are a number of language examples that 'realise' several function-types. Try to decide what functions are served by the various examples.

Group A: (1) A teacher conversing with a colleague says to a child who has interrupted the conversation, 'Not now, Bradley, we're talking. You can tell me about it later.' (2) Greeted at the family dinner table with her least favourite dish, Brussels sprouts, an eight-year-old girl turns to her younger brother and says, 'Uk-yay, I ate-hay russel-bay prouts-say!' (3) A citizens band operator radios his friend, 'Hey ol' buddy, this is rubber duckie, pushing out of Crow City and sendin' good numbers to sugar Daddy, a 10–34 on the superslab near the Eversdale turnoff.' (4) The opening paragraph of an article on quantitative psychology reads, 'The additive constant problem was originally formulated as the problem of finding a constant c, which converted the observed comparative interpoint distance between a pair of stimuli hjk, into an absolute interpoint distance, djk, in such a way as to minimise the dimensionality of the resulting Euclidean space in which the stimuli were to be represented.' (5) A middle-age woman, when asked by her best friend to give an opinion of a most horrible dress purchased by the friend, replies, 'Why ... yes dear, it's a most ... interesting dress.'

Group B: (1) A tribal chief utters curses on a mortal enemy and a Roman Catholic priest delivers an excommunication pronouncement on a sinner. (2) Without the verbs *bet, pronounce, dub, sentence* and *bequeath* being spoken, wagers could not be made, marriages would not take place, knights would not be created, prisoners would not be sent to gaol, and children would not receive their parents' estates. (3) An audience watching an old film break out laughing when the hero exclaims, 'You know me dear, a gay young bachelor!' (4) A Roman Catholic priest raises the Eucharist wafer and intones, 'This is my body.' (5) Rather than saying *cancer*, some people whisper the word or say 'a long illness' or say, as John Wayne did, 'the big C'.

Group C: (1) An angry worker threatens his foreman with 'I'll get you, mate!' (2) A student fails an examination and exclaims 'God damn it!' (3) Hitting his finger with a hammer, a weekend handyman cries, 'Ouch!'

Group D: (1) A devout worshipper fingers his rosary beads and prays 'Hail Mary, full of grace.' (2) Placing an academic hood over a student's head, a university chancellor says 'I confer upon you the degree, Bachelor of Arts.' (3) Most American schools commence the day with a recitation of the 'Pledge of Allegiance to the Flag' — to do so is a mark of patriotism for the American people. (4) 'Up there Cazaly' is sung by spectators at Australian Rules football matches.

We should not convey the impression that Jakobson's model of language function is merely a device for generating lists of functions. His model has been influential in the studies of Dell Hymes, a pioneer in the field of language and society. Hymes (1968) applies Jakobson's taxonomy of the various factors and functions (see Figure 6.1) in single speech events to the patterns of speech behaviour in whole communities. For Hymes, Jakobson's model has pointed the way to a study of language that deals with more than the facility that a person has in speaking the language code. There are social competences that a speaker brings to a communicative act; for example, the ability to choose the appropriate channel or a particular form of the language code to suit the occasion.

The Halliday model of language functions

A different functional perspective is that of M.A.K. Halliday (1973, 1975 and Kress 19). Halliday looks especially at ways speakers use language to carry out various roles within a social group, satisfying material needs and incorporating the value system of the group, and developing personality and integrating it with a world order. For Halliday, to say that a child 'knows' language is to say that he knows how to use language to perform these functions. Halliday sees seven distinct functions emerging early in a child's development:

1   Instrumental ('I want'): language as a means by which the child satisfies his material needs or requirements. This is one of the first functions to evolve in the child's repertoire. Example: (57) John: I could have your Easter egg.

2   Regulatory ('do as I tell you'): language used to influence and control the behaviour of others. Example: (35) Margaret: I know, let's write letters and (50) John: Get out my room!

3   Interactional ('me and you'): language as a means of maintaining ties with other people. It reveals the child's awareness of others and his relation to them; language used to get along with others; the language of social interaction, consolidation, inclusion and exclusion, humour and persuasion. Example: (51) *Rosemarie*: John. (52) *John*: Yeah?
(53) *Rosemarie*: Do you wanna write a letter?

4   Personal ('here I come'): language for expressing one's own individuality and for developing awareness of the self and of personality; the language of interest, pleasure, disgust and personal feelings. Example: (38) *John*: Yeah. They're mine. They're all mine.

5   Heuristic ('tell me why'): language as the means of exploration, both inside and outside oneself; language used to discover and learn about things. Language like this is used with a parent, but rarely with a sibling. Before entering school the child already controls a metalanguage for the heuristic function in the words and meanings of 'question', 'answer', 'understanding' and 'knowing'. Example: Four-year-old: 'Daddy, what are those things called again at the end of the flower?' Father: 'Roots! What are they used for?' Four-year-old: 'I think they're used to suck up things.' Father: 'What things?' Four-year-old: 'Water... erm... fertiliser... and soil.'

6   Imaginative ('let's pretend'): language used to create one's own world or environment, including meaningless sounds, rhyming and other linguistic play. 'Story', 'pretend' and 'make up' become elements in the metalanguage of the imaginative function. Example (not included in the extract): *John* (singingly of sister Rosemarie): Naughty, naughty, boydy, naughty Rosa.

7   Informative ('I've got something to tell you'): language used to communicate new information, to express propositions and to convey a message which makes reference to the world surrounding the child. The informative function does not

appear in the language of the very young child, but it is
sometimes regarded as the dominant function in adult speech.
Example: (66) *Rosemarie*: They are mine if you would like to
know.

Children use these functions to cope with their environment, to ensure
their survival and to take their place in the 'scheme of things'. Halliday
describes the functions of adult language in three 'macro-functions': the
ideational, representing ideas or experience; the *interpersonal*, expressing social and personal relations; and the *textual*, the 'enabling' function which breathes life into language and gives it its sense of realness,
cohesion and texture. The textual function is what makes the language
used in human interaction different from a word in a dictionary or a
sentence in a grammar book. These macro-functions work together in
individual utterances, giving rise to three kinds of structure. For example, Rosemarie's statement, 'They are mine if you would like to know'
(66), has an ideational function (asserting something about the world),
an interpersonal function (intervening strongly in the situation), and a
textual function (this is an appropriate form of words in this situation).

Halliday draws attention to three aspects of the speech situation which
influence the way functions are realised in particular instances. (1978)
The *field of discourse* refers to what is going on in the particular situation. This determines the grammatical patterns and vocabulary denoting
who does *what* to whom. It is, therefore, associated with the ideational
macro-function. The *tenor* signifies the role relationships of the people
involved in the speech situation (for example, the teacher-pupil relationship). This influences the kind of rapport between the people concerned,
and what speakers do to achieve this rapport. *Tenor* is related, therefore, to the interpersonal macro-function. The *mode* points to the channel of communication (whether written or spoken) and the rhetorical
forms of persuasion, didacticism, description, exposition, etc. It expresses the cohesion of language — how one sentence hangs together with
another within a stretch of language. Mode is linked, therefore, to the
textual macro-function. Taken together, field, tenor and mode are variables which provide the framework for the selection of meanings and
the actualisation of these meanings in structural forms. They comprise,
in Halliday's view, 'register', the study of which can reveal what linguistic forms will be determined by particular contextual factors.

We can use these terms to test whether these interacting variables
result in the kind of language used by looking at (44) to (49) of the
extract.

Field: No adults present.
Children's argument: arguing whether to play at
letter-writing.
— making bids as to whom children should write.
— suggestions and rejections of them.

Tenor: Intimate: young boy and two older sisters interacting.
— eldest sister in charge: making suggestions so as to determine course of action.
— younger children rejecting suggestions of older sister.

Mode: Spoken: unrehearsed dialogue.
— recommendatory/disapproving.
— pattern of bid-rejection unites discourse.

The Tough model of language functions

Joan Tough has focussed especially on the role of language in the socialising and self-relating elements in a child's experience. This interest was prompted by Tough's concern about the poor school showing of lower working-class children. Tough gathered examples of the language used by 'advantaged' children (those with professional parents — lawyers, teachers, physicians, etc.) and 'disadvantaged' children (those with parents having completed an education at a minimum age and working in unskilled or semi-skilled occupations) at the ages of three, five-and-a-half and seven-and-a-half. In her research, Tough poses the question, 'How is educational success related to the way different children use language to create a picture of reality?' She is especially concerned, therefore, with how language serves the purpose 'of expressing and constructing meanings, that is, language functions in relation to the child's developing conceptualisation of the world around him'. (Tough, 1977, p. 44.)

Maintaining a cognitive view throughout her work, she distinguishes four functions 'that can be recognised by the characteristics of four different modes of thinking that language serves to express and promote'. (Tough, 1977, p. 44.) These are the *directive, interpretative, projective* and *relational* functions. Within each function, Tough differentiates various *uses* of the language of the three age groups of children studied. For example, within the interpretative function, she finds the *reporting* and *reasoning* uses. She also uses the notion of *strategies*, that is, the various linguistic and non-linguistic devices the child employs to make meanings out of his experiences. For example, in the reporting use, such devices as 'reference to detail', 'comparison', 'labelling' and others, promote explicitness. Particular strategies can serve different uses and different functions. Unlike Halliday, Tough is not interested in building up a picture of language through the functions it serves. Rather, her functional labels represent a means of categorising the sense-making process of children so that teachers can evaluate and promote language skills.

Tough comes to the following conclusions after applying her functional analysis to the language of advantaged and disadvantaged children:

1 The Relation function — protecting self-interest, drawing attention to self-needs and maintaining self-status — underlies the speech of the disadvantaged group of children.

2 The Directive function — directing and extending the child's own action and obtaining co-operation with others — was used more often amongst the advantaged group than the disadvantaged group, who employed language as an 'accompanying', rather than 'controlling', medium.

3 The advantaged group used language serving the Interpretative and Projective functions — recalling past experience, reasoning, anticipating future events and imaginating — more than the disadvantaged group.

Tough's work highlights the insights achieved when a functional, rather than syntactic, approach is taken in the analysis of children's language. Not only does such an approach put the investigator in closer touch with what children have actually learned about using language; it also reveals much about how they interpret their experience. The form and structure of a child's language may be inappropriate or even inaccurate indicators of how the child can use and make meanings through language. In Tough's view, educationists who assume that syntactic differences in the child's speech and writing are signs of linguistic deficiency may devise unnecessary intervention or remediation programmes. For Tough, young children's use of language reveals the meanings which they have internalised and which shape the way they respond to situations.

Since advantaged and disadvantaged children differ in the meanings they have internalised, and the way they respond to the same situation, Tough proposes that the disadvantaged child's potential for meaning be developed. This is accomplished, she suggests, by the teacher encouraging the child to engage in teacher-pupil dialogues which extend, probe and give a focus to the child's experience, imagination and communicative capacities. Control over function, then, not vocabulary building or sentence drills, enables disadvantaged children to realise their full potential in school and to have greater opportunity of achieving success there.

The Britton model of written language function

Thus far, we have outlined several models of language function that deal primarily with spoken language. Now we turn our attention to a model of language function that describes the written word.

The British educationist James Britton, in the course of classifying 2122 pieces of writing from 500 boys and girls aged eleven to eighteen, developed his own model of language function. Although Britton intended these functional classifications to be employed in the analysis of all language, whether spoken or written, they have come to be used by Britton and his co-workers in the investigation of written language, especially of that produced by adolescents. Britton's model of language function can be diagrammed (adapted from Britton, 1970, p. 174) broadly as in Figure 6.2.

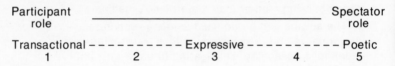

Fig. 6.2 The Britton Model

For Britton, the Expressive function (expressing personal attitudes, feelings, reactions etc.) is the 'starting point' in one's linguistic experience — the neutral ground from which one moves out to meet the demands made by larger language needs. We saw earlier that the expressive function was also called *emotive* and focussed on the addresser/speaker in the speech event. It is expressive speech, then, that is close to us, that contains our personalities and identities. It is the speech of egocentrism. Expressive speech is the means of communicating and exchanging ideas, gossip, values, news and opinions in a face-to-face situation. It is the instrument through which we make initial formulations, rehearse and test out ideas, explore likely possibilities. In short, we create solitary 'brain-storming' sessions in our use of expressive speech.

When the needs of the moment call for action to be taken, expressive speech gives way to the transactional function. In the transactional, we participate in informing, analysing, teaching, planning, arguing, persuading, or any other kind of activity where a practical outcome is to be achieved. The language expressed by this function will be explicit, logical and utilitarian; it will show a regard for cause-effect relationships and chronological order and will be sensitive to context — audience, background information, purpose, etc.

When the interest focusses on the form and shape of a linguistic experience for its own sake, rather than on what it accomplishes, we find expressive speech shifting ground to the poetic functions. Here, the spectator role is demanded. By standing detached from a linguistic experience, the observer can evaluate it in terms of the larger value system it holds for him. Thus released from the need to achieve an outcome or interact with another participant, the spectator can be free to attend to the linguistic experience *as linguistic experience*: the forms and structures of individual utterances and the discourse as a whole, the sequence of happenings in a narrative, the configuration of ideas and, in particular, the pattern of feelings represented. The language expressed by the poetic function might be called 'verbal art'.

Britton argued that these three functional categories can be applied to children's writing to distinguish the main function served by the piece of writing. For the child beginning to write, the Expressive function is a natural starting point. It is the dominant function in our daily interchanges with others. It suits the child's egocentric behaviour in that such demands as contexts, others' points of view, background knowledge, etc. need not be taken strongly into account. Writing in the Expressive function is largely a matter of transcribing speech, and since expressive writing reveals most fully the writer's personality, a meaningful relationship between writer and reader can develop. This is not to say that children grow out of the expressive function. Britton's model is not developmental in this sense. The Expressive function is to be seen as the 'matrix', the 'neutral point' from which a process of increasing differentiation would take place: towards the utility of the Transactional mode on the one hand or the self-consciously formal mode of the Poetic on the other.

In short, since children rely so much on expressive speech to interact with others, to make their needs known and to construct their versions of experience, expressive writing was seen by the Britton team as being crucial in the development of confidence and range in the writing of children.

Many of the features of expressive writing are illustrated by Mark, aged ten, in his journal entry entitled 'Fears':

> My biggest fear are nightmares and errie music. The dark
> scares me a little and so does big insects. Scary movies makes
> me shiver and when I'm about to get into trouble that makes me
> scared.

This writing is typical of what is found in journals, diaries, log books and many personal letters. The writing reveals language that is very much 'on the run', serving the shifting foci of thought and the demands made upon it by the writer, who can work out his feelings, attitudes, beliefs, etc. as his thoughts take him.

As the child moves out of the expressive toward the transactional, the writing becomes more suited to the context. It must be universalised, since unknown readers might wish to know more about the subject being written than about the person doing the writing.

For classifying writing which has not been differentiated for the Transactional or Poetic function, yet which shows signs of moving in either direction (see Figure 6.2), Britton proposes 'transitional' categories, that is, numbers 2 and 4 in the diagram. (Britton would see most primary-school writing as coming within categories 2, 3 and 4.)

To illustrate transitional category 2, we turn to a thank-you letter written by a Year-5 girl to a bus driver who had taken her class on a day excursion:

> St Josephs Primary
> 24th May 1979

Dear Uncle Arther,
    I'm writing this letter to thank you for a lovely time at Mundaring Weir on Wednesday. Most bus drivers are grouchy and mean, but you were really way out, you were really something else. I also want to thank you for helping us at the Musem with our answers, and playing games with us, and for not being grouchy and mean, but most of all I want to thank you for taking us to the Weir and bringing us back from the Weir.
    You never know I might see you on the 309 bus. Until then
      See you:
          With all my thanks   NICKIE!

Although Nickie's letter serves the purpose of acknowledging the bus driver's help, it particularises the day-trip experience and reveals to us as much about Nickie's personality as the experience itself.

The following write-up report on a broad-bean experiment, written by Rhonda, a Year-5 pupil, is an example of transactional writing:

> We first got a dry bean and a bean that had been left over night in water. Then we examined the dry bean. We looked at the wrincles and cracks in it and looked at how dry it was. Then we looked at the soaked bean and compared it with the dry bean. We found that the bean had been soaking if you squeezed it water would come out.
> We sealed the dry bean with wax from a candle on the scar because that's where the water came out and we put the bean in a jar which said sealed on it. Then we put the other bean in a jar which said unsealed. We left them over night and we were ment to take them out the next day but it was a holiday so we left them in till next Tuesday and they were to soaked so we threw them away.

Little, if any, of the observer's personality is revealed here. The role of participant has been made fully explicit to meet the needs of the role. Moreover, we find other features of transactional writing. Its validity rests on what it has to say rather than on who is saying it. The writing might produce a like response in the reader (acceptance, a challenge, suggestions for modifications, etc.), and it sets out a process in logical, carefully-planned language. Because processes must be carefully worked out in clear, concise language, instructions, directions, recipes, scientific reports, philosophical treatises, etc. are written in transactional language.

As the child comes to look at the language of his writing for its own sake, the child's writing may be said to move from the Expressive to the Poetic function. Whereas transactional writing can elicit a response suited to the participatory nature of the writing, in poetic writing we find that the response sought is one of experiencing, in spectator fashion, what is presented. Instead of creating a *process* for possible re-creative use later, a writer in the Poetic mode creates an *experience* which a reader can reconstruct for himself and enjoy as much as the writer.

An example of a transitional Expressive-Poetic function can be found in Jenny's (Year 5) fictionalised account, in diary form, of a nurse caught in a typhoid epidemic during the gold-rush days in Kalgoorlie. Only two entries out of a much longer passage have been extracted:

Wednesday the 21st of December

We have run out of medicine just when we need it. We always have precious little or no medicine at all. Four more died and got replaced with four more people. It is really sad watching the women, men and children suffer expecially when you cant do a thing to help them.

Sunday the 25th of December

This is the worst Christmas of my life. Three people died this morning, two children died an hour ago and the only two left are in great pain. I had no medicine or water. I was very sad I felt like crying. Half an hour later I heard something, it was the medicine cart and I got two bottles. I gave my patients two doses and they were saved but for how long?

We perceive much of Jenny's personality coming through the diary: her compassion, her feeling for what is unjust, her feelings of pity. However, she is creating a 'world', an experience, which she and we can stand off and observe. Moreover, she displays a sense of narrative pattern (the deaths and her reactions to them impel the 'story line' along), and irony (it is Christmas, yet a time of despair) and her use of auditory images for dramatic effect (she hears 'something' — the medicine cart) gives the experience an air of reality.

A child writing in the poetic function constructs a verbal object and makes use of the formal properties of language; for example, sound, structure and form. We know we are 'hearing' a story. In the first paragraph of her short story 'Claude,' Sarah, a Year-7 pupil, reveals the characteristics of poetic writing:

Once long ago, in medieval times, there lived a dragon by the name of Claude. He was a small plump, friendly dragon but he was very miserable. This was because nobody bothered to pay any attention to him. All the other dragons had scales that glittered when the sun shone on them. Claude has dull scales

because he had no mother to wash them. All the others were
brave but Claude was timid.

Many features of 'Claude' classify the story as Poetic: at the level of
language, Sarah uses 'inverted' sentences ('there lived a dragon'), 'poetic' vocabulary ('glittering'), and unusual forms ('by the name of'). At
the narrative level, Sarah marks her story with 'Once long ago', moving
to the more specific setting 'in medieval times', and patterns her story
to work from increasing conflict to climactic resolution. At the 'value
system' level, Sarah orders the narrative to reflect her belief that exclusion and social isolation can be overcome through understanding and
sympathetic acceptance.

Britton and his co-workers applied these categories to the 2122 samples of writing collected and analysed. They came up with several
results which were surprising in the light of the project team's emphasis
on the Expressive function. Of the writings assigned to one of the three
functional categories, 63.4% were found to be Transactional, only 5.5%
to be Expressive, and 17.6% Poetic. The remaining 13.5% was divided
between 'Additional categories' and 'Miscellaneous'. Confirming this
pattern of distribution is the Bennett Writing Survey in Western
Australia (Bennett, 1979). Assigning 2011 'scripts' written by children
15 to 17 to Britton's functional categories, the Bennett study found
86.9% falling into the Transactional category, 2.9% into the Expressive,
and 9.2% into the Poetic. (1.0% was classed as 'Other'.) Britton also
devised 'additional categories' for 'sense of audience' — related to a
reader's expectations of the writing — and 'special contexts of education'; but these need not concern us here.

There is much less expressive writing than other forms, according to
Britton's study; and when determined on a year-to-year basis, the expressive function dwindled to 4% in the final year of secondary school. Britton saw the poor showing of the Expressive function as regrettable. He
blamed the schools for fostering too much transactional writing aimed at
a teacher-as-examiner audience, rather than writing that shows independent thinking. But Britton's basic premises have been challenged by
Jeanette T. Williams (1977). She pointed out that with expressive writing favoured over the transactional in Britton's philosophy, harm could
be done if his project persuaded various subject teachers to use forms of
language unsuited or inappropriate to their subject area (for example,
science teachers using expressive writing).

Some of Britton's conclusions are controversial, but his categories are
useful in laying out for teachers three important areas of use for language in the written mode: language to get things done; language to
express self and to work one's way into understanding (in this sense,
Rhonda's transactional report on the broad-bean experiment was as valuable for her understanding of the concepts and processes involved as
anything expressive); and language to construct a reality. Nor should
any criticism hide the central need for children to gain self-confidence in

writing. This quality is achieved as children explore themselves, learning to nurture and harvest their thoughts and ideas, to develop their own distinctive writing 'voice', and to regard the implicit values of honesty and truth in all good writing.

Conclusion

The recent interest in language function signals a shift in linguistic study from the formal properties of language to the uses that speakers make of their language and the demands they place upon it. This interest might be summed up as a new regard for the *ecology* of language: a view that language does exists not in isolation but in company with a host of interlocking factors. Language is actualised through a web of relationships among speakers, surroundings and uses. A similar trend in the natural sciences has emphasised the rightful place of the organism in its native setting, rather than in the scientist's laboratory. Yet this comparison should not give the impression that language is a 'living' organism in the sense that a butterfly is. Whether the butterfly sits preserved in a lepidopterist's display case or flies about in its natural setting, it has an existence independent of its surroundings. Language, on the other hand, comes to life through the building-up of meanings which people create as they use language in specific contexts. If we say that language 'gains life', it does so only when people put it to such uses as talking about the weather, writing essays, reading poetry, teaching children to do sums, taking vows of marriage, filling out tax forms, or telling a joke. Like the 'Dance', which does not appear until the dancer makes it so, 'Language' does not assume a shape until people make it happen. And the realisation of this potential — whether one is 'Dancing' or 'Languaging' — comes through use and purpose.

The author wishes to thank Dr. A. MacGregor, Director of the Mount Lawley College language research team for making the recording tapes available for use in preparing the extract, and Mr. James Peterkin and Ms Susan Marville, the student researchers who produced the initial transcriptions of the extract. Also, the author is grateful to Mr. Bernie Hird of Mount Lawley College for providing the writing samples used.

Suggested activities

1   Consider the reasons why it would have been difficult to integrate Britton's transactional, expressive and poetic functions with those of Jakobson, Halliday and Tough. Where might Britton's functional model fit in the model in Figure 6.1?

2 Think of a situation where one might say to an obviously sick-looking friend, 'My, you're looking fit!' Is the statement a lie? Why or why not? What is the function of such a statement?

3 Using Britton's model of written language function, determine to which function the following script (written by a Grade 2 boy) belongs. Explain your choice.

The Six-eye Monster

Along time ago their lived a Monster and He
lived on Plootoy and He lived in a cave.
He had a invizabl dore and He is Big. He
was a nise monster. He never Rect Sitees
and Cars.

4 Transcribe every word and sentence of a ten-minute conversation with a friend. Which functions seem to predominate? Which do not appear? Why?

5 Look at typical examples of language from the classroom context, and analyse what functions they serve, and what functions of language are significantly absent.

Chapter 7　Ian Malcolm
Language and Social Context

'Many happy returns of the day!'

All readers of this book will have said or heard these simple words many times, and will have had no difficulty in understanding them. Most of us would regard them as perfectly normal English. But grammatically they are aberrant. There is no subject or verb. We also know that we cannot vary any of the words. We cannot say 'Many merry returns of day' or 'Quite a lot of happy returns of the day'. According to a recent comprehensive grammar (Quirk *et al* 1972) this expression belongs in 'a museum of oddments'. In this case we can explain the lack of a subject or verb as an example of ellipsis (leaving something out) which happens frequently enough in English. But why can we not vary any of the words? The rules say that we cannot affect the form of the language, but these do not seem to be rules of grammar. From this example we can suggest the hypothesis that English should be regarded as more than a linguistic system. It is governed by rules of speech use as well as rules of grammar.

If knowing English means knowing not only its grammar but also the conditions of its use, then we have a basis for understanding why we thought 'many happy returns of the day' was normal when, grammatically speaking, it is abnormal. The criteria for determining normality are not only linguistic but also social; and social meaning may be carried by linguistic forms to extend greatly, or even contradict, their literal meaning. Because you know the social meaning of English (at least to some extent), you know from hearing 'many happy returns of the day' that it is the birthday of the person who is being spoken to. You know also that the speaker knows him, and wishes to be seen to be expressing personal goodwill. If the words were spoken to you, you would know that you would be expected to acknowledge them with equal goodwill. If these words are spoken when none of these conditions applies, then a rule of speech use, or what we shall call a 'sociolinguistic rule' has been broken, and confusion and embarrassment result. Thus, the playwright Harold Pinter is able to create an unnerving situation at the

beginning of Act Two of *The Birthday Party* by having these words
spoken between strangers who share no goodwill, when it is nobody's
birthday.

In real life, of course, we cannot go around doing this sort of thing.
We have to obey rules of speech use, not only rules of grammar. Our
English — grammatical and ungrammatical — has to be employed
according to a sociolinguistic system. One well-known sociolinguist has
put it this way:

> Recall that one is concerned to explain how a child comes
> rapidly to be able to produce and understand (in principle) any
> and all of the grammatical sentences of a language. Consider
> now a child with just that ability. A child who might produce
> any sentence whatever — such a child would be likely to be
> institutionalized: even more so if not only sentences, but also
> speech or silence was random, unpredictable. For that matter, a
> person who chooses occasions and sentences suitably, but is
> master only of fully grammatical sentences, is at best a bit odd.
> Some occasions call for being appropriately ungrammatical.
> (Hymes, 1972 : 277)

Operating the sociolinguistic system

We all are subject to lapses in the way we operate our sociolinguistic
system, and we all know people who make us uncomfortable because,
from our point of view, they do not play the rules properly. Do you
know anybody who characteristically takes what you say the wrong
way, so that your joking remarks are taken seriously or your social
gambits are treated as hypotheses to be critically examined? After a few
unfortunate experiences, our conversation is likely to dry up in the presence of such a person if, indeed, we allow ourselves to be caught in his
presence again. The sociolinguistic system to which we have become
accustomed has such power over us that we are likely to be put on the
defensive as soon as we find its rules transgressed. Think, for example,
of how you feel when you answer the telephone and a voice at the other
end says 'Who am I talking to?', or when you answer the front door
and a stranger says 'Good morning and how are you?' Sometimes the
sociolinguistically inappropriate way to respond is to insist on the
grammatical or literal sense of what has been said to one. Let us consider, for example, another couple of exchanges from Pinter's *The
Birthday Party*:

> Do you mind sitting down?
> Yes, I do mind.

To answer the question literally is, in this case, to misinterpret it or to display antagonism towards the speaker. In the following exchange, the speakers know one another well and understand one another's very cryptic utterances, but McCann, because he does not wish to talk about what he has just seen, refuses to acknowledge the intent of Goldberg's words:

Goldberg : (to McCann who has just entered) Well?
McCann : (does not answer)
Goldberg : McCann. I asked you well.
McCann : (without turning) Well what?
Goldberg : What's what?
McCann : (does not answer)
          (turning to look at Goldberg, grimly) I'm not going up there again.
Goldberg : Why not?
McCann : I'm not going up there again.

Sociolinguistic units of description

Speech in context conveys a great deal more to us than the literal meaning of the words, and the social exchange that is language-in-use is an exchange, not of grammatical units but of sociolinguistic units, or 'speech acts'.

Social situations may be characterised by the kind of speech with which they are associated, and many speech acts, and combinations of speech acts, cannot be transferred from one social situation to another. The following utterances were recorded in various parts of Western Australia in a common social situation. On the basis of your familiarity with speech-use conventions of English, you will almost certainly be able to identify the social situation and, for each utterance, the speaker and the addressee:

1. Right, listening.
2. Philip West, sit up, thanks.
3. Mr. Roberts, can I have a turn 'cause I haven't had a turn.
4. Come on Dennis, quick.. Come on, we're waiting for you.
5. Okay, sitting up straight.
6. Miss Bentley, she drawed on my atlas.
7. Right, Brian, call out number four please.
8. I don't pick people who call out.
9. Pencils down and eyes here.
10. Mr Moss, my um social studies book's out in my bag.
11. I want to see every hand up.
12. Sir, I haven't finished it yet.
13. Well, you'd better get on with it.
14. Put a tick if you had that correct.
15. Whereabouts was the Batavia wrecked, Glenda?

Of course the social situation represented here is the classroom. The ease with which you recognised it from this evidence shows how close is the relationship between language and situation. The classroom is not just a social situation, but a *speech situation*, in that speech is inseparable from what goes on in classrooms, and the speech acts which occur there are in many cases peculiar to that situation. Note the very unusual (in terms of speech use in society at large) functions which speech in the classroom performs. It is used to compel participants' attention (1, 9 above), to regulate participants' posture (2,5) and their use of time (4), to ask 'quiz-type' questions (15) and to negotiate for respondents (3,8,11). A very large number of classroom speech acts have attached to them the name or title of the person to whom they are directed (2,3,4,6,7,10,11,15). Blunt directions may be given (7,9,13,14), and individuals may need to raise, in public, things which in other situations might be conceived as their own private business (10,12).

It is impossible, however, to understand the sociolinguistic patterning of a speech situation by considering isolated speech acts. A succession of events takes place in a situation like the classroom, and each event may be seen as a *speech event* in which speech behaviour follows a particular pattern. The rules of speech use are concerned not only with what speech acts may be used, but also with how they may be ordered. Note the significance of the ordering of the speech acts in the following exchange from a Western Australian classroom:

Mrs Reed	:	What do the Arabs mainly live in?
Class	:	(hands up)
Mrs Reed	:	Catherine
Catherine	:	Tents?
Mrs Reed	:	In tents,
		good
		Why do you think it's er necessary for the Arab to live in a tent?
Class	:	(hands up)
Mrs Reed	:	Dave?
Dave	:	There's no wood around?
Mrs Reed	:	That's right,
		there isn't any wood about.
		What, what other reasons .. there are also other reasons why the Arabs use a tent for living in.
Class	:	(hands up)
Mrs Reed	:	Robert?
Robert	:	Um they can put it up quick 'n take it down when they shift?
Mrs Reed	:	That's right.
		Good boy.
		It's easier for them to take it down 'n put up there when they're moving about, 'cause as you know they're always on the move, aren't they?

It is clear that, just as underlying rules govern the ordering of words in a sentence, so underlying rules govern the ordering of speech acts in a speech event like this one. The questions are all asked by the teacher and the respondents are all nominated by the teacher. Though only one respondent will be chosen for each question, the class as a whole is expected to offer to answer (by raising hands). The teacher both repeats and evaluates answers as she receives them, and is free to expand upon them. The children's role in the interaction seems to be more circumscribed. The children even give their answers a questioning intonation, showing that the content of the communication is seen to be something over which the teacher presides. In the extract we have reproduced here, it is easy to observe that the interaction proceeds by means of a cycle of speech acts repeated three times, each of which is initiated and concluded by the teacher. That is, as it were, the formula for the operation of this speech event.

We shall return later to the question of how speech use in classrooms may be best described. For the time being, this is simply an illustration of the broader issue of the sociolinguistic structuring of speech situations and speech events.

Sociolinguistic interference

Knowing how to speak English is, then, more than might appear on the surface. One needs to know not only the linguistic system that is English, but also the sociolinguistic system that governs the use of English in the speech community in which one wishes to use it. This knowledge is, like our knowledge of the linguistic system, acquired gradually from early childhood in the context of our daily experience. Progressively, as we grow older, we learn how to handle the speech-use demands of new situations. Life often forces this upon us — as when, for example, we start going to school, or move into employment, or take an executive position on a committee. Nobody, of course, is at home in all speech situations of a community, and, as we have seen, malfunctions in the sociolinguistic system at times cause embarrassment or confusion to us all.

The problems are, however, greatly magnified for some members of our community who have learned the sociolinguistic systems of other speech communities which contrast with that of the one in which they now must operate for a good deal of their time. The rules of speech use in different communities, like the languages and dialects, may vary markedly. When one's knowledge of one system hampers one in attempting to adopt or operate within another, *sociolinguistic interference* is said to occur. Sociolinguistic interference may affect the communication of migrant or Aboriginal Australians in general Australian society.

Some problems of sociolinguistic interference affecting migrant speakers in Australia have been investigated by Michael Clyne. In one study (1977), he tested the speech-use perceptions of four groups of sixty informants: three immigrant groups [Italians, Greeks and German speakers (Austrians and Germans)], and one non-immigrant Australian group. Each group was asked fifteen questions relating to possible areas of sociolinguistic interference; for example, 'Someone says to you "See you later" at the end of a conversation and you don't see him for several weeks. What do you think of him?' . . . . 'What do you think of someone who starts a conversation by talking about the weather?' . . . . 'If an Australian much younger than yourself (but of the same sex) addresses you by your Christian name, how do you react?'. Clyne found that, although most members of immigrant groups in his study had learned to adjust to 'Australian' rules, and even at times to overgeneralise them (for example, by reducing the frequency of handshaking to the point where they would do it on fewer occasions than most Australians), there were certain points where what he called 'communication conflict' was likely to occur.

Many migrant speakers were confused by the absence of any 'good appetite' routine at the beginning of a meal in Australian society. Some would have used such a routine in entertaining Australians, though none of the Australian group would have used it. A considerable proportion of the migrant speakers (the majority of the Italian and German speaking groups) would have said 'Goodbye' or a similar expression to a shopkeeper they did not know well after purchasing something from him, while the great majority of the Australian group would have said 'Thank you', or nothing. If they were eating in a restaurant and strangers at the same table left, the majority of Greek and German speakers would expect the people leaving to say 'Goodbye' or use a similar expression, while the majority of Australians and Italians would expect them to say 'Excuse me' or nothing.

German speakers and Greeks showed that they were much more likely than the Australian group to take offence at an ironical remark, such as 'Got a bit of a cold', addressed to them if seriously ill. Many Greeks, in contrast to the other groups, would have taken exception to being checked up on by the foreman at work. If they had not received a reply to a business letter, most German speakers said they would call into the office, whereas most Australians said they would make a telephone call. All immigrant groups said they would be more likely to employ written channels than would the Australian group. These findings show that in diverse areas of social interaction many non-English-speaking Australian migrants may use and interpret speech acts according to conventions learned in other speech communities. The problems, as Clyne has pointed out, may not lie at the level of specific acts, but at the level of more general rules of interaction. 'Communication conflict is likely to occur where the rule threatens the dignity of the individual — that is, on three types of issue: power, trust and solidarity' (1977:13).

In research in the Northern Territory, Stephen Harris (1977) has investigated the speech use of the Yolngu people of north-east Arnhem Land, and considered its bearing upon their behaviour in educational settings. The Yolngu are a traditionally-oriented Aboriginal group. Harris found that in their society the social context of speech use was distinctive in a number of ways. The Yolngu talk for social rather than utilitarian purposes, often punctuating speech with silences. They use the same kind of speech to both adults and children, but there are strict rules relating to speech between brothers and sisters and with one's 'in-laws'.

Outsiders to the Yolngu community are likely to be confused by a number of aspects of their speech use. Take, for example, planning and promising. An outsider would be mistaken if he interpreted a 'promise' by a Yolngu as an unconditional commitment. It was seen by the Yolgnu as subject to his feelings and other obligations at the time. Outsiders might also misinterpret Yolngu behaviours with regard to the expression of thanks. It is assumed by the Yolngu that one person helps another either because he wants to or because it is his obligation (on the basis of a kin relationship). In either case, any speech act expressing gratitude would be redundant. Outsiders might interpret the absence of such a speech act as ingratitude. Again, the Yolngu differ from European Australians in the rights they accord to speakers and hearers. Everyone has the right to speak, and also the right not to listen! To the Yolngu it is not offensive to make no response to a direct question; nor is it rude, when in the audience, to be restless, to interject, or to carry on one's own conversation.

On the other hand, the Yolngu are likely to take exception to certain speech behaviours which are assumed in non-Aboriginal society, and in particular in schools, to be 'normal', such as the use of an impersonal debate form and the asking of hypothetical or 'Why?' questions. These findings relate to one remote Aboriginal cultural group. However, a survey of Aboriginal speech communities Australia-wide (Malcolm forthcoming) has shown that they correspond in many respects to what speakers expect and do in a large number of Aboriginal communities. Apparent communication failure between Aboriginal and non-Aboriginal Australians may often (even in close-contact communities) be attributable, at least in part, to sociolinguistic interference.

Sociolinguistic variation in language

Our discussion thus far has developed from two assumptions: language structure implies a linguistic (or grammatical) system, and language use implies a sociolinguistic system. English is, on one level, a linguistic system. It does not, however, exist (except in theory) independently of speech communities which use it. Thus, what English is like in a given place where it is used will depend on the social factors which prevail.

We have seen that three social factors which will have a bearing on the form which English will take when it is used will be the speech situation, the speech event, and the influence of other systems on the speaker. It is necessary for us at this point to refine further what we have been saying about variation in language in general and English in particular.

When we look closely at a language in the contexts in which it is used, we begin to see that it is a multi-layered phenomenon. To call our language 'the English language' is to give it an extremely gross categorisation which tends to cloud the reality of its many distinct but interrelated manifestations. It is normal for linguists to refer, therefore, to sub-categorisations of language, and the most general term referring to these is *varieties*. English, as we use it, is a large number of varieties which are appropriate in different social situations.

How many varieties of English are there, and how many might one speaker command? We shall probably never be able to answer the first of these questions, since no two individuals are entirely alike in the way in which they use English, and therefore every speaker has his own individual variety or 'idiolect'. Every speaker will also have his own particular repertoire of varieties, depending upon how language has entered into his experience and what functions language has had to perform for him. One way of classifying the kinds of linguistic variety we may find is to consider those varieties which are associated with different *users* and those which are associated with different *uses*. (Halliday, *et al*, 1964). The former have been called *dialectal varieties* and the latter *diatypic varieties* (Gregory and Carroll, 1978).

Dialectal varieties may vary on a basis of individual difference (idiolect), period in history (temporal dialect), geographical location (regional dialect), social class (social dialect), and range of intelligibility (standard or non-standard dialect). Diatypic varieties may vary on a basis of the user's purpose (for example, technical/non-technical), medium (for example, spoken/written), personal relationship to the addressee (for example, formal/informal), and functional relationship to the addressee (for example, didactic/non-didactic). Speech use rules are responsible for the individual's selection from among the varieties in his repertoire, and for the associated speech acts and routines. Some speech acts and routines 'belong' to certain varieties. For example, the kind of bantering which Australians associate with Bazza McKenzie cannot be carried out in a formal variety, and some of Dave Allen's jokes are not funny without the Irish accent.

If, as we have suggested, each individual has his own repertoire of varieties, the members of a speech community will always have different levels of familiarity and confidence about which speech to use at a given time. Different varieties (and associated speech-use rules) are associated with different domains — that is, particular contexts. Domains associated with distinctive language use are, for example, the home, the school, the church, the workshop and the office. We differ in the different domains we are exposed to and in our experience and status within them. Those who best meet the speech-use demands of the workshop may be inarticulate in the office (and vice versa). The child who only mumbles monosyllables in school classrooms may be garrulous at home and in the peer group.

It is also possible that a person's repertoire of varieties may be affected by different kinds of experiences in particular domains. One theory is that children may have differential access to the varieties required in school because of predispositions acquired as a part of their socialisation within the home. Bernstein (1972) has claimed that the role relationships in working-class homes in England differ from those in middle-class homes, and that these role relationships determine the forms of communication which will be used. The working-class family, according to this view, is 'positional' in that it typically orders its behaviours according to the roles associated with status or position within the family. The associated communication system is 'closed'. The middle-class family, on the other hand, is seen as 'person-oriented', in that the ordering of behaviours is associated less with the statuses than with the personal qualities of the family members.

The communication system which results is 'open'. Children accustomed to a 'closed' communication system use a language variety which Bernstein calls a 'restricted code', and children accustomed to an 'open' communication system use an 'elaborated code'. (See also Chapters 2 and 9.) For the working-class child, going to school involves a shift from the use of a 'restricted' to an 'elaborated' code, and this may put him at an educational disadvantage with respect to the middle-class child. Some support has been lent to this theory by studies of the ways in which middle-class and working-class mothers talk to their children. For example, Robinson and Rackstraw (1972) reported:

> Bernstein's thesis is supported in several predicted ways: working-class mothers reporting how they would answer their children's questions produce responses with a higher incidence of 'no answers', inaccurate and lesser amounts of information in a 'noisy' linguistic context, restatements of questions as answers and appeals to simple regularity and authority. We infer that these mothers are using a restricted code whose function is to specify the form of the mother-child relationship rather than to teach the child about other matters — as Bernstein's theory demands. (Pp. 156–157.)

As we have seen, however, it is difficult to accept the view that, even in his pre-school experience, a child is limited to a single variety.

The evidence for the existence of restricted and elaborated codes is not conclusive (see Stubbs, 1976; Robinson, 1978); and to depict children as single-variety speakers may in itself be educationally damaging.

Rather than classifying children linguistically according to social class, schools might appropriately see it as a part of their role to investigate carefully the repertoire of varieties used by the pupils they serve. Such investigation, ideally, might be expected to precede the development of language arts policies and programmes within the school.

Conversational analysis

When even the simplest segments of natural conversation are intensively examined, it becomes apparent that, throughout the course of an interaction, the speakers are constantly making decisions about how they will participate. Interactions do not just happen; they come into being as the joint accomplishment of the speakers, operating according to specifiable (though usually implicit) rules or 'maxims'. As Erving Goffman, who has contributed greatly to the development of this conception of interaction, has put it,

> The socialised interactant comes to handle spoken interaction as he would any other kind, as something that must be pursued with ritual care.

> (Goffman, 1972:36)

Our understanding of how conversations are organised has been gained as a result of studies in which a large body of examples of naturally occurring interactions has been scrutinised for its regularities. Set against a background of similar cases, a conversational segment which, at a first glance, we would regard as unregulated, shows itself to be highly organised and rule-governed.

There are various ways in which such rules may be described. Two kinds of rules according to which speakers constantly monitor what they say have been called rules of alternation and co-occurrence (Ervin-Tripp, 1972). Rules of alternation say which of a number of words or phrases referring to the same reality a speaker will choose in a given situation. Take, for example, the question of forms of address. Should you call the person you are talking to 'Sir', 'Mr. Brown', 'mate', or nothing at all? (See Chapter 2.) The implications of the possible choices which English generally allows have been made explicit by Ervin-Tripp (1972:219). Once you have made the first choice, you have limited the range of further choices open to you in the conversation, since co-occurrence rules will apply, according to which your speech needs to be consistent. Once having called the person you are talking to 'mate', you will find it difficult or awkward to close the encounter by saying 'Good afternoon'.

People in an exchange are also bound by rules of sequencing. Take, for example, the case of a telephone conversation. As Schegloff (1972) has shown, such conversations begin as 'summons-answer' sequences which are always ordered in the same way. The answerer must speak first, and after he speaks the caller must speak again, providing the first topic for the conversation. If the order or nature of the turn-taking is altered, the interaction breaks down.

Once a conversation is in progress, it may continue only as the participants observe certain rules with regard to the taking of turns. It has been observed (see Sacks, Schegloff and Jefferson, 1974) that, at least in American society, one participant in a conversation speaks at a time, and that his turn continues until a point of 'transition relevance' (such as the end of a sentence) is reached. At this point, there are three possible ways in which the turns may change: the current speaker may select the next speaker, for example, by asking him a question (and the selected party must take the turn thus offered to him); or, if this does not happen, another participant may 'self-select', or the current speaker may continue.

When it comes to closing the conversation, this turn-taking cycle must be interrupted. As Schegloff and Sacks (1974) have pointed out, this means lifting the 'transition relevance' so that no participant feels obliged to take the next turn. This is achieved when a person uses his turn to utter a 'pre-closing', like 'We..el...' or 'Okay...'. This signifies that he sees the end of this topic as having been reached, and wishes to proceed with no new topic. Appropriately, the pre-closing may be followed with a 'terminal exchange'. This will take the form of an 'adjacency pair', where the first part of the pair, such as 'Goodbye', must be followed in the next speaker's turn with the second part of the pair, such as 'Goodbye'.

The complexities of interaction revealed by conversational analysis have scarcely been hinted at here, and the reader is recommended to consult some of the source papers, one of which appears in the Book of Readings.

Sociolinguistics and the classroom

The perspective we have taken in this chapter has brought two fundamental understandings about language to the fore. First, language use (like language) is meaningful and systematic; secondly, a necessary and significant feature of language is that it varies according to speaker and context. Let us consider very briefly some of the implications of these understandings for the classroom teacher.

Teachers and schools will not be able to found adequate language education programmes on a less-than-adequate understanding of language and the way in which it operates. If English contains many varieties, as we have suggested, it should not be regarded in schools as a single unvarying system. So teachers should not expect children in the playground to speak as they would in the classroom. Nor should they make universal pronouncements about right and wrong language from grammar books or dictionaries; and they should not equate children's language development with what they can produce in classroom test situations. In the real world, a child who speaks sentences which are perfectly grammatical but socially inappropriate would be 'institutionalised', so teachers cannot hope to succeed if they have a programme designed to produce such a speaker.

As our earlier discussion has shown, classroom discourse can be understood within a sociolinguistic framework on the same basis as any other verbal interaction. Insights gained from the sociolinguistic study of many other speech situations will be relevant to the understanding of what goes on in classroom discourse.

Here is a young male teacher in his second year of service taking a creative writing lesson with a Year 3 class in a rural school, and, by his own admission, 'not getting very far':

1.	Mr. A.	:	Who else can tell me something else about.. the circus?
2.	Several	:	Oh!... oh!
3.	Mr. A.	:	Thora.
4.	Thora	:	When we went to the circus, Mr. A..., we seen camels.
5.	Mr. A.	:	You saw a camel! That's a rather interesting animal to see at the circus. What would a camel be doing at a circus?
6.	John	:	I know!
7.	Mr. A.	:	Freda's not thinking very hard... Kevin's not. Noreen.
8.	Noreen	:	(pause) What did you ask?
9.	Mr. A.	:	Oh.. you must be deaf. What would a camel be doing at a circus? In fact I could ask that about any animal. What would any animal be doing at a circus?
10.	Several	:	Oh!
11.	Mr. A.	:	Some boys are not thinking at all hard. Freda. Oh I think we'll have to say it again for Kenny.
12.	Freda	:	They're trying to do tricks?
13.	Mr. A.	:	They're trying to do tricks.. But *why* are they trying to do tricks? For what reason?
14.	Bill	:	I know!
15.	Mr. A.	:	What reason are animals at circuses other than doing tricks?
16.	Bill	:	Oh.. I know.

17.	Mr. A.	:	I'm gonna..
			Put your hands down..
			I think we're not getting very far.
			Sit down, Bradley..
18.	Bill	:	I know.
19.	Mr. A.	:	Now I'll ask this question again, and think.
			Firstly, put your hand up if you've been to a
			circus.
20.	Class	:	(hands up)
21.	Mr. A.	:	Right,
			hands down.
			Now put your hand up if you know why we put
			animals at circuses.
22.	Class	:	(hands up).
23.	Mr. A.	:	Melvin.
24.	Melvin	:	To show people what they can do?
25.	Mr. A.	:	To show people what they're they're, what they
			can do, what kinds of things they have been
			taught...

In the light of the observations we have made about language use in general, we may draw attention to a number of distinguishing characteristics in the above discourse. First, it is apparent that one participant (we'll call him Speaker A) performs a role which is quite distinct from those of the other participants and from any role performed in the kinds of conversation analysed in the previous section. Speaker A is always the initiating speaker, and he tends to initiate with questions (see utterances 1, 5, 9, 13) or directives (see utterances 17, 19, 21). Since he commonly uses the first pair part of an 'adjacency pair', Speaker A tends to control what other speakers will say. When people provide the second pair part, Speaker A tends to repeat it (for example, utterance 13), and he may modify it (for example, making 'we seen' into 'you saw' in utterance 5) or extend it (for example, utterance 25).

Speaker A also is concerned with participants who do not respond to him, and equates a lack of response to his initiations with failure to think hard (utterances 7, 11). It is apparent that, to Speaker A, the interaction which he has initiated is supposed to be 'getting' somewhere. He reacts to responses in accordance with this expectation. That is, whatever their relevance to his initiation, they are given no positive acknowledgement if they do not lead towards his intended end point (see utterance 13).

The obvious quandary of all participants apart from Speaker A is that they do not *know* his intended end point. This is a kind of conversational blind man's buff in which everybody is blindfolded except Speaker A. The game, however, has some appeal, in that speakers repeatedly signal their desire to have a go (in the words 'Oh!' or 'I know!': utterances 2, 6, 10, 14, 16, 18). Paradoxically, Speaker A, who criticises people who make no response to his initiations, often ignores the offers made by others who want to respond. (It is apparent that, in this conversation, a desire to respond to Speaker A has to be signalled and approved before the response may be made.)

We could go on, but enough has been said to demonstrate that this is no ordinary conversation. Classroom discourse clearly is a special kind of discourse with its own specific operational rules. It is necessary, then, for us to go further, and suggest how it may be systematically studied with a view to showing its basic structure. Three approaches which are consistent with the understandings developed in this chapter might be followed up with profit.

A system devised by Sinclair and Coulthard (1975) is based on a rank scale model. That is, it tries to describe classroom discourse as built up in successive levels or ranks of discourse units, with each rank except the lowest having a structure which may be expressed in terms of the units in the rank below it. At the lowest level are speech acts, of which Sinclair and Coulthard have identified and defined twenty-two. Acts may be combined in certain ways to form Moves. Exchanges are structured out of Moves, and in turn combine to form Transactions. A Lesson is an unordered series of Transactions. Let us look at the first Exchange in our extract from Mr. A's lesson according to Sinclair and Coulthard's system.

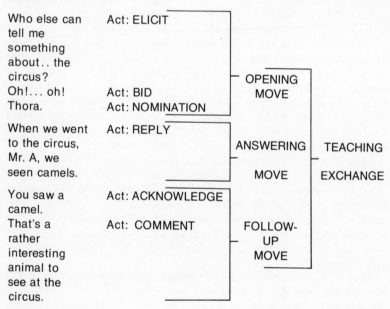

Fig. 7.1

This analysis helps to make apparent the so-called 'IRF' (Initiation-Response-Feedback) structure which has been found to characterise classroom discourse in many parts of the world. Sinclair and Coulthard's system was devised to cope with data gathered in formal teaching situations. It has not always been found useful in the study of less formally structured classroom interactions.

Another approach, developed by Hugh Mehan (1978, 1979) at the University of California, has been described as 'constitutive ethnography'. Mehan has attempted to capture the interactional work which is engaged in by teachers and pupils to 'accomplish' the classroom events we call lessons. He sees teacher and pupil as working together to achieve a symmetry in the interaction. Symmetry is achieved when an eliciting act receives its replying act (completing one adjacency pair) and when these in turn are followed by an evaluation (completing a second and linked adjacency pair). These three-part sequences of communicative acts are the stuff of which lessons are made. Mehan calls them 'I-R-E' sequences (see IRF sequences above).

They are always initiated by the teacher. Some sequences are directive, some are informative, and some form topically-related sets. A lesson is structured in three phases. The first or opening phase is composed of directive and informative sequences (in that order); the second, or instructional, phase is composed of sequences in topically-related sets, and the third, or closing, phase is composed of informative and directive sequences (in that order). When the basic pattern is not maintained, Mehan claims that a number of 'improvisational strategies' may be employed by teacher and pupil. Thus, for example, the teacher may employ 'the work of doing nothing', by ignoring a child's response when it has been made out of turn, or the teacher may 'open the floor' to anybody when the required response is not forthcoming from the nominated child.

Malcolm (1979, 1979a) has developed a system to deal with data recorded in classrooms with Aboriginal pupils in Western Australia. He sees classroom interaction as composed of speech acts with seven basic functions (eliciting, bidding, nominating, replying, acknowledging, informing and directing). He distinguishes 125 ways in which these functions may be realised by teachers and pupils (including some which specifically characterise Aboriginal children's behaviour). Speech acts may be combined in many ways to form routines (see the 'repeated cycle of speech acts' illustrated on page 123). Different routines are associated with different speech events. Thus, such classroom speech events as 'imparting content', 'revising content', 'news', 'reading instruction', etc. may be characterised on the basis of their discourse structure. Classroom communicative problems may be related to the ways in which speech acts and routines are realised by teacher and pupil. In the following sequence, the teacher is attempting to follow an

'Individual Discussion Routine', in which individuals are nominated to interact according to a basic IRF pattern with the teacher. The Aboriginal children, however, do not fulfil their turns in the anticipated way, and the teacher is forced to modify the requirements of the routine:

			Acts
			(TE = teaching eliciting act,
			CR = child replying act, etc.)
			etc.)

Mrs H.	: Who can tell me something about mustering?	TE	Eliciting
	Do you know what they do, Diane?	TN	Nominating
	You tell us..	TN	Cueing
	Listen carefully. Diane is going to tell us too..	TD	Retrieving audience attention
	Diane,	TN	Nominating
	what do you think they do?	TE	Multiple eliciting
	Listen..	TD	Retrieving audience attention
Diane	: (no reply)	CR	Declined replying
Mrs H.	: Do you know, Beryl? You tell me what you think they do when they go mustering.	TN	Nominating
	Do you know?	TN	Cueing
Mary	: They take de-	CR	Unsolicited replying
Mrs. H.	: Ssh.. Let Beryl have a turn	TN	Upholding priority
Beryl	: (very quietly) Sheep	CR	Replying
Mrs H.	: They get the sheep, do they? What do	TA	Acknowledging
	they.. how many horse d'you think they'd use if they do the-	TE	Eliciting
Several	: Three! Two! Three!	CR	Unsolicited replying

It is, of course, impossible to convey in a page or two an adequate idea of systems of analysis which, in each case, have required an entire volume to present. However, from what is presented here, it may be seen that teacher and pupil talk in classrooms is describable in sociolinguistic terms; and that, if teachers take the means that are to hand to look at their own classroom speech in sociolinguistic perspective, they may well be able to trace and eliminate flaws in their classroom performance.

Conclusion

According to the understanding on which this chapter is based, language implies not just talking but also acting in social situations. Meanings reside not in words but in people, and language is part of the system, or set of systems, whereby people in society exchange meanings. To be able to handle a social situation successfully, a person needs to be in control not only of linguistic rules but also of rules of speech use. Experience in one culture, or in one social situation, does not necessarily hold good for the speaker when he moves into a new culture or into a new social situation. This affects the behaviour of children in classrooms, and if teachers are aware of this fact, they may better understand and deal with communication problems with their pupils.

Suggested activities

1. Make explicit the social knowledge which might be entailed in the correct interpretation of the following linguistic fragments:

    > Kitchen door up right.
    > The covers were off.
    > Baby want a bikkie?
    > A crash on Wall Street.
    > Seats lost in landslide.

2. Record an exchange with someone you know very well. Transcribe it, and write down beside the transcription the social knowledge assumed by both of you in interpreting one another.

3. Take a modern play in which deviant language use conveys an impression of absurdity or nihilism. Account for the effect obtained on the basis of rules of speech use.

4. Test out Hymes's claim that, by speaking with linguistic accuracy but sociolinguistic normlessness a person would be 'institutionalised', by systematically breaking sociolinguistic (but not linguistic) norms.

5. Label the fifteen speech acts listed on page 122 according to function. Take another speech situation in which speech is used differently and list some of its characteristic speech acts. Label them according to function.

6. Describe (in terms of the sequence of speech acts) the routine being followed by Mrs. Reed and her class in the extract on page 124. Transcribe and analyse interaction from other lessons, and compare the patterns.

7. If you have access to immigrant groups other than those surveyed by Clyne, test them for sociolinguistic interference on features like those isolated by Clyne.

8. Make a sociolinguistic profile of yourself, noting your repertoire of varieties. In what speech situations are you unsure of the speech rules, and why?

9. Draw up a list of sociolinguistic principles for language management in the classroom.

Chapter 8   Ian Malcolm
Authority, Instructions and Control

The controlled conversation of classrooms

We noted in the previous chapter that it is possible to view the talk which goes on between teachers and pupils in classrooms as a kind of conversation, but that it is no ordinary conversation. In terms of the distribution of conversational rights, teacher-pupil conversations in classrooms are decidedly lopsided affairs. We saw that one speaker in such conversations (always the teacher) has the right to compel the other participants' attention, to regulate their posture, to give them blunt directions and receive from them what, in other circumstances, would be private information. The teacher initiates the conversation, and evaluates participants' contributions in terms of how they approximate to the end point which he wishes it to arrive at. If this is a conversation, then it is different from other conversations in that it is 'controlled'. Both the intended end point and the means of getting there are in the hands of the teacher. At times, teachers exploit to the full the potential which the classroom offers them for controlling the conversation. Take, for example, the following exchange which was quoted in the previous chapter:-

Mr. A. :	Now I'll ask this question again, and think.	
	Firstly, put your hand up if you've been to a circus.	
Class :	(hands up)	
Mr. A. :	Right,	
	hands down.	
	Now put your hand up if you know why we put	
	animals at circuses.	
Class :	(hands up)	

Here the teacher has relieved the pupils of the responsibility even of speaking. Their part in the interaction is to put their hands up when told to and to put them down again when told to. Extended interactions cannot be conducted in this way. Teachers tend to resort to this approach in emergencies, when their control of the classroom discourse has been threatened.

There is no guarantee that the class will comply with the pattern which the teacher wishes to impose. Let us look in on a lesson where teacher and class are clearly pulling against one another in the way in which they are operating the interactional system. The teacher is in his second year of service and in his first term of appointment to this country school. He has a Year 4/5 class of mixed European and part-Aboriginal composition. It is an afternoon session when the children often have informal work, but today the teacher wishes to revise work in social studies. As he addresses the class, he is sitting on the blackboard ledge at the front. The desks are arranged in rows, facing him. (Participants' names have been changed in the transcript).

1.	Mr. W. :	Remembering on a little bit further, we had all the explorers .. well, not necessarily explorers, but various people sailing around the place and, bumping into Australia, specially up in the North-West. After that ..
2.	Simon :	(miming bumping into something)
3.	Mr. W. :	(quietly) If you're going to be silly, Simon, you can remove yourself for five minutes until you quieten down.
4.	Bill :	Yes!
5.	Mr. W. :	(to Bill) Now that's the last time I'll talk to *you*.
6.		After that, we had a few people who actually came out and had a good look at Australia, until finally, Captain Cook came out,
7.	:	and what was *his* job?
8.	Joe :	'E was .. 'e was .. I know.
9.	Mr. W. :	He had a job ..
10.		Joe?
11.	Joe :	'E was chasin' a pig?
12.	Class :	(hilarity)
13.	Mr. W. :	All right ..
14.		Joe,
15.		I think you've got the wrong lesson. We're doing social studies here, not um ..
16.	Barry :	Jokes.
17.	Mr. W. :	joke time.
18.	Class :	(continuing laughing)
19.	Mr. W. :	Right,
20.		come on.

21.		'Ey, no, look.
22.		I'm just not at all happy with some people in this room at the moment..
23.		Okay,
24.		you've had a hard day, you've had tests and things..
		I still want you to listen.
25.	Bob :	(non-verbal bid)
26.	Mr. W. :	Bob?
27.	Bob :	Um, starting a settlement?
28.	Mr. W. :	Starting a settlement,
29.		No, it wasn't that quite 'is job before.
30.	Andy :	(non-verbal bid)
31.	Mr. W. :	Andy.
32.	Andy :	Can I go to the toilet?
33.	Class :	(another burst of laughter)
34.	Mr. W. :	Quick,
35.		go round that way, I'll (unclear word) for you..
36.		Righto,
37.		that's enough..that's enough.
38.	Linda :	(non-verbal bid)
39.	Mr. W. :	Linda
40.	Linda :	To see what sorta land it was?
41.	Mr. W. :	To see what sort of land it was,
42.		why?
43.	Linda :	To see if it was better than England so they could come out to live there, see if people could live there 'n um they could send some of their people there?
		(Nancy has not been paying attention).
44.	Mr. W. :	Nancy,
45.		What did Linda just say?
46.	Nancy :	(no answer)
47.	Mr. W. :	You don't know.

After a number of further exchanges, the teacher determines that the discussion should cease and written work should begin:-

48.	Mr. W. :	What I want to do now,
49.		very quietly..
50.	Class :	(noise of voices and taking out of books)
51.	Mr. W. :	(long silence)
52.		What I want to do now...
53.	X :	(an unidentified pupil is singing in the background)
54.	Mr. W. :	Whoever it is that's doing the singing, would you stop.

55.		There's singing tomorrow afternoon.
56.		Quietly take out those Pioneers books, please.
57.	Class :	(noise of voices and taking out of books)
58.	Mr. W.:	Freeze!
59.		The very first word I said was quiet.
60.		Let's do it quietly and show me that you know what quietly means.
61.		Most of you wouldn't have a clue.

In the course of this interaction, the teacher is trying to employ what in the last chapter we called an 'IRF' pattern, where he initiates by asking a question, children put their hands up to offer replies, the teacher chooses a respondent, the selected child replies appropriately, and the teacher evaluates the response. He is dependent on the children, however, to make this pattern work. From them must come the offers to reply, the appropriate replies, and the attentive audience behaviour. Insofar as they have the power to withhold these essential behaviours, or to use them to subvert the teacher's intention, the children are able to compete with the teacher for control of the classroom conversation. We might sum up the ways in which, in this extract, the children bid for control or independence and the teacher reacts, as follows:-

Inappropriate Pupil Behaviour	Teacher Reaction
Inappropriate offers to reply:	
8 Verbal bidding	9, 10 Delay in nominating
30 Bidding to request rather than to reply	31 Nominating to reply
	34 Regulating time
Inappropriate replying acts:	
11 Irrelevant replying	15-17 Treated as a joke; mildly reproved
46 Failure to reply	47 Interpreted as ignorance
57 Responding to directions noisily	58 Demonstrating authority
	60 Demanding quietness
	61 Making personal evaluation of children
Inappropriate audience behaviours:	
2 Miming during teacher speech act	3 Reproof for being 'silly' Threat of expulsion from room
4 Audibly expressing concurrence with teacher	5 Reproof. Threat of action.
11, 18, 34, Laughing when the teacher's intention has been frustrated	19-21, 36-37 Calling class to order 22 Evaluating behaviour
	23-24 Persuasion, reasoning
43 Failure to listen to other pupils' replies	44-47 Nomination to repeat replies missed

50 Failure to listen when teacher is speaking	51 Pause for attention
	52 Repetition of directive
53 Singing in the background	54 Request to desist
	55 Mild sarcasm

The first pupil bid to wrest control of the interaction from the teacher comes in act 2 where Simon makes a kinesic response to the teacher's suggestion of explorers 'bumping into Australia'. Simon is diverting attention away from the teacher, and in order to maintain the single-focus speech event which he has set up, the teacher has to disallow what Simon has done. The teacher's threat to remove Simon from the room (act 3) does not mark a point of 'transition relevance' (see previous chapter, page 131). That is, it is not a permissible place for the speaking turn to pass to another class member. Bill's 'Yes!' (act 4), although it expresses concurrence with the teacher, therefore occasions a further reproof from the teacher. (We might wonder if Bill is accustomed to hearing the teacher making threats of this kind and is trying to goad him into action. The teacher, as we see from the rest of the extract, has an extensive repertoire of verbal means of asserting control, and is continually nagging rather than taking action.)

In act 6 the teacher makes an elicitation — 'What was his (Captain Cook's) job?' — to which, forty speech acts later, he still has not received an acceptable response. The problem lies partly in the teacher's (unexpressed) criterion of acceptability of response, and partly in the pupils' deliberate resistance to his questioning. The acceptable response (if one can judge from the teacher's own response to his question, given later but not included in this transcript) was 'To found a colony'. The actual word 'colony' was crucial, in that Bob's suggestion of 'starting a settlement' (act 27) could not be accepted. The children showed little interest in the teacher's question. Having put the question to the class, he received at first only one bid to answer, and that (act 8) was expressed in an unconforming way ('calling out', instead of raising the hand). The teacher did not respond straight away to this bid (act 9), thus signifying his awareness of its illegitimate form, and perhaps hoping for another offer. Joe, given the floor (act 10), showed that his reply, in common with his bid, was an act of non-compliance. By answering irrelevantly (act 11), he frustrated the teacher's intention and earned the approbation of his class-mates.

The teacher's control of the classroom discourse at this stage has been undercut progressively by several deliberate acts of the child: first, Simon's mime, then Bill's uncalled-for concurrence; and now, in the face of class resistance to his elicitation, Joe's inappropriate bid and wildly irrelevant response. The class is showing itself as responsive to these various acts of non-compliance as it is unresponsive to the teacher's questioning. It is highly likely that another bid for 'pupil power' will be forthcoming soon, since there has been a progressive escalation in the pupils' attempts to defy the teacher's control. At this point, the teacher acts in a somewhat conciliatory way. He treats Joe's irrelevant response rather indulgently as a joke (acts 13-17); and, as the class's hilarity continues, he tries to reason with 'some people' (act 22), sympathising with the 'hard day' they have had (act 24) and seeking their attention, if only to make him happy with them. At first the strategy seems to work, in that a 'regular' exchange ensues (acts 25-29).

However, it is followed by a further disruptive act by Andy, who exploits the ambiguity of the act of hand-raising in order to produce further hilarity. Knowing that the teacher will interpret a raised hand as a bid to respond to his elicitation, Andy raises his hand and then, when nominated, asks 'Can I go to the toilet?' (act 32). Despite the uproar it produces, the teacher accepts the act at its face value, granting Andy the permission he requests, though, as is customary, qualifying that permission by enjoining speed (act 34). One further regular exchange follows (acts 39 43); but, as Linda is replying to the teacher, Nancy is talking and giggling. This breach of procedural rules is not allowed to pass by the teacher. Rather than repeating or acknowledging Linda's reply, he turns to Nancy to retrieve it from her (acts 44, 45). Nancy is unwilling or unable to reply (act 46) and her silence is taken as an expression of her ignorance (act 47).

The interaction from acts 1-47 can be interpreted, on one level, as an exchange between teacher and pupils on the subject of Captain Cook's commission. It is, however, much more than this. It is a succession of initiatives, on the part of teacher and pupils, to manipulate an exchange of speech acts to their own advantage. It is a power struggle, where power is shown in the ability to control the discourse. Successive members of the class have entered the fray on behalf of their fellows: Simon, Bill, Joe, Andy and Nancy. The success of their efforts is attributable not only to their own acts but also to the consistent support they receive from the class as a whole. In acts 48-61 the teacher is in combat with the whole class. The class fails to yield him silence when he speaks (act 50) and when they carry out his instructions (act 57). The teacher employs various devices: pausing (act 51), repeating (act 52), mild sarcasm (act 55), emphatic commands (act 58), and deprecatory personal evaluation (act 61) in attempting to strengthen the impression that the interaction is under his overall control.

Since teaching depends on personal interaction, and no individual can make an interaction without the compliance of another, teaching always depends upon an interpersonal agreement between teacher and pupil or pupils. Control of classroom discourse does not finally rest with either teacher or pupil, but is always subject to ongoing negotiation. Where the parties concerned do not readily recognise their interdependence, or where they do not agree in the meaningfulness or worthwhileness of the speech event, they may antogonise one another by aborting one another's discourse initiatives. The result may be much talk to little effect. This is what has happened in Mr. W's social-studies lesson. Mr. W's main mistake in this lesson was to start it off without any measure of interpersonal agreement (the children were expecting informal activities and he subjected them, without explanation, to a formal revision lesson), and to proceed in such a manner as to minimise the chance of reaching interpersonal agreement. (An early mistake was to refer to a row of unresponding pupils as a 'pack of deadheads'.) It was apparent to the children that communicative rights were to be achieved by confrontation rather than friendly negotiation. If this seems to bear comparison with industrial relations in the adult community, the parallel is not coincidental. An unruly class, like an unruly workforce, may be symptomatic of a basic human-relations breakdown.

The language of the school bureaucracy

Bureaucracy is an important form of social organisation within our society whereby many of the functions of government are carried out. The characteristics of bureaucratic organisation have been summarised as follows:-

1. The detailed subdivision of labour, to be performed by many different highly trained specialists;

2. General rules and regulations to ensure objective and impersonal treatment of the organisation's clients, and to coordinate the efforts of the organisation's specialist workers to promote an orderly, systematic and rational means of providing services; and

3. Hierarchical relationships designed to ensure the coordination of the specialists' efforts by providing clear and rational allocation of authority and responsibility.

(Brubaker and Nelson, 1974:64).

Schools, like the educational systems of which they, in most cases, are a part, are usually organised as bureaucracies. Their day-to-day functioning is according to explicit rules and regulations, and there is an hierarchy of power and responsibility, according to which each individual's accountability is defined. In Government schools, teachers and principals have their responsibilities spelled out in weighty volumes of regulations. Specific regulations require teachers to know their regulations and to comply with them. The language of regulations is remote from the language of social interaction:

57D. (1) This regulation applies, pursuant to paragraph (e) of subsection (1) of section 9A of the Act, to the reimbursement of efficient schools in respect of interest paid by those schools on money borrowed by them for prescribed purposes, such reimbursement being hereinafter referred to as an 'interest subsidy'.

(Education Act Regulations 1960, Education Department of
Western Australia)

In everyday language we might perhaps express this as 'This regulation applies to "interest subsidies" which the Department may pay to schools to reimburse them for interest paid on their special purpose loans.' Note how bureaucratic language differs from everyday language. In some ways it is less explicit and in some ways more explicit. The main concern of the regulation is reimbursement, but we are not told who does the reimbursing. At the same time, we are given a far heavier cross-referencing within the text, of which the regulation is a part, than we would normally require in speech. This is achieved by the use of certain cohesive expressions which are normally used only in writing: 'pursuant to', 'in respect of', 'such' (meaning 'this') and 'hereinafter'.

Teachers and school administrators are not only on the receiving end of bureaucratic language: they also employ it in dealing with parents and children. The language is, of course, distinct from the legal language we have just been considering, but it is also distinct from the language of most of our day-to-day interaction. The language of the school bureaucracy may be expressed in lists of school rules, or rules for particular areas of the school, such as libraries, in written communications with parents, in announcements on blackboards or notice boards, or over the public address system. We may illustrate this language by reference to regulations and announcements made or in force in a particular high school at the time of writing. Five chief distinguishing characteristics of the language may be observed:

1.   Lack of personal addressee reference.

Unlike most person-to-person language, the language of bureaucracy usually does not envisage an individual person as addressee. Accordingly, a generalised addressee may be incorporated into an instruction as its subject; for example: 'Students who are ill or have been hurt should report (or be reported) immediately to the Principal Mistress.'

Alternatively, the instruction may be given an impersonal subject; for example:

'All clothing and property must bear owner's name and class.'
'It is not necessary for parents to visit the school to enrol students.'

Most commonly the addressee is eliminated from the surface of the utterance by the use of the passive voice; for example:

'Valuables must be carefully treated' (instead of 'You must treat your valuables carefully')
'School bags should be left where they do not obstruct access.'
'Food and drink must be consumed in the main school area.'
'Students are warned that lockers are not burglarproof.'

2. Ellipsis.

Words or parts of words are often left out of instructions and announcements; for example:

'No running in main school area.'
'Short assembly for Yr. 9 under tree near R. 20 after recess 10.45.'
'Icecream containers still needed — to Mrs O'Malley or Miss Jones.'

(In this, school rules may be compared with instructions on packets, in recipe books and in other instructional manuals).

3. Imperatives.

The language of the school bureaucracy is full of commands, but it does not have many imperatives — verbs in the form which expresses a command. In polite conversation it is normally unacceptable, at least between equals, for imperatives to be used. For example, it might cause offence for one speaker to say to another 'Give me that book' or 'Open the window'. This problem is overcome by the use of various linguistic devices ('Could you possibly...', 'Please, would you...', etc.) to 'mitigate' the blunt command. Commands may take various forms in school regulations and announcements; for example:

Unmitigated:	'There are ample rubbish bins — use them.'
Mitigated:	'Please return the completed form to the main office.' 'Would the following please see Mrs Adams at the beginning of lunch time: Mary Jones, Beryl Thompson, Sue Bridge.'
Employing 'will':	'Amenities and Sports Fee will be $9.00 per student.' 'With the exception of Line 7, all students not at regular lesson will report to the library.'

4.   Emphasis.

Written instructions are often given a force which they would, if spoken, receive by means of volume and intonation, by having auxiliaries or negators in capitals or underlined; for example:

'Stick ices MUST be eaten in Canteen area.'
'Students are not to leave school without the knowledge of Deputies or the Principal.'

5.   Particular collocations.

Certain collocations, or groups of words, only occur in the language of instructions and announcements; for example:

'Out of bounds': 'Bicycle racks are out of bounds except when a student is arriving at or leaving school.'
'Late comers': 'Late comers must fill in a form obtainable outside the Principal Mistress's office.'
'Absent themselves': 'Students must not absent themselves from classes.'

The school, then, faces the child with at least two different kinds of imposed language use. Because it involves classroom instruction, it imposes the 'controlled conversation' of the classroom, and because it is organised overall in a particular kind of way, it imposes the language of the 'school bureaucracy'.

The language of educational control

Another approach to the consideration of language use in schools is to focus on the socialisation function performed by the school. Schools cannot properly be considered in isolation from the society which has ordained their existence. The social forces which prevail in the wider society prevail also in the school, and underlie the assumptions which are made there about teacher and pupil roles and curriculum and instruction.

A basic question is, if education is concerned with pupils gaining knowledge, how direct is the pupil's access to knowledge in the school? What is knowledge, as the school conceives it, and how is it controlled and mediated? It has been argued (for example by Delamont, 1976) that schools are structured according to the assumption that access to and control of knowledge are in the hands of the teacher. This may be seen to be the assumption underlying the 'IRF' discourse pattern (see previous chapter) according to which the teacher defines what will be talked about by the questions he asks, and then makes judgments as to the adequacy or otherwise of the pupils' contributions. If this is the dominant discourse mode of schooling, then it could be assumed that knowledge is perceived to be a commodity which the teachers (who have it) dispense, bit by bit, to passive students (who lack it).

Education so conceived betrays a 'hidden curriculum' (see Chapter 9) which makes quite clear judgments about such matters as the nature of the learning process, the value of the child's extra-school experience and learning, the significance of the children's relationships with one another, and indeed the nature of knowledge itself. If this is what education is all about, then, as Barnes (1976) has pointed out, a teacher's preoccupation will be with the 'transmission' of knowledge rather than with its 'integration' into the child's existing understandings. As far as language is concerned, the child may well be viewed in terms of what he lacks rather than what he possesses. Use of his most familiar, informal variety (see previous chapter) may be denied him, in that learning will be in large groups dominated by the teacher and his instructional register. Access to the knowledge of the subject may indeed be only by way of the specialist language which is associated with that subject or with the educational domain.

It has been suggested (Bernstein, 1971) that schools exercise educational control by the way in which they *classify* and *frame* educational knowledge. Schools classify knowledge by sorting it out into separate subject areas and keeping the subject areas distinct. They frame knowledge by determining what will be taught, when, and in what way. The school curriculum shows what the school has defined as valid knowledge; its pedagogical policies show how it has determined that the knowledge should be transmitted; its evaluation procedures show how it judges whether children have acquired that knowledge. A school in which separate subject areas are kept completely distinct has strong classification, whereas a school which favours integrated learnings has weak classification. A school has strong framing if the 'uncommonsense knowledge' of school learning is kept distinct from the 'commonsense knowledge' of experience and if the selection, pacing and mode of presentation of educational content are predetermined. A school has weak framing when the nature of school learning is more open to definition by the pupil. According to Bernstein, strong classification and framing of educational knowledge have generally prevailed in the European educational tradition; and as a result, education has been seen as something removed from everyday life. Such a situation puts arbitrary barriers of language between everyday experience and schooling, which may work to the disadvantage of many pupils in their efforts to learn.

Not only may teachers in a school have access to educational knowledge which is not directly available to the pupil, but they may also have access to what has been called 'guilty knowledge' — that is, private knowledge about the pupil (Delamont, 1976). One source of such knowledge is educational testing. The teacher may have, for a class, test scores relating to I.Q., language development, reading age, and other abilities. Often, these scores have been regarded as 'facts' about the children, as much a permanent part of them as their blue eyes or red hair. Recent study of testing encounters as social events has shown that, by concentrating on test results and making a number of assumptions about the interactional aspect of testing, educators may often have been misleading themselves and doing an injustice to their pupils.

Hugh Mehan (1973) was intrigued by the fact that children in remedial classes displayed abilities which, according to test results, they were not supposed to have, so he undertook a study of the testing event as an 'interactional accomplishment', closely studying videotapes of children being tested and asking them afterwards why they gave the answers they gave. He found that test instructions were not always interpreted according to assumptions which were common to tester and child. Incorrect test answers were often meaningful within the context of the testing event and should not have been attributed to faulty reasoning or ignorance. For example, given the task of circling the appropriate letter, out of D, C and G, as the first letter of the name of a medieval fortress which was shown in a picture, some Year 1 children incorrectly answered 'D'. The correct answer was 'C' for Castle. But Mehan found that the children circling 'D' had identified the picture as Disneyland. In questions requiring children to touch pictures, he found that the testers were constantly having to make judgments as to whether to interpret ambiguous gestures on the children's part as right or wrong. Depending on the way in which the tester's voice responded to incomplete answers, children might complete them (and get them right) or leave them (and get them wrong). And the children sometimes asked the testers questions, or interrupted their instructions.

The point Mehan was demonstrating was not that tests were poorly administered, but that tests are inevitably interactional events, dependent upon continuous interpretative activities by both tester and child, and that much of the meaning of a test result may be lost when one considers only the score. If this is so, then the control over pupils which teachers possess through knowledge of test results may have an unreliable basis. In more recent studies (1978) Mehan has shown how counselling sessions in schools may work to the disadvantage of some students because of the interactional strategies adopted by the counsellor.

The language of textbooks

In most classrooms, textbooks of some kind are used by the students, and in the secondary school the students may receive a large part of their instruction from textbook rather than teacher. Other chapters in this volume have dealt with the ways in which written and spoken language differ and with the skills involved in the reading process. It is clear that, if a student is receiving a large part of his instruction in the written mode, he needs to develop strategies to enable him to cope with verbal material which carries a much higher information load than spoken language. Students need to learn to read textbooks both selectively and at varying rates. A good textbook helps the student here, suggesting what is essential and what is optional for some readers, and providing clear headings and layout. However, the teacher needs to help as well. Textbook-reading skills cannot be assumed to be present without instruction. Some texts provide barriers to the learning they seek to impart:

> Many seem to be written by people who have only read other textbooks; they may have been bigger and more difficult but they were textbooks none the less. The authors or compilers handle a grubby second-hand or umpteenth-hand language which they have accepted as part of the 'content' of the subject. They show little awareness of what pupils will make or fail to make of their language beyond some crude notions of easy and difficult vocabulary and shorter sentences. (Rosen, 1972: 123)

Students, especially at high-school level, must be expected to encounter specialist language in textbooks. It should, however, be the object of the book to mediate meanings rather than to obscure them. The text should anticipate the reader's problems with vocabulary. It should also, as Rosen implies, simplify linguistic structures on a principled basis. (See also Chapter 9.)

At the primary-school level, workbooks are in common use. These may be set out largely in question-answer format, designed to allow the child to work with minimum supervision. However, to some children, the taking of instructions from an impersonal, written source is neither natural nor straightforward. The problems are compounded where the questions or exercises have no apparent function except that of eliciting answers. Although workbooks may be useful in preparing primary school children for learning from textbooks, their use should be accompanied by intensive oral interaction with the teacher or with class-mates.

Modifying classroom structures

We have seen in this chapter how, in various ways, schools employ language in seeking to control the behaviours of children. If we accept that society needs schools, many of the consequences we have observed must follow. But even a teacher who basically accepts the prevailing structures of power may ask whether some things might not be changed in the interests of pupils. Where the child's access to knowledge is being hampered by the role assigned to him in classroom discourse, or by the way in which knowledge is classified and framed in the school, or by the inadequate account taken of the linguistic facts associated with testing, counselling, using textbooks, or organising a bureaucracy, there would seem to be need for some change.

Perhaps the hardest area in which to introduce change is that of class-room discourse. Part of the problem lies in the lack of awareness on the part of teachers of the nature and effects of their linguistic dominance in the classroom. Even when teachers think they are liberalising classroom structures, they may be changing very little. Take, for example, the case illustrated in the following transcript, where the teacher has allowed the pupils to take over the lesson. The class, from year 4/5, had been engaged in project work, and the group which had been investigating Singapore was invited to present its findings:

Mrs. W	:	Right,
		who's organising Singapore over here?
		Arthur?
		Facing this way everybody please,
		because Arthur might want you to
		point something out.
		We'll just make it informal,
		Arthur,
		just make it a chat.
Arthur	:	Well,
		today we're gunna talk about Singapore.
		Um, is Singapore a very big country?
Mrs. W.	:	If anybody has an answer to make,
		put your hand up so that..
Arthur	:	Where is Singapore?
Mrs. W.	:	Put your hand up and Arthur will call you by name to answer.
Arthur	:	Lois?
Lois	:	In Western Asia.
Arthur	:	How do they do the er they make batik?
		Bradley?
Bradley	:	(inaudible)
Arthur	:	What do the people use to eat their food?
		Robin?
Robin	:	Sticks?
Arthur	:	What type of food do they eat?
Bill	:	Fish
Arthur	:	Daniel?
Daniel	:	Vegetables?
Arthur	:	What else?
Daniel	:	I dunno
Group	:	(bids to answer)
		Fish..egg..fish

Arthur   :   How much price fine do you get if you drop a
              piece of paper?
              Warren?
Warren :   A hundred dollars.

Although Mrs. W. has handed over the session to the children, she still
determines just what goes on. She calls the class to order and nominates
Arthur to speak. Then, although she invites him to make it a 'chat', she
twice interrupts to determine procedures. Children are to put their hands
up to answer, and Arthur is to call people by name to answer. Thus we
find that this 'chat' follows the basic interaction pattern of the classroom,
with Arthur becoming an extension of the teacher, who, everybody
knows, is there in the background. (Arthur, we note, has not perfected
the pattern, as he fails to give any evaluations of the answers he
receives.)

Established patterns of classroom discourse are, then, firmly
entrenched. Can they be changed, and if so, will learning take place? In a
study intended to find this out, Barnes and Todd studied the interaction of
high-school students in small-group learning situations in the absence of
the teacher. They found that, when the teacher was not there, the pupils
did take their learning tasks seriously, and began to treat one another as
learning resources in a way not possible when normal discourse conventions prevailed (1977:31). The fact is that speech-use behaviours will
change when we change the social situation, and that to reduce the
teacher's dominating role may not be to reduce the learning potential. As
Barnes has noted elsewhere (1971:244):

> The intimacy of the small group makes it possible for the talk to
> be hesitant and exploratory, full of hints and false starts, lacking
> in overall plan yet allowing the exploration of first-hand
> experience. The full class, however, demands a public style
> which must be explicit, well-planned and perceptive of the needs
> of non-intimates.

One of the best ways of changing classroom discourse patterns is to
change the 'participant structures', or the structural arrangements within
which pupils interact. The addressing of the whole class by the teacher is
only one possible structure. Another is interaction between the teacher
and a small group. Another is individual desk work, with the teacher
available for one-to-one consultation. Another is group work with the
teacher excluded. In a study in American Indian classrooms (Philips,
1972) it was shown that under the first two of these structures, pupil
participation was far less ready than under the last. The same is true in
many Aboriginal classrooms. (Malcolm 1979). It will indeed be to the
benefit of all pupils if the teacher can employ a variety of participant
structures. The reality is that absolute control of classroom interaction by
the teacher is neither possible nor compatible with the learning objectives

of the school. To recognise and accommodate to this understanding is not to weaken the position of the teacher in the classroom but rather to place it on a firmer foundation.

Conclusion

Language functions in schools as a medium for the regulation of teacher and pupil behaviour. Schools impose patterns of communication, both in classroom discourse and in administrative messages, in which the structures of control are embedded. The school also shows, by the way in which it organises knowledge, the extent to which it assumes that pupils should have open access to it. Linguistic control may be exercised by schools over pupils in the way they obtain and use test and interview data, and in the way they use textbooks. To change patterns of language use it is normally necessary to change patterns of social organisation and control. There are limited ways in which with a view of improving child learning such changes can be effected in schools as we know them.

Suggested activities

1. It has been suggested (Woods, 1976) that the laughter of pupils in classroom is sometimes 'subversive', in that it attempts to undermine the authority structure of the school or the status of the teacher. Look back at the first transcript in this chapter. Would you say that the children's laughter was 'natural' or 'subversive'? Why? What does the teacher take it to be?
2. Martyn Hammersley has noted (1976:108) that a teacher sometimes asks a question 'not to get an answer but as a summons, and also to imply to the pupils that he knows when they are not attending even though he may not always show it'. Can you find an example of this in the transcripts in this chapter?
3. When children ask permission to leave the room, why do teachers so often qualify the granting of permission with a directive to be 'quick'?
4. Must schools be organised as bureaucracies? Can you find an example of a school without a 'language of the school bureaucracy'?
5. According to one anthropological perspective (Burnett, 1973:13), the school, in a pluralistic culture, derives its organising principles from one reference group within the community — 'the reference culture of a school culture is the one from which the school and its personnel draw the *rule-guides*, standards of behaviour and relationships for the activities that characterise that school.' If this model holds for the society you know, what is the favoured and what are the less

favoured cultural groups within the society (with reference to the school)? What are the implications for language use in education?

6. Examine some of the curriculum and syllabus documents you, as a teacher, will be expected to use, and infer from them whether educational knowledge is given 'weak' or 'strong' classification and framing.

7. It has been said that 'basalese' is the artificial language of basal readers often used in junior primary classes. What are the linguistic characteristics of basalese? What are its pedagogical implications?

8. Take a workbook intended for use by pupils in one of the primary grades. Make a selection of the tasks it sets for pupils, and ask a number of pupils of the appropriate grade what the book is telling them to do. How effectively might pupils work on this material without supervision?

9. Make a list of possible participant structures which might be engineered in classrooms with a view to varying discourse patterns.

Communication and Mind

Chapter 9 Bob Hodge
Language, Thought and Culture

We all use language to communicate with; but equally important, we use language to think with. Language is not a passive vehicle for thoughts, it is part of their very texture. To use a common metaphor,it is not a clothing to thought, it is like flesh itself. Thoughts without language would be disembodied skeletons. So the study of language forms is inseparable from the study of thought. Real thinking leaves innumerable traces on the surface of language. Language patterns show patterns of thought. The characteristic patterns of thought are learned through language, and remain embedded in linguistic performances. So it can be said that 'language' determines thought, to emphasise the point that general habits of thought learnt through language influence the form of every particular thought (see Whorf 1956: Kress and Hodge 1979). Different forms of language often reflect different typical patterns of thinking which are characteristic of a particular group. Where there are differences in these basic patterns of language and thought, direct translation will be impossible or at least misleading. Not only will the thoughts and concepts be different; the orientations will be different too. How can you translate an orientation?

The importance of all this for educationists is evident. Education is concerned with thinking. If the study of language is like a kind of X-ray vision into underlying patterns of thought, teachers will naturally be interested in language. They need to understand the thought processes behind children's words or silences. Where differences in patterns of language and thought exist, the consequences are incalculable. There will be communication breakdown of the most far-reaching kind. Efforts to transcend such barriers will therefore be educative on the same scale, requiring challenges to unexamined assumptions of one's whole culture.

If language is such a sensitive record of general thought processes, it becomes illuminating to look at pieces of language from this point of view. Take the following essay, written by a 14-year-old girl:

Discovering Sex

When discovering sex you find that many people Help you to discover 'SEX'. THE DIFFERENCE of a woman is that a woman has Breasts and a VIRGINA, and men have only a pelvis (----) with sackes of spearms Below the pelvis and in it goes and Boom Pregnant.

Discovering Pregnancy

When TRYING to Discovering Pregnancey of a woman many x rays and blood samples are taken from the Woman and are tested by a special machene or By Doctors that know what to look for under microscope. Then the woman comes back and is told that she is pregnant in 9 months time.

Discovering a Birth //// a Baby

When TRYing to discover a Birth of a Baby many Doctors go into a room and Discover the Birth
Sometimes the Baby Dies then

Discovering a Death of a Baby

When trying to Discover a Death of a Baby the doctor takes a Blood sample from the Mother and the Dead Baby this is how some people know that a Baby Died from a Disease.

Discovering a Disease of a Dead Baby

When TRYING to discover a Disease of a Baby that Died at Birth the Doctors take Blood samples from the mother, the father and the Dead Baby. Then check under a Microscope. Then look at a book or tell the parents of the baby what caused the Death.

(Example collected by Sue Willis)

Everyone would make the general judgment that this girl is not well informed about human reproduction, and that some of her attitudes are more morbid than a health education teacher would like. But the language tells us more than this about the intellectual categories and processes she brings to bear on this and other problematic areas of experience.

Take vocabulary first. This girl's understanding of technical terms is clearly different from that of a standard English speaker. *Pelvis*, for instance, probably means *penis*. It may not seem to matter to the quality of her thinking if she uses *pelvis* or *penis*, and *virgina* for *vagina*. But what does this girl think when she hears people talk of *Elvis the pelvis*? And her speaking of *Virgina* suggests she sees some connection between *virginity* and *vaginas* — which there is, of course, but the connection is not direct. The mistakes suggest the possibility that even when she uses a word that seems correct, she may understand something different from it. For instance, *X-rays* and *blood-samples* are appropriate words to use, but what does she understand by them? She says 'many x-rays are taken *from* the woman', suggesting that she thinks x-rays are something a woman possesses until a doctor removes them.

What we have, then, are two sets of terms: her language, and the language of biology. Sometimes she refers to the same part of reality by a different word, and sometimes she refers to a different part of reality by the same word. In general, since the set of terms she has is so restricted and vague compared with the full set of biological terms, her understanding of what is told to her, in the correct terminology, will obviously be very different from what her teacher intends — and the teacher and the student will probably underestimate greatly how wide a gap there is.

She uses the word 'discover' in an unusual way. Sometimes it seems to mean 'find out about'; sometimes 'detect the presence of'; sometimes 'understand the causes of'. Since she has just one word for what a fuller form of English would regard as three distinguishable concepts, it seems possible — not certain on this evidence, merely possible — that she does not make the distinctions which would be normal for speakers of standard English. So we can compare the two 'languages', hers and standard English, at this point as shown in Figure 9.1.

GIRL   STANDARD ENGLISH

discover   see
find out (discover)
understand
(what and why)

Fig. 9.1 Comparison of 14-year-old girl's and Standard English

The circles may cover the same ground, but standard English makes several distinctions between active and passive looking; between seeing and understanding; and between understanding phenomena and understanding causes, what's and why's. Not to make such crucial distinctions is clearly a serious inadequacy of thought. If this girl cannot make these distinctions, she will not be able to 'understand anything, because she will not know the difference between seeing something and investigating the nature of the phenomenon and its causes. Of course, on this evidence alone we could not make so drastic a judgment. She might use a single word on this occasion, but show herself able to appreciate the distinctions at other times. In fact, in this extract she uses both *see* and *look for. See* is crossed out, showing both that she can distinguish between the two, and that she initially conceived of the doctors' action as *seeing*, not *looking for*. However, this actually confirms the suspicion that she uses *see* differently from how a standard English speaker would have expressed himself: he would not have put *see* in the first place. So there may be some actions she would think of as 'seeing', which a standard English speaker would describe as 'looking for', if she used these words to cut up reality in different ways.

The girl is talking about processes and causes, so it is important to see how adequately she represents these two aspects of her understanding of reality. Processes involve people or things acting, alone or on other things. Processes in English are represented through physical process clauses which are either transitive, with action flowing from an agent to an object (for instance, *a doctor takes a blood sample*), or intransitive, where there is no object but only a subject which is involved in the action (for example, *the woman comes*). See Halliday (1971).

When we look more closely at this essay, we do not find her representing physical processes involved in sex very often: just *In it goes and boom pregnant*. This is an intransitive (*it goes*) followed by the vivid *boom*, and then the seemingly inevitable fact: *pregnant*. The intransitive form is not as clear or explicit as the transitive is about how actions flow on from agent to object. In this example *it goes* does not say whether anyone is responsible for 'its' movement, or what is affected by 'it'. The girl's use of the form shows how vaguely and imprecisely she is thinking of this action. The vagueness might come from intellectual limitations, but on this occasion it is also likely that this is a subject the girl cannot bring herself to talk about explicitly.

The form of *pregnant* similarly suggests that she is evading utterances she actually could produce in other conditions. This is a transformation from a more comprehensive underlying form: *the woman is pregnant*, or *she becomes pregnant*. The surface form implies this underlying form, so we can assume that this is what she is thinking. However, the surface form also shows her not saying this more comprehensive form. *The woman is* has been deleted. This deletion reveals what she is thinking. It also suggests how she feels about what she is thinking. In fact, she has a strong tendency to remove herself, and women generally, from the surface of her utterances. She does the same with the base, too. Take the series of agents of *discovering*. The agent of *when discovering sex* has been deleted, but from what follows we can supply *you*: *when you discover sex*. This *you* is an impersonal *you*, standing for anyone like the girl who is engaged in a kind of self-discovery. The next agent of *discovery*, however, is unclear. Who is *trying to discover pregnancy*? The woman, or the doctors? By the time the third discovery (*discovering the birth*) has been mentioned, there is no ambiguity any more. The doctors are doing the discovering, and the woman is only a passive object of their act of discovery.

If we look at the form of the clauses, we find a consistent pattern along these lines. Overall, the majority of clauses describe not physical actions with women as an important class of agent, but mental processes or actions which reflect mental processes, with doctors as the main class of agent. Generalising from this, we can say that this is a world of thinking, not acting, where women are the passive objects of expert acts of male cognition (assuming that this girl assumes that all doctors are male).

We can also ask what kind of sense of causal processes this girl has. She has arranged her essay in a tight sequence: sex — pregnancy — birth — death — post-mortem. This is a chronological sequence. Does it also show a grasp of causality? One place in which to look for grasp of causality is in the use of conjunctions and prepositions. The most common conjunctions this girl uses are *when*, *then*, and *and*. *Then* is used to show a sequence of events: this, then that. *When*, however, is used by this girl with a present continuous: *when discovering / trying to discover*. The *-ing* form indicates that the main action is happening during the same time as the action in the *-ing* clause. This girl characteristically sets two simultaneous events alongside each other; one giving the purpose of the other, the doctors' actions and their motives. So she is extremely interested in causality, but the causality that she understands only links the motives of the doctors to their actions. It does not link the actions or motives of lovers or potential parents. The key events *she* is involved in are simply presented in strict sequence, without any indications of causal links.

This girl has, if anything, an excessively powerful sense of causality at work. She uses *sometimes* once, to indicate that babies do not inevitably die at birth, but she does not have a rich set of words to indicate whether her statements are true of all cases all the time or only describe what is possible or probable. She does not have any *ifs*, or *buts*, or *sos*, and has only one *or*. She does not use modals like *may* or *might*. She only uses the general present. The overall impression is of someone with an excessively simple and powerful sense of causality, unable to conceive of complex or hypothetical links of cause and effect. With an image of causality of this kind, it is natural to feel passive and helpless, since the sequence of events seems to be an inescapable progression. This sense of helplessness is shown by her sentence structures as well, where women are typically in the object-position in transitive sentences.

What we have been doing is to look at this essay both for its particular content, and for what it suggests about the writer's general ways of thinking, and how well she is able to think about this subject matter and other similar problems. The essay is the product of thought. It is evidence of how the writer thought, on this occasion, about this subject. The essay we have is affected by at least three factors: the girl's knowledge and experience (she seems to be disturbingly uninformed), her basic pattern of thought (she seems inclined to simplistic and rigid patterns), and the particular situation (she probably has suppressed many of the things she knows or believes on this topic, out of embarrassment). It would be wrong to emphasise any one of these exclusively. If a teacher merely tried to correct her misinformation, only the surface of the problem would be touched. She would feed the new information into the same rigid causal scheme, and would be hardly better equipped to understand the complexities of human sexual relationships. Outside this area of experience she may be less rigid. In talking privately to a sympathetic person she might be able to be more explicit, personal and insightful. Generalisations can be dangerous. But it is likely that the repeated forms of language and thought in this essay will be found elsewhere in the writing of this girl. They have a significance which goes beyond this piece of work, even though we do not know how far beyond. Forms of language reflect forms of thought so sensitively, and reinforce certain patterns over others so strongly, that attention to style shows a concern with what educationists are most interested in: the basic processes of thinking.

Language and thought of textbooks

School textbooks are written by adults to communicate to students. Typically they select and translate the content which is thought necessary, putting it into terms which will be accessible to younger, less informed and less intellectually powerful minds. But even though the language is English for both writer and student, the problem of translation still applies. Along with the particular content, textbooks convey more or less of a particular way of thinking about that content. These ways of thinking are crucial to a full understanding of the subject, since no subject is simply a set of facts. And these forms of thinking, and the forms of language that carry them, can be so habitual that they seem easy, natural and effortless; whereas for the inexperienced user they are difficult and sometimes incomprehensible.

The following extract is from a science textbook designed for students aged 12–14.

> It is sometimes necessary to consider carefully the problems of survival of the individual organism, and also the problems encountered in the continuation of the particular type, or *species*. Reproduction is an important process which occurs as a result of stimuli in order to preserve the species from becoming extinct. All living organisms must be able to reproduce, although this process does not help the parent.
>
> Reproduction is a production of offspring which will grow into adults, and finally produce young of their own,......Reproduction in which two sex cells come together is known as *sexual reproduction*. Usually, in this kind of

reproduction, a male and a female of the particular type of organism become attracted to one another and each provides a sex cell: the female an egg, and the male a sperm. When combined, these develop into a new individual of their species.

— R.A. Criddle, W. Izett, and Ryan, C, 1975:33

This writing has a number of characteristics which are typical of textbooks. A first characteristic is impersonality. The first sentence says *It is necessary to consider carefully* . . . For whom is it necessary? Who should be doing the considering? The writer, or the reader? Who says so? In the next sentence, who says reproduction is important? In the following sentence, who says living organisms *must* be able to reproduce? This information is systematically removed from the surface of the language. It is an automatic transformation process for this style of writing, though it would be possible for a user of English to have said either *I sometimes need (or feel the need) to consider problems carefully*, or *I want you children sometimes to consider problems carefully*. The effect of writing in the impersonal style is that the authority of the utterance is concealed, left to be understood. In this form it is invisible and therefore dificult to challenge or argue with. It is interesting to compare the effect of this feature with the girl's self-effacement. She has learnt an impersonal style, too, which she uses to hide behind. Impersonality can be an attempt at objectivity, or it can be an evasion. Teachers who insist on an impersonal style ought to be aware of the habits of thought and attitudes that they are enforcing.

A second dominant feature is the use of nominalisations, that is, verbs turned into nouns. Take as an example *the problems encountered in the continuation of the particular type*. This is a transform of a more comprehensive form that could be represented as the *particular type tries to continue, and encounters problems*. The verb *continues* becomes a noun: *continuation*. The relation between the two clauses, which is a complex and vague one, is represented by the preposition *in*. This is the same relationship as the girl's *when*. She could have *In pregnancy tests* instead of *when trying to discover pregnancy*. By using nouns linked by prepositions, a writer is able to tie a number of distinct events or facts into a single complex structure. Take, for instance, *Reproduction . . . . occurs/as a result of stimuli/in order to preserve the species/from becoming extinct/*. This is the result of transformations which link together distinct sentences into a single unit. The result is more complex than the girl could produce. In this example, if we probe we might find that the causal links do not work perfectly. Does reproduction occur as a *result* of stimuli, or as a result of fertilisation of an egg which is a consequence of stimulus-response chains? Does it occur *in order to preserve the species*, or is preservation of the species simply a consequence of reproduction? Or is this need the main stimulus (for higher animals)? And so on. The linguistic forms allow complex structures to be produced but they do not guarantee that the thinking is watertight. And since the causal links are so hard to see, it would not be surprising if normal students failed to grasp them.

A major difference between this passage and the girl's essay is the level of abstraction. The nominalisations help here. If you say *reproduction*, for instance, you do not have to say who is doing the reproducing. If you use a full sentence, English requires a subject which in this case could be men, women, birds, bees, plants etc. Simple, active sentences to describe physical actions or processes require you to be concrete and definite about who or what is the agent of the action. Sentences using lots of nominalisations can avoid saying who is doing what, though in order to understand every individual nominalisation, you need to be able to supply some kind of agent. The style of these textbook writers, which is typical of textbooks, is compressed and abstract. The price of this is that the processes themselves are not presented directly or concretely. If students do not have a grasp of the processes in their concrete physical reality, they will not be able to interpret the sentences, and will never understand these processes. Something like this seems to have happened to the girl we looked at.

There is a number of specialist terms these writers use which are almost indispensable to what they want to say. *Reproduction* is one. The single word covers the complex phenomenon being described. It refers to both animal and plant reproduction. It is more general and abstract than *having children* or even *having young ones*, since neither of these refers to plant reproduction. *Species* and *individual* are other key terms, since it is important with this topic to distinguish between the benefit of reproduction to the species and the possible problems to individuals. The distinction can be translated into everyday language but only with difficulty. When these writers try to put the point in easy terms, they lapse into imprecision. 'All living organisms must be able to reproduce, although this process does not help the parent', they say. But it is not every individual organism that must be able to reproduce — worker bees do not, for instance. It is the species that must have some means of perpetuating itself, if it is to continue. That point is very difficult to make without the word, and concept, of a species as opposed to the concept of an individual. Naturally a reader without a grasp of the concept of *species* will not get the point, and the attempt to make it vivid that we have quoted above will hardly help.

We have looked at how complex causal relationships are conveyed in this style of writing: not through conjunctions, but through prepositions linking nominalisation. With the girl, we noted her tendency not to limit the scope of her generalisations, so that she presents everything as certain, not as possible, probable, or hypothetical. These writers have the same tendency. They use one *sometimes*, one *usually*, but otherwise no statement is modified. The tense used is the general present, with the exception of *will grow* and *(will) produce*. But most of the statements could be qualified. The offspring, for instance, only *might* grow into adults. Sometimes, as the girl observed, they die. The girl had the impression that pregnancy and birth followed inexorably from intercourse. These writers would only confirm that impression. They use no ifs, buts, or ors, no mays or mights or coulds. Either they are not capable of hypothetical or nuanced thinking, or they do not think their readers are or ought to be capable of it. Whichever the reason, they are reinforcing simple and rigid patterns of thought in students like the girl.

The qualities of style of this passage are typical and deliberate. They represent qualities of thought which are valued in the discipline. This kind of language is capable of presenting complex relationships at a high level of abstraction. It is impersonal, removing writer and reader from the surface of the language. Concrete particular descriptions are heavily transformed, so that they are often vague for writers, and even vaguer for readers, whose chances of understanding the text depend on their already knowing all about the particular processes at issue. A number of important mental operations is largely absent: speculation; criticism; weighing of alternatives; doubt. Teachers need to be aware of the power of the modes of thought carried through this kind of language, which is very compressed and abstract. They also ought to be aware of the valuable kinds of thinking it excludes, which can be carried through different forms of language.

Language and social class

Differences of language sometimes — not always — reflect differences of thought. In Chapter 2 we saw how value-judgments on language forms often reflect social prejudice. If this is based on external features like accent or pronunciation, we can call it mere prejudice. No sound, of itself, is more intelligent than any other sound; but qualities of vocabulary and syntax are another matter. Fundamental differences of language are likely to reflect different patterns of thinking. These different patterns may be better or worse for particular purposes. Obviously we need to discount claims for one language type over another which merely reflects prejudice. But there are differences, and teachers have to make decisions about those differences.

In Chapter 2 we noted the influential argument of Bernstein (1971) that English in England includes two languages, which correlate with the two main social classes. One he calls an elaborated code, associated with middle-class speakers. This is language which is capable of abstraction, hypothetical thinking, and self-reflexive, critical thought. The other kind of language is particular and context-dependent, emphasising social solidarity rather than role differentiation. Bernstein calls it restricted code. Both main classes have access to restricted code, but for lower-class speakers it is their only language. Elaborated code is like intellectual capital, or the intellectual means of production, which is controlled by the dominant class, just as it has expropriated material capital. On this argument, the lower classes are linguistically and intellectually deprived. This deprivation reinforces their other disadvantages, and keeps them in a subordinate role.

This is a controversial argument. In Chapter 2 we saw that there are commonly two poles describing the range of language forms in a community — high and low forms — whose use corresponds to the status of the speaker and the occasion. The high-status language forms are usually presumed to do with prestigious qualities of mind. However, we saw that some of the markers of status are not really proofs of high qualities. And some of the low-status markers signify other qualities which are valued by the society, such as vigour, energy, and warmth. It is possible that Bernstein may have been taken in by the attitudes to these two kinds of language in the community, and that his opponents, who argue for the vitality of low forms, may simply be asserting the covert prestige values of low forms. However, in this chapter we have argued that different forms of language *do* reflect different patterns of thinking. We need to clear our minds of stereotype attitudes to these forms of language and see what mental habits they carry and reinforce, and what some of the inherent strengths and weaknesses are.

Bernstein illustrated what he meant by the two codes through an experiment in which children looked at a picture and described it. Restricted code users tend to be dependent on the context. Their descriptions rely on the hearer being able to see the picture. They gesture rather than elaborate. Elaborated code users have fuller descriptions which would communicate effectively and impressively outside the context. Here is material from the same experiment repeated with 16-year-olds. They were shown a newspaper picture of an unhappy child on his first day at school. Here are two responses:

R.

It's the first day at for the boy. He is somewhat nervis because he has to go to school alone. He stands there frightened, wondering, what will happen when he gets to school. 'Will I meet anyone when I get there or will I be just be ignored as if I wasn't even there'.

On his way to school he sees lots of other children about his age with their mothers. Seeing them with their mothers he begins to feel sulky, till he feels someone tapping on his back, he turns around and see's another boy by himself and says to him 'hello', then the other boy says back to him 'hello'. So they continued on to school together talking about what was going to be like at school. They remained friends from then on.

E.

The forlorn look on the small boy's face was heightened by the stance which he had struck. This stance was pitiful — shoulders slumped as if, in defeat, they had drooped like a wilting flower; school bag clutched piteously between two small white-knuckled hands. All were overshadowed by the eyes. Eyes of misery, crying out for salvation and love. The large, dark irises framing the pupil which appeared to be bottomless, like a dark, mysterious pool.

Small tears trickled from the ducts at the corners of his eyes and, when he blinked, these tears coated his eyes with a gleaming film which tended to add towards the look of utter dejection and depression.

The boy, whose name was Paul, may have been dressed in the same type of clothes as the other boys who were in Grade One with him, and his hair was neatly combed like some of the other boys, but, even so, he was a loner.

(Examples collected by Andrew Sooby)

These two pieces were produced by boys of the same age. E's social background is middle-class, R's is working-class. First, make a general impressionistic judgment on the ability of the two . . . Which did you think was the better student? Most teachers would judge E to be the superior performer. He would be regarded as more fluent, with a wider vocabulary, more complex syntax, more imagination, generally a more sensitive and perceptive student. His description does not depend so much on your seeing the actual picture. If what he is writing is elaborated code, then there is no doubt that elaborated code forms are more highly valued, and are seen as evidence for desirable qualities in the student, though in this example we have not attempted to match the two boys for IQ. E might be much more intelligent than R. Then again, he might not.

There is one way in which E is objectively superior to R. E is much more productive. We have only reproduced a third of what he wrote in the same time as R's whole output. E produces about four times as much as R. If production of words is what writing is all about, then E has four times the productive power. But we do not know why R produced less. It might be because he simply cannot produce much: he has inferior equipment. But it might also be that in this situation he feels that what he could produce would not be valued, so he is inhibited, reluctantly producing small amounts of the kind of thing he does not want to say, instead of larger quantities of what he really does want to say and could say but would not get credit for.

What is E good at producing? One marked difference is the number of adjectives. E has 15 to R's four. E also has two adverbs, where R has none. E has a greater number of nouns: 37 to 16. R, however, has more pronouns, 18 to 5, mostly 'he'. Including both nouns and pronouns, there is not much difference between the two: 42 for E, 34 for R. If we divide the nouns into concrete and abstract, adding pronouns to concrete nouns to see how often they refer to concrete reality, we have 31 for E, 31 for R.

We can now ask what is implied by these figures. Taking the combined figure for concrete nouns plus pronouns, we can say these two are referring to physical reality about as often. But R uses many more pronouns, which indicates that for him physical reality is much more taken for granted, pointed to rather than described explicitly. With a word like 'he', you assume that the hearer knows more: at least that the 'he' is young. Another difference between nouns and pronouns is that nouns can take adjectives. It is awkward to say 'The small he'. E has many more adjectives per noun. These are mostly descriptive, suggesting precise observation. R's nouns tend to be more general and repetitious. He only refers to six different nouns, where E has 16. R keeps referring to 'school' or 'boy', and does not mention particularities like shoulders, bags, or 'small white knuckled hands'. So we can see why E seems much more observant and perceptive. He particularises reality more, and he makes more judgments on those particular details. He is translating more of the picture into words — he is more word-oriented — which is why his description is more self-contained. And he intervenes his judgment more often. Adjectives like 'forlorn' and 'pitiful' are not neutral descriptions; they are judgments, about the boy's state of mind or the attitude of an onlooker.

Does all this show better powers of thinking or observing in E? Take the phrase 'two small, white-knuckled hands'. This initially seems very precise observation. In fact it is too precise, because E is describing a newspaper photo which does not have sufficient quality to see whether the boy's knuckles *are* white. White knuckles are a cliché, like the dark eyes, which would be reproduced as dark by the newspaper photo whatever their colour. The apparently precise observation is an illusion, on this occasion. The language is doing E's seeing for him, producing perceptions that he would not be able to produce on his own. Similarly with the small tears from the ducts at the corners of his eyes: could he really notice the ducts? Or was it just that he knew the word, and knew that there are ducts there, and perhaps liked the sound of the scientific term? But he is right that there are ducts there, and he has mentioned details, such as the shoulders, the bag, the quality of the boy's clothes, and his hair. Some of the precision may be illusory, but he is still more precise than R; and though the judgments may be conventional, he does not make them.

Another source of the vividness of E's language is his use of comparisons: like a flower, like a pool. There are not any flowers or pools in the photo, of course. E is showing a capacity to leave the particular situation and imagine other situations. However, pools and flowers are rather conventional images. E has not an original imagination, but at least he does have an imagination. R makes no comparisons; though he uses one 'as if', as does E. What he does is to imagine a story, involving another boy who befriends the first one. This is just as much an alternative reality as pools or flowers, and arguably it is a more constructive alternative reality, though its quality is very different. Pools and flowers are static. R's story is active. In his narrative he has 19 verbs or participles describing actions, E has 12, R's verbs are vague and general — go, see, feel, say — but they are referring to active agents. His boy has a greater range of reactions: fear, resentment, then a coming to terms with the new situation. E pulls out the emotional stops on behalf of his boy, but does not try to understand what this boy might do, or how he might cope. E has a richer set of judgments and responses in his repertoire, but a relatively poor set of models for actions. E seems from his language to be interested in feelings rather than actions, the inner rather than the outer world, and he seems to have attributed these qualities to the boy, too. Neither E nor his boy sounds like a forceful ruler of society.

This discussion is meant to bring out the complexity of the issues in this area. Language does reflect thought; and different forms of languages, associated with different social classes, do indicate different habitual patterns of thinking. But the prestige form is not always superior in every respect. We saw some of the defects of the science text. E has different strengths and limitations. Both E and the scientists have some features that could be regarded as elaborated code. Similarly the girl and R have restricted code features, but the girl represents herself and others as helpless and passive, whereas R is concerned with active agents. R is a male, the girl a female, which may also have some bearing on the matter. And R is still at school at 16, which makes him better educated than some others with his social background.

Prestige forms are not as total a guarantee of higher thought processes as many people think, but they do have prestige, and that is an important social fact. And they do enshrine important and powerful modes of thought, as well as carrying limiting tendencies. Individuals use the language they are given more or less creatively, transcending some of its limitations or failing to use some of its resources adequately.

So what is a teacher to do for the best when faced with examples of language which fall clearly into one or other category? A difficult balance has to be struck, between respecting the forms of language and thought that the student finds natural, and helping the student to go beyond the limitations of those modes: between knowing what forms are valued by people of power in society, and seeing the real qualities of thought behind everything a student writes or says.

Language and culture

So far we have been talking about differences within one language. If we take two very distinct languages and their corresponding cultures, the scope for difference and for radical misunderstanding increases many times over. In fact a writer like Bernstein draws heavily on the theories of B.L. Whorf, a major thinker whose area of research included the language of the Hopi, an American Indian tribe (1956). Whorf's work had major if indirect implications for education policy. At the time he was writing, the Hopi were undergoing what amounted to cultural genocide, through a policy of enforced schooling for Hopi children in white schools. Hopi children were taken by bus to school, at gunpoint if necessary, Whorf said nothing about this policy. He simply attacked the assumptions on which the policy was based — the arrogant assumption of white Americans that their language, way of life and culture were superior in every way to the Hopi's.

Whorf looked at some of the basic features of Hopi grammar, taking these as indicators of different habits of thought, and even different possibilities of thinking. From some analyses of this kind he argued that the Hopi would find some of the concepts of Newtonian physics more difficult to grasp than would English speakers, but they would find some of the most difficult concepts of Einstein easier than the average European would. Newtonian physics is important, of course, but so is Einstein's theory. How could an education system insist on stamping out a language and way of thinking that finds Einstein congenial — that Einstein therefore would presumably find congenial — even if it finds Newton more difficult? Whorf's fundamental point has a wide application. Languages which seem 'primitive' are as adequate in their own domain as more 'advanced' languages. If there are some areas where one language is more simple, there will be other areas of life and thought where it is more complex and discriminating. Members of a dominant culture are likely to think their ways of speaking and thinking are superior in every respect, and that anything different must be inferior. It is salutary and educative to recognise the opposite, and see the inbuilt limitations of one's own habitual assumptions and languages. And of course it is important for teachers to realise where something that seems simple and clear to them is surprisingly difficult for a student from a different background of language and culture.

To take just a fairly simple instance, many Aboriginal languages have several words for 'we' or 'our', where English has only one. For example, Malak malak has three words for 'we':

> yanki — I and you (single person addressed)
> yawot — I and others (not person addressed)
> yerkit — I, you and others

Malak malak speakers are sensitive to whether 'we' includes the person spoken to or not. In English we are not. Try to imagine the greater subtlety and precision of Malak malak. If I were saying 'In English we aren't' to you, just you, I'd say 'In English we (yanki) aren't'. If I were addressing a large group comprising only English speakers I would use 'yerkit'. But if I were talking to an Aborigine I would have to say 'yawot'. We can see the connection between language and perception here. Malak malak forces the speaker to notice carefully who is being spoken to, and whether the statement applies to them. In English we (yerkit?) can be inattentive and vague about all this. Or take a more complex example: Djeebana has five words for 'our'.

1   yours and mine (inclusive, singular) *ngadda*
2   mine and his/hers, not yours (exclusive, singular) *njadana*
3   yours and mine, and his/hers, but no one else's *ngadana*
4   ours, lots of us, but not yours (exclusive, plural) *njaddabirra*
5   ours, lots of us, including yours (inclusive, plural) *ngaddabirra*

Djeebana speakers make complex judgments about social relations and relationships of possession every time they use a word for 'our'. This may seem surprising to European Australians, who often have the patronising assumption that Aborigines have a simple, childlike, undeveloped notion of possession. It is English which has the simple linguistic form in this area. We might ask, 'How can this be in our culture which is notoriously obsessed with possessions? Does the language suggest the opposite of what is true of the culture?'. Part of an answer to this may come from a look at my use of *we/our* in the foregoing sentences. I am happy to say 'our culture' because I do not know who is reading this book, and I need to be vague. Or a teacher might say to a class 'We don't want a mess in our classroom, do we?' Is this focusing on just one child (ngadda)? Or does 'our' mean that the classroom belongs to the teacher and school (njaddabirra)? Or does the statement include everyone (ngaddabirra)?

In English we like to be vague because it is so convenient. The vagueness it allows is a kind of unintentional dishonesty since what the teacher often means with this phrase is '*I* don't want a mess in *my* classroom'. The Djeebana are required by their language to be more precise and explicit and therfore more honest, at least in this respect. It is not that English speakers cannot make the discriminations Djeebanas do, but that Djeebanas make these judgments automatically, as a matter of course. English speakers do not make these discriminations habitually, and they do not really notice when others do not make them. Whorf's judgment on English versus Hopi applies to Aboriginal versus English, on this point at least: 'Does the Hopi language show here a higher plane of thinking, a more rational analysis of situations than our vaunted English? Of course it does. In this field and in various others, English compared to Hopi is like a bludgeon compared to a rapier'.

Conclusion

Language reflects thought, so typical features of language reveal typical patterns of thought. Teachers need to be interested in *how* students think as well as in *what* they think, since how they think affects both what they will be likely to think and how they will interpret what they read or hear or see. Teachers also need to realise that the language of educators — their own language, the language of textbooks, the language students are required to produce — carries particular patterns of thought and assumptions about the world. These patterns of thought and assumptions are an important content, so teachers in any subject ought to be aware of what habits of thought they are transmitting, what some of the main strengths and limitations are, and where they might be difficult or alien for students. And teachers need to realise that some of their students may come from different social or cultural backgrounds, with ways of thinking and speaking that do not mesh in directly with the dominant modes used in schools. In such a situation the teacher has the difficult task of standing between two languages and two ways of life, trying to achieve a harmonious and rich resolution of the differences that exist.

Suggested activities

1. Take an essay, on any subject; look for systematic preferences of clause types (transitive/intransitive), kinds of agent (such as human/non-human, abstract/concrete) and kinds of action (such as physical process, mental process), and reflect on the significance and functional value of these preferences.

2. Take a textbook description of a topic, and try to translate it into explicit, concrete terms. What is lost or what may be difficult in the translation?
   How would you help students to move between concrete and abstract language forms in this case?

3. Take a conventional form of writing required of students (for example, laboratory report, mathematical proof, history essay). Describe the forms of language required in detail, and bring out the forms of thought carried by the linguistic forms.

4. Compare two pieces of language which might be regarded as elaborated and restricted code respectively, looking for strengths and limitations in each.

5. Use a description of a grammatical feature of a language other than English (Aboriginal, Asian or European) compared with English, to explore the distinctive ways of thinking behind the English and the other form.

6. If you know a language other than English, take a short but significant text in the other language, attempt to translate it, and focus on where the two languages are different. Try to explore what this suggests about ways of thinking.

Chapter 10   Bob Hodge
Language and Development

All children in the average classroom can speak their own language
fluently. The major developments have all taken place by the age of
five. From then on, some development will occur, but this is minor
compared with what happens in those first five years. So why should a
teacher try to understand the basic processes of language development,
especially a teacher at secondary level? Why not take advantage, grate-
fully, of what has been done, and concentrate on the job in hand?

One good reason is the sheer success of this initial act of learning.
Language is a formidably complex skill, taught by amateurs (as most
parents are) to individuals who are commonly regarded as barely teach-
able in other spheres of intellectual activity. What is the secret of this
miraculous success story? What does it suggest about the process of
education, and the mind of a learner?

To get closer to this major educational event, look at this transcript.
Two mothers are talking to their 19-month-old children, Mark and
Christie:

Mother A	:	Just one more
Mark	:	Wumore
Mother A	:	O.K., one more. O.K. and no more after this
Mark	:	This
Mother A	:	After this no more
Mark	:	Wumore
Mother A	:	Only one
Mark	:	O One
Mother A	:	Say thank you mummy
Mark	:	Ankyou marmmy
Mother A	:	Good boy
Mother B	:	Do you want another one? Please?
Christie	:	Ah ah ee
Mother B	:	Please
Mark	:	Arwun unyum
Mother A	:	Well just one more each, O.K.? And that's all.
		Ta?
Mark	:	Ta

Mother B	:	Ta from you too? You've lost yours haven't you? Half way between thank you and ta and I don't get either at the moment.
Mark	:	Ar yun.
Mother A	:	No. No more onions now, darling, that's enough onions for one little boy.
Mark	:	Aryun.
Mother A	:	No more onions. What about carrot? Carrot.
Mark	:	Aryun.
Christie	:	Um um.
Mother A	:	What else have you got on there, Marko?
Mother B	:	Uh?
Christie	:	Ahahz heez.
Mother A	:	Cheese yeah.
Mother B	:	Would you like a little bit of bun too Christie?
Christie	:	Un.
Mother B	:	Do you want some bun? Please?
Christie	:	Pees
Mother B	:	Please, good girl and — would you like some of this bun?
Mark	:	Dumartos.
Mother A	:	No you can't have tomatoes darling because your sore feet, love and your sore face. Do you want some bun? Look at this nice bun, you like that don't you?
Mark	:	Ik that.
Mother A	:	You like that, yes that's nice bun isn't it?
Mark	:	Arbu.
Mother A	:	Yes, yum yum, nice bun. There you are. Do you want some more drink?

Simply to arrive at this transcript was a difficult job. The sounds were indistinct to my ears, and it was often hard to tell whether a particular phoneme was interpreted correctly or not. This is only an extreme form of what happens when we listen to other adults. The sound they produce may not be exactly right. For instance, a long 'a' as in 'father' may not be much different from the more frontal vowel in 'further'. As adults, what we do is re-interpret what we hear so that each sound falls into a distinct class, distinguished by at least one feature that makes it different. So long as the 'a' in 'father' is a bit more open, a bit lower in pitch and a bit further back in the mouth, we treat it as a good enough 'a', completely different from 'er'. To do this, we rely on the other adult having the same system of sounds. With a child, we cannot rely on a common system. The child may not distinguish between 'a' and 'er' (these two children do not). So what they produce slides between one and the other. They have exactly the same problem with adult sounds, but in reverse. To them, there is no distinction between the two vowels, because they have not the categories to distinguish them. They may perceive the difference, but the difference is not significant for them. It cannot be significant until they see the point of it.

Let us go further back in a child's confrontation with language. For a year she has heard this huge, loving being speaking gibberish, a stream of indistinguishable sounds. The child scans this mass of sound for a pattern. The first pattern that emerges will be intonation patterns. The child will then come to make the elemental contrast between vowels and consonants, vowels being the resonance of the voice and consonants being an interruption of the voice. This is the first system the child has — and every child, of every race, probably has it. Note that it's a system: the sound of the voice has been divided into two classes of sound by a single principle. This principle will probably be used to make a sharp distinction between vowels and consonants, so the representative first vowel will probably be a back vowel, like 'a', and the consonant might be produced by the lips, at the front of the mouth — a 'p' or 'b'.

Roman Jakobson (1968) has argued that the way phonological systems are built up has a universal logic. Children from different cultures have the same physical attributes, and they produce systems with a common form, although the languages they ultimately speak will have many sounds which are not found in English. The system builds up by the application of some distinctive feature which contrasts two classes of sound. An early stage of the system might appear as in Figure 10.1.

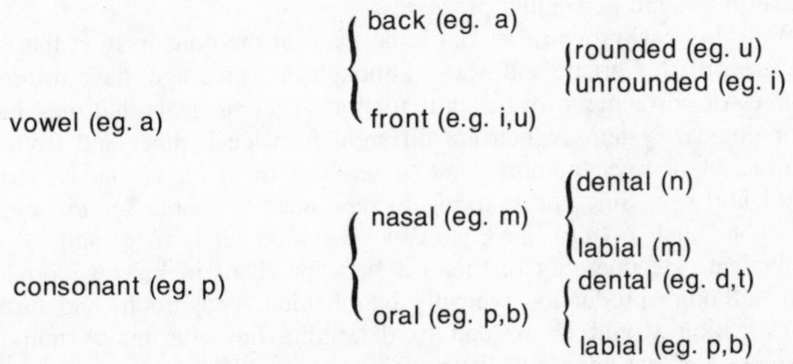

vowel (eg. a)
- back (eg. a)
  - rounded (eg. u)
  - unrounded (eg. i)
- front (e.g. i,u)

consonant (eg. p)
- nasal (eg. m)
  - dental (n)
  - labial (m)
- oral (eg. p,b)
  - dental (eg. d,t)
  - labial (eg. p,b)

Fig. 10.1 An Early Language System

The system grows *as a system* until it corresponds to the relevant adult system. So sounds are not acquired in isolation, by imitation. Each sound can be used — recognised and produced — only if the child can contrast it, in a consistent and therefore principled way, with another sound. As the system gets more extensive, each individual sound is classified by more features. So 'a' initially was simply a vowel, contrasted with consonants generally. Later on it is a vowel produced with the jaw open (low, or open), the tongue towards the back of the mouth (back) and the lips unrounded (unrounded), and must be produced so that it does not merge with, for instance, a low front rounded vowel, if there is one in that language. That means that although 'a' might sound much the same for the child as for the adult, it actually has a different value because it is part of a different system. The child might still think he is producing 'a' when it has become a different vowel for the adult.

Jakobson claims that sound systems emerge in this uniform way, with their own internal logic, and that they dissolve following this order in reverse. In aphasia, or loss of speech functions, people lose the capacity to produce or recognise the minimally contrasted sounds first. Jakobson also suggests that the same principle works with colour. The meaningful colour spectrum is built up in a step-by-step way, with dark-light followed by the emergence of a chromatic colour (red), and further primary colours build up following the same lines. The complete set of basic colours is built up in the same kind of way as the set of sound terms, so the two systems seem — to some individuals at least — to be parallel to each other. So rounded vowels like 'o' and 'u' are 'dark', and unrounded vowels (e and i) are 'light', and back vowels (like a) are 'red'. Whether the parallels are seen or not, there seems to be a widespread law for the development of colour terms in different languages which demonstrates the same principles as phonological development. (Berlin and Kay, 1968). This suggests that there is something about the way children come to recognise and learn sounds that is congenial to the human mind and perceptual processes.

With this background, we can look again at the conversation that has been recorded. Christie and Mark, although the same age, have different degrees of correctness in their articulation. That suggests that they have phonological systems which are different from each other and from an adult's. Mark says 'numore' and 'o one' — or at least, that is what I heard him say. Since he is trying to reproduce the same sound, ow, in 'no more' and 'o (nly) one', we can guess that for him 'u' and 'o' are equivalent. He does not distinguish between them in his own production, although production typically lags behind recognition, and further investigation would be needed to determine how far his system has developed. What he is not distinguishing is the difference between middle and high vowels. He seems not to have reached this stage of refinement of his system, though the basis for it is already there. Christie, however, struggles over a and i when she tries to say 'please' (ah ah ee). She can distinguish them, but it is an effort. i is a front vowel, said with the mouth fairly closed, the lips unrounded: a is a back vowel, with mouth open, with lips unrounded. That means these two vowels are strongly contrasted. If Christie has difficulty with them, then her vowel system must be rudimentary. Most of her vowels will be barely distinguishable from each other. She may have a third vowel — the feature 'rounded' may give her o or u — but we can predict that that will be the limit of her system.

We can now attempt to contrast the two children, at this stage of their development, and characterise Mark's achievement. He has been able to analyse one aspect of physical reality, human sounds, into an hierarchy of categories rapidly and automatically to give a multiple specification of a particular aspect of that reality. He is able to use this abstract scheme to connect together physically different sounds, since his mother's 'Mummy' would be different from his own in pitch and in many other properties if analysed. His reward for this feat of intuitive system-building is that he has more words, and conceptually simpler words, to understand. Since Christie has so few distinct sounds, many words must sound the same for her. For instance, she says 'onion' very like 'I want'. She probably says and hears 'a bun' and 'iron' and 'only one' and 'even' much the same. How can you make sense of the world when the adults around you seem to be suggesting that all these things are to be included in the one word? Christie's ability to understand is probably ahead of her ability to produce sounds, but compared with Mark she will have more difficulties in uncoding words.

In acquiring the sounds of a language, the child is obviously trying to imitate the adults around him. Mark repeats 'this' apparently just to get the sound right. But imitation is not a passive process. It is based on a complex analysis of the sounds that are heard. This analysis into distinctive features creates the thing which is imitated, because it is the features which are reproduced, not the sound itself. Children do not *sound like* their mother, or their father: they reproduce the same sound system and are therefore understood as if they are producing the same sound.

Syntactic development

Syntax means the ordering of elements in an utterance, so syntax is not possible until the language user is producing utterances of two or more elements. The first stage in a child language development consists of one-word utterances. But are these really without grammar or syntax? Take Mark's 'onion'. This single word corresponds to a whole sentence. Adults also use one-word sentences. What food do you prefer?' 'Onion'. Here the single word can be understood as part of a full sentence, '(I prefer) onion', where the bracketed part has been deleted from the surface because it is already understood. Why should we not analyse the child's use of one-word utterances similarly? The question draws attention to the speculative, hypothetical nature of the enquiry. A grammar is not an observable fact. The only observable facts are the sounds produced by the child. But these facts are interesting only for what they imply about the inaccessible mental processes going on behind this overt behaviour.

In this case, Christie uses only one-word utterances. Mark uses one-word utterances differently from Christie. He distinguishes 'onion' by different intonations, for different intentions. If he has a heavy stress, he means something like '(I want an) onion'. With slower delivery and less emphasis, he probably means '(This is an) onion' if he has a wide pitch-range, he means something like '(Look at this) onion!' Mark's 'onion' is clearly more advanced than Christie's. It might be regarded as already syntactic, with two elements, word and intonation combined. Or it might be seen as a proto-syntax, a stage preceding true syntax.

This is partly a matter of definitions. But behind the problem of definitions is a substantive issue: whether it is more helpful to emphasise the similarities or the differences between early forms of language and later forms. For some purposes it is important that a form that looks the same in both child and adult language — for instance, a one-word utterance — should be understood as very different because the two systems are so different. But adult language does emerge from child language, and without continuities this progression would be inexplicable. In the case of the movement from holophrastic (one-word) sentences to two-word sentences, this intermediate stage, where there is a number of significantly different intonations, gives a model for the second stage. There is a small set of intonation markers, which can be attached to any word the child knows, to modify its meaning. So the basic form at this stage is modifier plus modified. In the holophrastic stage, modifier (intonation) and modified (word) are simultaneous. At the next stage, the same structure is repeated but now the modifier is a word, too.

This is the break-through into syntax proper. But the form of syntax at this stage is still both like and unlike the adult form. Take Mark's two-word utterances 'one more', 'no more' and 'only one'. In each of these, Mark is repeating words used by his mother, so imitation is occurring; but he only imitates what makes sense in terms of his grammar. He does not, for instance, repeat 'more after' or 'this no', which occur together and could as easily be copied. There are principles behind what he copies and how he copies. That is, he has a grammar.

In each of these phrases he puts a stronger stress on the first word. This word modifies what follows, just as intonation modified the single word at the previous stage. 'One' and 'no' are two words which function in this way. The child might say 'one onion', 'one cheese', 'one tomato', or 'no onion', 'no tomato', 'no please'. We can describe Mark's grammar in terms of its basic categories and its rules. There seem for him to be two classes of word: a small number of modifiers, and a larger number of words that can be modified. Some writers have claimed that this development is a normal one for children and they have called the two classes of words 'pivot-words' and 'open-words'. The pivot-words act as a kind of fulcrum, a small set of words that provide a framework, and the open-words are a larger set which is constantly expanding, as new words are added. (Brown and Bellugi, 1964).

Mark is just at the beginning of this stage, so we do not have any unusual examples of sentence structure in the transcript. But if he follows the normal course of development, he will use this simple grammar productively, to produce forms which are quite regular and predictable in terms of his own grammar but which he could not have heard because they are ungrammatical for adults. Later on in this recording he said 'more plate'. This has the meaning 'another plate', but it is ungrammatical, and we can be reasonably sure he has never heard it. He is not copying, then he is producing a new utterance in accordance with the rules he has derived from the adult language that he has heard.

All this has general implications for learning theory. In learning language, children do not simply accumulate new items. They go from system to system. Each system builds on the previous stage, incorporating structures and elements into a more comprehensive order. The child is making successive hypotheses about the total system, as well as guesses about particular syntactic forms. In later stages we find the phenomenon of over-generalisation, where the child grasps a simple rule (such as: the past form ends in (e) d, t; or plurals end in (e) s/z), and applies it where adult speakers would not (for example, camed, fighted: or geeses, teeths). Children go through the same kind of powerful theory-building as scientists do in major periods of scientific revolution. (See Kuhn 19.) Each movement from stage to stage is a major linguistic revolution. Stability is reached when the child has acquired the basic system of the adult language. The child is an active agent in this process, making daring guesses about the form of a grammar which is never spelled out and is not even known consciously by most adults. So language is not acquired piecemeal, although particular words are learned by experience, and the hypotheses are reactions to what is presented by experience.

There is scope for different emphases in the account of this general process. Some writers, the 'nativists', focus on the child's contribution and the universality of the general forms of human languages; but this emphasis should not be carried too far. Human languages have an irreducible variety, and children are attempting to learn the particular language used by adults around them. There is no doubt that different environments affect the development of language. However, it is also clear that children are not simply passive receivers of language. A decisive argument against a simple empiricist or behaviourist view is that children learn rules as well as words. These rules form a complex system which they are never taught and never come to learn consciously. Until a linguist comes along to explain them, these rules exist only inside people's heads, below the level of consciousness. So how could they be part of the environment acting on the child? Yet how could they reach the child unless they are somehow implicit in the world and experience of the child?

Language and thought

Language develops. Thought develops. But what is the relationship between these two developments? A short answer is: important but complex and difficult to determine. Language and thought are separate in the early stages of life. Before the child can speak he is thinking. He recognises some significant parts of life's reality and tries to act on them. At the next stage, the development of a phonological system, we have seen that the child is engaged in a complex analysis of one part of reality — the sounds made by adults — into a small set of elements, organised by an hierarchy of categories. This is an impressive act of thinking. It precedes language and is the prerequisite for it. The development of this system is virtually complete by four years old, at least in outline, at a stage when children are, according to cognitive psychologists, capable only of elementary thought processes. A similar paradox arises with grammar.

We have seen the child using the hypothetic-deductive method on a formidable scale in acquiring grammar at the age of two and three. Yet Piaget sees adolescence (12 plus) as the age at which this kind of thinking emerges first, in an explicit form (1955). Many individuals who speak grammatically, and therefore were budding Newtons at the age of three, hardly use these modes of thought as adults. So the thinking *behind* language seems to have gone well ahead of thinking *in* language. Yet the thought implicit in a natural language, including many of the concepts underlying words they hear or use, go well beyond the apparent grasp of children. In acquiring language, then, they acquire forms of thought which go beyond what they can understand. To give just one example: children up to the age of seven have the word 'because' but cannot complete 'because' sentences consistently to express what adults would regard as a cause (Piaget, 1955). So insofar as language is ahead of thought, it seems a kind of pseudo-thought — like adult's clothes on a child frame, which the child will grow into.

In practice it is difficult to decide whether language is or is not ahead of thought, because it is so difficult to define and isolate thought, and see where language ends and thought begins. Consider one example used by Piaget (1967). Children by the age of ten can usually arrange three elements — A, B, C — in order, on the grounds of size or colour. But ask a child this question: 'Edith has darker hair than Lily. Edith's hair is lighter than Susan's. Who has the darkest hair?' Up to the age of eleven the answer is likely to be that Lily has the darkest hair, and Susan the lightest. But what does this show? That their thinking in language lags behind their other strategies for understanding reality? Perhaps. Certainly, language is not helping them to solve this problem. But why do they find this problem so difficult? (Adults also find it difficult.) Let us look at the form of language used in the question.

If we take these sentences transformationally, we start with two simple sentences about Edith. 'Edith has dark hair. (Lily has dark hair). Edith has light hair (Susan has light hair).' These are then transformed by a comparative transformation: 'Edith has dark*er* hair *than* Lily (has dark hair). Edith has lighter hair *than* Susan (has light hair).' The parts in Italics are added by the transformation, and the bracketed parts are deleted. The deleted parts contain precisely the wrong answers the under-elevens give, suggesting that it is the difficulty of the transformational operation which is interfering with their ability to solve the problem. Uncoding the transformation is itself an intellectual task, which has to be performed before the given problem can be solved. Even to get the answer wrong in the way Piaget's subjects did requires a complex operation.

So Piaget's test may simply be showing that thought deployed on decoding language is unproductive in problem solving. Language here is using up too much of the child's intellectual capacity. While a language form is unfamiliar it will attract too much attention and will be a hindrance to thinking. So language will only enhance thought after it has become familiar and habitual. We can expect that language development will have to come before a cognitive development which depends on it in some way. It is also obvious that a cognitive task that has to be presented or revealed through language cannot be tested for independently of language, even though the capacity for its performance may already be present in the child.

However, language is not irrelevant to thinking about serial order. I asked Christine, a ten-year-old girl, the Piaget question. After much hesitation, she answered correctly. I then asked her: 'Compare three people, saying ways in which they are different.' She wrote the following answer:

Jodie Cathy Mum

Cathy and Mum have bad tempers sometimes where as Jodie
hasn't much. Jodie and Cathy are much more cheerful than
Mum is to me. Jodie is good at sport and Cathy and Mum aren't
really. Jodie and Mum are not shy at all, but Cathy is a bit.
Jodie and Cathy sometimes brag and show off, but Mum
doesn't. Mum is kind but the other two don't really like to give
things to people much.

Christine's judgments are built up by applying a single category which distinguishes one of the three people from the other two. This is the same process that builds up the phonological system, though Christine's categories do not seem to be an ordered set of features. Since she was writing this, she had time to carry out further modifying operations. The first judgment — 'Cathy and Mum have bad tempers' — is a simple judgment. Later she inserted 'sometimes' and 'much', to make it a more complex and relative judgment. The second judgment, on Mum's cheerfulness, adds 'to me', again making it a complex relative judgment. Piaget sees seven as the normal age for the break-through from egocentric thinking. Christine's 'to me' refers to herself as contrasted with others, so she has gone beyond egocentric thought, which does not distinguish between self and others and takes the self as the centre of its world. The linguistic form 'to me' is a simple one, well within the capacity of a much younger child; but used as a modifier, as here, it is the instrument of a mature thought form in Piaget's scheme.

None of her examples shows serial thinking: A > B > C. Nowhere does she attempt a comparison of this form. However, she has a rule for the ordering of the names, Jodie > Cathy, Jodie > Cathy > Mum. Since Jodie is younger than Cathy (Christine is the younger sister of Cathy, and friend of Jodie), the order goes from youngest to oldest. Christine has ordered these people in reverse age, giving the list at the top of her answer, and she follows this order throughout even while she is concentrating on her other acts of judgments. Clearly she can handle serial thinking effortlessly, but this achievement lies behind her organisation of language and thought, not on the surface.

Because the basic forms she uses are familiar to her, language is helping Christine to make complex, relative judgments, not hindering her as in the hair question. But what about her conceptual development? The concepts she uses are relatively simple: 'bad-tempered' etc. But if we can regard 'Mum', 'Cathy' and 'Jodie' as concepts, their significance is a complex bundle of features. Mum, for instance, is —

$$+ \quad \text{bad-tempered}$$
$$- \quad \text{cheerful}$$
$$- \quad \text{good at sport}$$
$$- \quad \text{shy}$$
$$- \quad \text{bragging}$$
$$+ \quad \text{kind}$$

The list, no doubt, could be extended. As a concept, 'Mum' seems to be an unstable aggregate of qualities. Vygotsky has argued that in children's thinking there is a progression (1962). They start with what he calls complexes, which refer to heterogeneous items loosely specified by a collection of features. They then progress to concepts, which are stable and abstract collections of features. The stability of the concept in Vygotsky's view comes from the organising presence of an adult concept. Because there is a word for 'Mother', a child's complexes are likely to be guided in that direction. In these terms, 'Mum' is a complex, not a concept. It might be the basis of a concept, presumably 'Mother', just as 'Cathy' might be generalised to become 'sister', and Jodie might become 'friend.'

In Vygotsky's scheme, complexes come before concepts, but one merges into the other. For the child, the concept has to become concrete to be meaningful, just as the complex has to become stable, coherent and part of an interpersonal system of meanings. The complex, in this progression, still has a vital function. Christine probably has the concept 'Mother', which as a stereotype would be likely to be associated with 'good-tempered' and 'cheerful', as well as 'kind'. So the complex might be implicitly critical of the general concept 'Mother', and of this particular mother for her lapses from the stereotype.

Abstract thinking is generally regarded as the highest stage of development. For Piaget, a crucial development in language and thought comes when the thinker can manipulate propositions and think through these, rather than through direct observations using concepts closely tied to experience. Piaget sees the final break-through in this ability coming during adolescence. This girl is not yet old enough for that, but her thinking is concrete and complex, and effective and subtle in its own terms.

In this piece of thinking, concepts may be hovering waiting to be born, but they have no regular name. What about concepts which come to the child from outside, from the teacher for instance? Vygotsky distinguishes between 'spontaneous concepts' and 'scientific concepts'. Spontaneous concepts develop out of complexes, guided by existing terms in the adult language. By scientific concepts Vygotsky means the systematic terms which are used in the language of instruction. Below a certain age, abstract concepts will be incomprehensible. In Chapter 1, we saw how the seven-year-old girl reacted blankly to the word 'education'. From seven to twelve, however, children develop some capacity to respond adequately to abstracts even though their understanding of them will be less than an adult's. So, should a teacher use them for children at this stage? There are different educational philosophies at stake here, arguing for opposing courses of action. If it is seen as important to encourage children to discover their own concepts, the teacher is in effect relying on spontaneous concepts which are likely to be richly concrete, immersed in diverse experience, and confused, since they have grown out of complexes.

Learning will still be a social process, since the language gives ready-made terms which model the concepts that emerge. So this kind of teacher is relying on language itself to guide students' thinking along generally agreed lines. But what about those abstract concepts which, after a certain stage, become invaluable tools of thought? Vygotsky showed that between seven and twelve, children had a better grasp of causal processes in relation to concepts learned through instruction (scientific concepts) than with spontaneous concepts. The language of instruction, by being in advance of spontaneous or everday thinking, acts as a stimulus to the development of higher forms, though both forms are essential for development.

In working its slow way upwards, an every day concept clears a path for the scientific concept and its development. It creates a series of structures necessary for the evolution of the concept's more primitive, elementary aspects, which give it body and vitality. Scientific concepts in turn supply structures for the upward development of the child's spontaneous concepts toward conscious and deliberate use. — (Vygotsky, 1962:109)

To see a child in this 7–12 age group using scientific concepts, here is Christine again, responding to the question 'What is education, and what do you think of it?'

Education is when you go to school or to a university to learn things. I think it is a useful thing for when you get older.

This is clearly a competent answer. The concept is significant to her, as it was not to the seven-year-old. She uses a general 'you', responding to the intrinsically abstract nature of the term. 'You' is in effect sub-categorised again, to give two levels of education, corresponding to the age of the student: 'school' and 'university'. This is the same principle she used in her spontaneous thinking to order the three people she compared; chronological age. This principle is also used in her justification of education. Education is useful 'for when you get older'. Here the general 'you' links her future experience with other people's present experience. We can see from this example how the two kinds of concept are complementary. The nature of the term forces her to go beyond her immediate experience of school, to include the experience of herself and others at different stages of life. The term has forced her out of narrow, egocentric thinking. But the experience invoked by the term is given order by spontaneous concepts which are key ones for her in making sense of her everyday reality. A healthy development of language and thought draws on both kinds of language and both kinds of thought.

Functions of language

Another perspective on language development is the functional approach. This was the subject of Chapter 6. There we saw that there is a wide variety of technical terms for language functions used by different theorists, but we can usefully describe the kinds of things done through language in informal terms. Here is a list of the main stages of early language development, in terms of the main functions at each stage:

1. Reflex sounds (cries etc.) These have a function for the mother. They are signs that the baby needs to be fed, changed or whatever. But though they indicate the baby's state of mind and regulate the mother's behaviour, the baby has no functional control over them.

2. Babbling. (3–6 months). Babbling is highly functional for the baby, who is acquiring control over the means of language, and creating patterns. We can call this an aesthetic function, or a metalinguistic function, since it is concerned with the medium of communication. So these are the first functions to appear. The babbling may also be expressive, though probably only of feelings, not of ideas.

3. One word speech (10 months). The child here is acquiring vocabulary. Words label reality, so language is being used to make sense of the world, another crucial function. Words are used also to create counter-realities: the imaginative function. Social functions are also prominent. The child can get adults to do things on his behalf. The child's behaviour is also controlled through the language of adults. Language is a primary mode of interaction at this age, and that becomes a major function served by language.

4. Two word utterances (18 months). This major structural advance is not associated with a dramatic increase in the number of functions. All the previous functions are present, but enhanced. In particular, since language is more creative, it can be used to project alternative realities, and focus behaviour of the self and others more efficiently.

Halliday makes a number of observations on the functional differences between child and adult language (1974). Children early on acquire a wide range of functions, most of the functions available to an adult, but typically each utterance serves only one function. Adult language is multifunctional. Every utterance does several things at once, in an integrated way. There is also a shift in the balance of functions. Social functions predominate for the child. For the adult, language used to inform is more prominent, and comes to seem the major use of language. So extreme is the shift that there is a tendency for some of the other functions to atrophy. So although adult speech (or the speech of adolescents) is multifunctional, the social functions may be not so manifest as in younger children. The paradoxical reward for the development of the informative function is sometimes a less flexible and effective means of influencing the behaviour of others. The young child can get its mother to do things more readily than some well-informed adolescents can achieve with a teacher.

Another way of categorising language development is in terms of kinds of discourse. Speech begins by being interactive, a kind of dialogue, and this affects both structures and functions. In this early dialogue, the child typically incorporates and re-uses elements from the adult's language. So language functions to socialise thought as concepts and instructions are internalised. Dialogue develops into a kind of monologue which Piaget has named collective monologue (1955). This form of speech is both individual and social. It is like a running commentary on the individual's thoughts, actions, or environment. Vygotsky has stressed the importance of this phase in regulating the individual's behaviour (1962). It is a kind of self-regulation that is also an incorporation of actions and experience into a public world of meanings.

Although the child is not talking to anyone in particular, other people are necessary as background. Around the age of seven, collective monologues slowly disappear. Vygotsky sees them becoming interior speech, which is socialised thought available to the private individual. Language, therefore, functions to give meanings and forms of thought to individuals which aid thinking, and at the same time it gives a sense of social sanction to these private thoughts. Robinson Crusoe on his desert island felt less lonely because his diary and his dialogues with himself created a shadowy but comforting sense of a society within. Language here is functioning to create complex illusions, so it takes some time before this function is acquired.

As well as the functional evolution of kinds of oral language, there is the development of written language. The forms and functions of mature writing grow essentially out of monologues, which have incorporated into them the presence of an abstract audience. So one function of writing is to create an image of the absent audience for the writer, and an image of the absent author for the reader. This is a complex speculative act, possible only if the communicator can conceive the communication situation in an abstract way. This complex social function of writing is so basic for self-motivated acts of writing that without it, productive writing is not likely to occur.

This development is dependent on cognitive development. A relation between functional and cognitive development of this kind is important for understanding linguistic development. For instance, children have the regulatory function, but their understanding of the complexities of social relationships is undeveloped. The informative function cannot emerge until children realise that in spite of being god-like and all-knowing, adults may not always know what the child does. A further refinement of the informative function is to attribute meanings to the other, either aggressively ('when did you stop beating your wife?') or more positively, as when a teacher completely rephrases a child's answer, where the relation between informer and informed is manipulatively reversed. Again, this development requires a complex model of social relations and a sophisticated sense of the relation between message and communication process.

Development and context

Although language learning is not simply a passive process of imitation which totally depends on influences from the environment, the environment does matter. Children may be acting like incredible little super-scientists, deducing the grammar of their language from a small and inadequate sample of it, as Chomsky has suggested; but we can still ask: 'What are the best conditions for these super-scientists to work in?' Everyone with normal faculties acquires language, but teachers must be interested in the different levels of mastery of the language. What lies behind these differences, and what social conditions favour language development?

In acquiring the sound system, the child, like any good scientist, needs good data in large quantities to work on, assuming that nature has provided good equipment (ears and vocal apparatus). That means an attentive, present parent-figure. Child-rearing patterns associated with different socio-economic classes or races can be expected to have an influence on linguistic as on other development. Children in institutions with limited adult attention will be disadvantaged at every stage. Contrast their situation with that of Christie and Mark in the first transcript in this chapter. These two, the only children of middle-class parents, receive a lot of attention. Take the mother's response to Mark's request for onions. 'No, no more onions now, darling. That's enough onions for one little boy. No, no more onions, what about carrot? Carrot?' Mark continues to repeat 'onion' in various forms, during his mother's speech. She has repeated the word three times, to match his three interventions. She is providing excellent feedback, which allows him opportunity to refine his hypotheses about 'onions', as a sound or as a word. This mother also gives an emphatic stress to the most important elements in her sentences, giving Mark valuable clues about what to attend to. Mark is linguistically advanced. Part of the reason probably lies with his mother's helpful collaboration.

The feedback given by mothers is important. In a famous article, Brown, Cazden and Bellugi noted that parents only rarely corrected grammar. Mostly parents accept the child's grammatical forms even if they are incorrect (as they typically are). They correct only for the truth-value. The authors conclude wittily: 'Which renders mildly paradoxical the fact that the usual product of such a training is an adult whose speech is highly grammatical but not noticeably truthful.' (1967:58) This finding certainly casts doubt on the need for constant correction of grammar in acquiring language. The typical maternal behaviour can also be justified on other grounds. Any linguist studying child language knows that as far as her own child is concerned, mother often does know best.

What happens is that the mother learns her own child's grammar and sound system. She does not correct the child's errors because she is hardly conscious of them. They are not errors in terms of the child's grammar, which the mother has acquired as one acquires a foreign language. Her feedback is therefore more precise and relevant for the child, who is building up an earlier model of grammar and is not, at this stage, even hypothesising the forms of a full adult grammar. Mark has someone who understands what he is trying to produce in its own terms. That is more helpful than someone trying to correct him by adult standards before he could grasp the grammar that made sense of these particular corrections. In simple terms, we see again the value to children of an attentive and present adult who can become an expert in their unique language. This mother is not talking baby-talk; she is using adult forms with an intuitive sense of her child's capacities, presenting him with forms which are both correct and appropriate to his grammar.

Children will obviously benefit linguistically from the right kind of adult attention. Adults can provide high-quality input for their children's hypotheses about language. They can also create a stimulating environment, one that the child will want to explore and talk about. All this is commonsense. Clearly the lack of this will be a disadvantage, even though the child will still acquire all the main forms of his adult language. There is a number of kinds of environment which are likely to be disadvantageous. Institutions are one such case. Some institutions may be better than some homes. Decisive here are the ratios of adults to children (1 to 4 seems to be the optimum for young children) and the attitudes of these adults. An institution has to be well funded to achieve these optimum levels. The staff are likely in practice to be too hard pressed to maintain the desirable level of attention for each individual child. The natural mother is not indispensable to the child's linguistic, emotional or intellectual growth, as the experience of the Israeli Kibbutz shows; but a consistent quantity and quality of adult care does seem to be.

Outside institutions, children in large families will tend to receive less attention, together with a lower quantity and quality of linguistic input. The average size of families of lower socio-economic groups in Australia is larger than for higher groups. Some ethnic or religious groups also have larger average family sizes. This raises the contentious issue of ethnic and class differences in modes of child rearing which potentially have effects on language development. Some researchers in America in the 1960s argued that children from low-income families, especially black children, were exposed to inadequate forms of language, so that their development of language was retarded. (Deutch *et al* 1968.)

We saw in Chapter 2 that judgments of this kind are liable to be affected by linguistic prejudices. The language presented to the child may be a non-standard form which is regarded as defective by the researcher, whose tests of language development might be similarly biased to measure competence in standard English, and affected by the child's confidence in test situations controlled by middle-class whites. In the case of urban blacks, Labov and others have argued that the environment these children grow up in is richly verbal, providing all the linguistic material a speaker needs for linguistic development — in non-standard English. This perspective is a valuable corrective to research which fails to take account of social stereotypes in evaluating the total situation of a child from a different background. However, there are consequences of poverty which do affect language and other development. Alcoholic, indifferent, or largely absent child minders are not conducive to the child's development of his or her full potential. For Australia, studies of poverty show that urban Aborigines are the group most severely affected.

Conclusion

The acquisition of language is a remarkable achievement, with many implications for understanding how people learn. Children are born with a basic propensity for language. They acquire the sounds of the language through a slowly evolving system, not simply through imitation. They acquire grammar in a similarly abstract way, intuitively grasping underlying, unstated rules to interpret and produce utterances. They progress through different grammars till they arrive at the adult grammar, the whole process taking place almost entirely without direct instruction in rules at any stage. Capacities for language and thought develop with maturity, but the relation between the two patterns of development is not a simple one. The child becomes increasingly able to use abstract thought, and produce and understand language of this kind; but sometimes the complexity of linguistic processes detracts from the capacity for equivalently productive thinking at that particular stage. As well as development of the structures of language and thought, there is development in control over the functions of language, with children growing able to use language to perform more complex tasks in more complex situations. But though the development of language relies on innate capacities of human individuals, linguistic powers emerge in particular contexts, which may be more or less conducive to children developing to their full potential.

Suggested activities

1. Listen carefully to the sounds produced by a young child below the age of two, and list the sounds he/she can produce against a list of the full sounds of English, to see what distinctive features he/she possesses, and does not possess. Use the scheme to predict what sounds will be difficult for the child, and consider the consequences for comprehension of not being able to distinguish these particular sounds.

2.   Collect a sample of two-word utterances of a child at the two-word stage, and attempt to divide the words into pivot (basic) and open. Then write the grammar of the child's language. What does the grammar suggest about the child's understanding of the world?

3.   Ask children of different ages to explain the meaning of an abstract term, and attempt to assess the different capacities at each age.

4.   Give children of different ages the task of comparing three different people, things or situations and see what spontaneous concepts they use.

5.   Look at children in different situations, and attempt to give a complete list of the things they use language to do, with examples of each function. Then consider the same children in the school situation, to see how many of these functions are or might be used.

The Study of Communication

Chapter 11   Bob Hodge
Uses of Grammar

What should a teacher do when faced with grammatical errors in students' work? How might grammars, of various kinds, be illuminating for the general teacher; and how can conscientious teachers find out what is useful for them from various grammars that are available?

These questions start from the ordinary classroom teacher's needs and assumptions. This chapter will try to give a helpful framework for these questions, setting them in the context of some modern concepts of what grammars are or can be. Chomsky, for instance, sees a grammar as a theory about a language. Halliday insists on the functional basis of that grammar. It has the form it has because of the functions language has to serve in a given society. For Whorf a grammar enshrines a metaphysic, a theory about the universe which is specific to a particular cultural group. Between them, these three propositions given an importance to the study of grammars and grammar. But what is their relevance and value for the classroom teacher faced with a piece of work which is written in ungrammatical English?

Take the following essay, written by Michael, a 15-year-old Aboriginal boy:—

'Two Minute Warning'

This person live in london and is nane was Mr Joe Brown one
day when Mr Joe Brown came home from work he found the
parcel at the   of his appartment he was a member of parliament
in the Gover-ment he go by the name Governor General Brown;
will he pick the parcel up and then he walk over to the table
and put the parcel down on the table and then he walk over to
the langesweet and sat down and then he stard to think who
sent him the parcel.   and what was in the parcel then he that
back about a year later then he remember that a capl of
member in parliament was sent a parcel like Mr Joe Brown as
got and the members of parliament was bloing to smitheres
and the phone rang Mr Joe Brown Jump to he feet and then he
went and answer the phone in a beep voes someone side you
have two minute to git out of the bluing Mr Joe Brown stode

dumfonder wandring what to does but the two minute was up and their was a isplocaen and Mr Joe Brown was kilde.

Here, for comparison, is the same boy discussing this piece of work with an interviewer:—

I.   Do you find that talking about something before you write helps, or is it better, like this one, to remember something that you saw?

M.   This one here, they read a story before this, talking about someone who lived in London who got a parcel, and we just had to add words on. They just wanted to know what was in the parcel, they just put a parcel and you had to say what was in it, whether it was a bomb, a birthday present, or something like that.

I.   I see, so that's how it started off, and when she started asking those sorts of questions, you suddenly remembered the film you'd seen in Perth?

M.   Yeah.

I.   Did that, that piece of writing was done in how much of a period? How much talk at the start, about five minutes? Did it take the whole period?

M.   She wrote some words up on the board, and was talking as she was writing it up and said we had to write about a bloke who lived in London, that received a parcel and just say what was in the parcel, and that took almost five minutes and then we had the rest of the period. I finished it all except for the last four lines at the end of the period. I wrote the last bit after the period finished.

(Bennett 1979)

An educated speaker of English would immediately judge the writing to be ungrammatical at many points, and full of errors. This judgment would be made automatically by most qualified teachers, without need to refer to a grammar book. So far so good for the concerned teacher. We can assume that everyone already knows all the grammar needed for this first operation. But what is the teacher doing when making this judgment? And what judgment exactly is being made? And what constructive actions can follow from it?

Since we are concerned with where Michael's grammar departs from the grammar of standard English, we can start from the 'errors' we originally noted. The majority of these are errors of spelling and punctuation. The spelling errors are mostly close to the spoken form; for example, 'gover-ment' instead of 'government'. Even standard English speakers often slide over the 'n'. Michael had asked the teacher how to spell some words. For others, he had relied on the closeness of written to spoken forms — unwisely, in a high number of cases. If all these errors had been marked, he would have been made even more aware of the difference between writing and speech. In this short passage there are 23 spelling errors (including crossed-out attempts), plus a number of words which were no doubt spelled out for him by the teacher. His sense of the difference between the written and spoken codes would act as a filter, if he aimed at correctness. His usable vocabulary would shrink right down to the few common words he could spell correctly.

Punctuation, for him, almost does not exist. Yet if we look at the transcript of his speech, we find he is able to organise blocks of language appropriately, indicating the boundaries of the units of meaning. The transcript has commas, etc., in the right places, which suggests that Michael has the functional equivalent of punctuation in speech. He merely does not know how to translate his intuitions about pauses into punctuation marks, or does not trust his intuitions. So he has opted out of the whole business of judgment, but this has not saved him from being judged. If he had put commas all the time, he would have been right sometimes. As it is, he will be judged as wrong, for the written language, all the time.

The most consistent grammatical error concerns the verbs. He often uses the verb stem on its own: 'live' instead of 'lives' or 'lived', and so on. This, in standard English, is known as the infinitive: that is, it is not limited to any particular time or modality. But we cannot assume it is an infinitive for Michael. One hypothesis we might try is that Michael's spoken language is a non-standard form which has no tense markers, so the written form is close to his spoken form. A glance at the transcript shows that this is not so, though he may still use non-standard forms at home. We might hypothesise that the opposite relation holds for Michael between his spoken and his written forms: writing is so incomprehensibly different for him that he does not dare to guess what tense to use. So as with the punctuation, he uses none. This may turn out to be the case, though he does also use the past tense. But first we ought to look more closely, to see if there is any consistent pattern that emerges.

The judgment that a linguistic form is right or wrong is an important one, but it needs to be refined. It is a relative judgment — right or wrong for that language, used at that stage in its development, in a particular social context. Shakespeare, for instance, used double negatives, which would now be ungrammatical; but it would be wrong to call the form ungrammatical for Shakespeare. The English language in the 16th century allowed a form which is now judged ungrammatical. A number of non-standard dialects of English allow double negatives. Since this is systematic for speakers of these dialects, it is grammatical for them. Many speakers of standard English would call these forms ungrammatical, but in fact they are simply registering the difference between the grammar of standard English that they have internalised, and the grammar of that dialect Since so many dominant speakers in the community attach such importance to the standard language, the judgment of ungrammaticality is representative and important, and a teacher cannot ignore it. But the distinction between an ungrammatical form and a non-standard form remains a necessary one, as the basis for appropriate judgment and constructive reactions by the teacher.

One extreme reaction to this piece of writing would be to mark every error, put in the correct version and require Michael to write out the corrections ten times. In this case, such a reaction might be unproductive. According to his English teacher, Michael usually produces only half a line of continuous writing in a period. This piece, produced over a period and finished in Michael's own time, was an exceptional achievement for him. Too heavy a hand, experienced teachers would think, might simply turn Michael off writing completely.

So for the moment, let us look at Michael's writing to try to understand what is going on in his writing and thinking processes generally, without committing ourselves to any particular strategy for correcting the errors. A grammar is a theory of a language. The grammar is a hypothetical set of rules that account for why some sentences are judged grammatical, and freely produced, and why others are not produced, or are judged ungrammatical if they are. In trying to guess the grammar of Michael's writing, initially we need to regard everything as grammatical, since it has been produced. Later on we can refine the hypothesis. At first, we simply look for patterns.

There are two distinguishable occasions when the infinitive form is used: for general propositions ('this person live in London'), and for vivid narrative incidents ('will he pick the parcel up'). The past form is used for particular events in the past. One exception to this seems to be the verb 'to be', where 'was' is used both for general propositions about the characters, and for particular events ('their was a isplocaen'). Leaving aside the exceptions, this gives a structure of tenses as follows:

$$\left\{\begin{array}{l}\text{infinitive}\\ \\ \text{past}\end{array}\right. \quad \left\{\begin{array}{l}\text{general truths}\\ \text{immediate present}\\ \text{specific, remote event}\end{array}\right.$$

Fig. 11.1

What is normally called the present in standard English corresponds to this structure, with the -s present (example: 'Joe Brown lives in London') usually general and timeless, with the -ing form used for a vivid narrative ('Now he is picking up the parcel'); though the -s present is also used for sports commentaries ('Buhagiar weaves out of trouble, Sewell fumbles but recovers and shoots for goal —'). From this example it is clear that the rules for the correct use of the present tense in English are complicated and obscure. Learners of English find it hard to grasp the rules for correct usage, and speakers of English who make no mistakes themselves still find it hard to explain what the rules are. Try it for yourself!

The position is equally complex when we consider written language. The -s present occurs more frequently in writing than in speech. It is normal form for expository prose that lays down general truths — as in a book like this one. Use of the past in such prose indicates that the statement is particular, and that it is distant for the writer. I could equally well write 'Michael was an Aboriginal boy' or 'Michael is an Aboriginal boy'. The -ed form is cooler and more limited in its claims. Now at the time of your reading this, Michael may not be an Aborigine, or a boy. The -s form will be claiming that Michael is both, when he will certainly no longer be a boy if this book survives a hundred years. It will communicate a sense of certainty and immediacy about the fact, even when the fact is no longer true. The written language, we can see, adds a further dimension of complexity to an already obscure and difficult form.

There is one isolated error which is, perhaps, revealing about Michael's grammar in written English. He writes 'wandring what to does', using the -s present instead of the infinitive 'to do'. There is only one other infinitive, 'to git', but this is used correctly, in a piece of quoted speech. In the transcript, however, he uses the infinitive form correctly four times. The pattern here seems to be that in writing, he converts -s present to infinitive and vice versa, but uses both standard forms correctly in speech. That is, he seems to be assuming that the written language reverses the rules of the spoken language. If that is so, his errors follow the systematic principle that written language inverts the rules of his own spoken language. It is as if he has invented a rule: When going from spoken to written language, change all -s presents to infinitives and all infinitives to -s presents. This is a particular rule expressing the general though vague principle that the written language is typically different from spoken language. This principle is not right, on this point, but it is often right. Whether or not our particular hypothesis is correct here, Michael has had to interpret a complicated and confusing linguistic situation. He initially learned non-standard/ Aboriginal English, which has its own grammar and forms of pronunciation. The European community then presented him with both colloquial and formal English, each with a distinguishable grammar, but there would have been no support from family or peers for him to produce standard English forms.

Writing, then, would present itself as a difficult, doubly alien code, with unique forms of grammar and vocabulary. Michael would learn that the vocabulary and grammar of his natural language have to be transformed or filtered to become acceptable standard English, and that standard English is further modified in the written code. Faced with the vagaries of English spelling, which departs even more from his normal pronunciation than from standard Australian English, he might easily over-generalise, and conclude that written forms are *normally* unlike spoken forms. So, in this piece of writing at least, he has made a creative but erroneous guess about written English. He has forced himself to distrust his own natural forms of speech more than is warranted.

The writing uses very few tenses. From this we might conclude that he has a very limited grammar of tense and modality. However, in speech he can say 'She wrote some words up on the board, and was talking as she was writing it up'. That is, he has a tense-system that can present two events from occurring simultaneously. This would give the syntactic basis for a much more complex narrative than appears in the writing, where events seem simply to follow on one from another. If Michael has ruled out this tense, and this structure, as impossible or dangerous for written discourse, he has restricted himself unnecessarily.

What have Michael's classroom teachers learnt from looking at the grammatical errors? And what might they do? One thing they should appreciate is just how difficult and alien writing is for Michael. Michael's science teacher said he thought that 'Michael could write, but would not. He was disruptive'. In a sense this is right, in that Michael's distrust of the written code prevents him from using acceptable grammatical forms that he knows. He had extended his difficulties with spelling on to grammar, and developed his own anti-grammar especially to make writing even more difficult for himself than it already is. This general insight, if it could be communicated to him, might be a liberating and encouraging one. His grammatical strategy for writing has been based on a hypothesis that is partly wrong, and that might be changed. He is right to think that English spelling is often arbitrary and weird, but if there were no penalties for mis-spellings, or if strategies could be arranged to remove spelling as a problem as he is composing, he could concentrate on evolving a form of written expression which is more adequate to the scope of what he thinks and can say.

Grammar and individual growth

Not all pieces of writing a teacher receives are full of errors. Here is a sample of writing from Christine, an intelligent ten-year-old from a white middle-class home:

Chilly & Bam Bam

Chapter One
Chilly was a brown and Black female dog, with one spot of white on her forehead. Bam Bam was also a dog, but he was black all over from head to toe, without one spot of white, brown or any other colour anywhere. Even his tongue was bright black.
The two dogs lived apart from each other. Chilly, the two year old, lived on Mr. Marcus's farm while Bam Bam lived on Mr.

Spick's farm. Mr. Marcus was a nice man with a good family of
four counting himself and his wife. The two children were 8 &
10 years old. The youngest was Mary and followed by her big
brother Mark. On the other hand Mr. Spick was a bachelor with
no-one to talk to except Bam Bam and the two were a good
matched pair. Bam Bam had learned many tricks and he did
what ever Mr. Spick wanted him to. Mr. Spick was not actually
Spick and Span either, being a bachelor, the house was a
horrible mess but surprisingly the sheds weren't. Bam Bam never
showed he was lonley, he seemed to enjoy it, but Mr. Spick
wanted to go and live with his mother in Spain, his only excuse
was the farm, he just couldn't bring himself to leave the Farm.

This piece of writing does not have many errors. There is the occasional comma where there should be a full stop (for example, 'being a
bachelor, the house was a horrible mess' although the problem here may
be a hanging participle). The basis for the relevant rules is an understanding of where one thought ends and another begins, as conventional-
ised in English punctuation. There is also a small number of minor
errors of usage. 'Bam Bam was also a dog' should be 'Bam Bam was a
dog, also'. 'Good matched pair' should be 'well-matched pair'. 'Followed by her big brother Mark' should perhaps be something like 'the
next youngest'. In this case, as in the previous one, most teachers
would be able to identify these as errors and produce the correct form.
But how should the teacher react to the grammatical errors and achieve-
ments of this girl in a way that is helpful and illuminating?

If we tried to write a grammar that accounted for most of the sentences Christine produces, it would have as a dominant component a
description of basic sentences with the form 'Something was a . . . . .
(noun)' or 'Something was . . . . . (adj.)'. Christine uses this general
form very productively, especially the adjectival form; for instance,
'Chilly was a brown and black female dog', which combines the noun
and the adjective by the use of three adjectives. She makes this first
sentence even more descriptive by adding a with-phrase. In the passage
quoted she used two more similar with-phrases and a without-phrase.
Michael had used no adjectives, and no with-phrases.

This may make Christine's grammar sound basically simple, but there
are some complex things she does with this basic form. Take 'Even his
tongue was bright black'. The basic form here is 'Something is (adjective)'. 'Even' signals that this sentence repeats a previous structure —
('something is black') in this case. And it contrasts the new element
('his tongue') with what has gone before. Having a black tongue is
more surprising than being black from head to toe. She then makes the
contrast sharper by adding 'bright'. What she is doing is writing a cohesive text. Each sentence of the 'Something is . . . .' form is a judgment.
'Even' indicates that this is a judgment whose form specifically recalls
other analogous judgments.

The same can be said of her error with 'also'. 'Bam Bam was a dog also' is a sentence which refers back to an earlier sentence in this case, 'Chilly was a dog'. The form she actually used — Bam Bam was also a dog' — refers back to a previous sentence: 'Bam Bam was .... (intelligent, hairy etc. or, a friend, a companion etc.)'. Christine has not yet quite mastered this particular form, but it is clear what she wants to do with it. In this instance, she is making a double judgment: one, the also-sentence, linking the two dogs; the other, the but-sentence, contrasting them. The contrast is a form of negative. She has lots of negatives, in different forms: buts, excepts, withouts as well as nots, nevers and no-ones. Prominent in the grammar we might suggest to describe her language is negation, used for purposes of contrast. The importance of this form to her can be seen in her use of 'On the other hand', which is not quite an error but is rather too emphatic as she uses it. The errors, if we call them that, throw light on parts of her grammar which are growth points in her development. Because of the ways she thinks, she is making demands on her grammar which are not quite adequate for her to cope with yet, although what she can do is already potentially complex and sophisticated.

The analysis I have given so far is an hypothesis about the basic rules she uses most, and how she uses them. It is also an hypothesis about how she characteristically copes with experience. She is concerned predominantly with structures of judgment, building up from simple comparisons and contrasts to complex judgments. She is using language to articulate these judgments, and to practise the act of judgment itself. The passage comes from a nine-page story she did in her own time, so presumably the act of writing, and the acts of mind she performed, were personally satisfying to her. As with Michael, we have used an analysis of her grammar to gain a deeper understanding of what her intellectual needs are. In Christine's case there is no need for remedial attention. Perhaps she would profit most from being persuaded to experiment with more complex judgments, contrasting more than two people or things, where she would reach out for even more complex syntactic forms naturally, in the process of thinking and writing. Or perhaps she needs to be persuaded to develop other aspects of her language and thought, if these are less developed: representing actions and events, for instance. A teacher can decide on the basis of wide knowledge of the student, but the decision itself will be better for the teacher having tried to understand Christine's grammar, its limitations and potential for growth.

Using grammars

What help in this process of understanding can be gained from books, by teachers who are not specialists in language? A first place in which some might look is traditional grammars. Formal teaching of grammar is out of favour even in the subject English, so other subject specialists will hardly want to take it on themselves. But since the demise of such teaching has been blamed for contributing to general illiteracy and weakening the nation's moral and intellectual fibre, it is as well for all teachers to understand something of the reasons. Formal grammar teaching based on traditional grammar texts was found not to improve the average student's ability to read or write grammatically, comprehend better, or think more logically, as once had been claimed. This was partly because most children's practical grasp of the structures of their native language goes far beyond what traditional grammar texts contain. A computer programmed only according to these texts would speak gibberish, and would not understand the language of a five-year-old.

The main activity associated with these grammars was parsing: labelling parts of sentences. The knowledge acquired in the process was simply the labels and what they applied to. Naming of parts does not necessarily help you to use them correctly. However, the reaction against grammar may have gone too far. These grammars may be out of date in some of their details, but terms like *noun*, *verb* or *adjective* are still essential to enable students and teachers to talk and think about language. Christine, for instance, uses nouns and adjectives with great facility, but she is not so sure in transforming adverbs to adjectives (for example, 'a good matched pair'). Michael does not use adjectives in writing, but he does in speech. In order to sort out his problems with verbs, it would be very helpful if he knew the basic tense system of English, along with the names of the different tenses. There are many basic observations about grammatical forms which any teacher ought to be able to make, and every student should understand; and this provides a very practical reason for everyone to know the basic set of terms provided by traditional grammars.

Another useful kind of reference is guides to usage. The most authoritative one is Fowler's *Modern English Usage*. Such guides are frankly prescriptive. This is their value. They are more useful than prescriptive grammars because they record the judgments of an authoritative ideal speaker of the language as to what is currently acceptable. These judgments are social-linguistic facts, which can be explained in other terms but not ignored. Fowler's merit is that he gives judgments and commonsense reasons for them. Christine's use of 'also' might have been referred to Fowler if a teacher was in doubt whether it was correct. Fowler as an ideal speaker represents the norms of the standard English of conservative adult speakers. But language is constantly evolving, with different levels and dialect versions. Fowler is no help here. With Michael's language, Fowler would often be inapplicable or even misleading. The use of Fowler's English as an inflexible standard is a kind of linguistic imperialism.

Dictionaries are another resource for teachers. Dictionaries tend to be conservative, and are less full and authoritative on contemporary uses of words, or slang terms, though most modern dictionaries attempt to come to terms with this area of language. There is also a circularity in dictionary definitions: they explain one word by another. Another limitation of dictionaries, especially for learners of a language, is that the meaning of words is determined through context. Some dictionaries give examples of use; but even so, a dictionary is not the place to go to, to acquire new vocabulary.

However, what a dictionary can give is a precise account of meanings, and standard spelling and pronunciation for words that have already been met in context. Both Christine and Michael should be able to make use of dictionaries. Michael's need is greater. A dictionary could unlock large stocks of vocabulary which exist for him only in spoken form. Instead of getting the teacher to spell words on the board as requested, which makes him dependent on the school context, he could make use of a dictionary. There would still be problems — 'langesweet' would be hard to track down, but Michael would own and control an authority on language higher than that of his teacher — a key to the arbitrariness of the written language.

A teacher who wishes to go beyond these aids and make use of modern theories of grammar must be prepared for some hard work. The major theories are not easy for the non-specialist to follow. In what follows I shall summarise some key ideas of two important schools, to suggest their relevance to teachers; but these summaries are no substitute for the originals.

Noam Chomsky developed a form of grammar known as Transformational Generative Grammar. His two major works, both difficult, are *Syntactic Structures* (1957) and *Aspects of the Theory of Syntax* (1965). Chomsky was a structuralist, concerned with the structures of language. In his account of language, he sees the child as a kind of scientist, hearing noises and guessing at the system of rules that structure the noises into meaningful discourse. These rules, for Chomsky, are guessed at, not taught directly. The writer of a grammar simply makes these guesses explicitly, accepting the judgments of reliable speakers of the language as to whether or not a particular form is grammatical. This is essentially what we did with Michael's and Christine's language. Since Chomsky's method as a linguist is, he would claim, essentially the same as every language learner's, it can be used, informally, by anyone attempting to understand language structures, their own or those of others.

In describing the form of a grammar, he insists that it should account for the creativity of speakers. All speakers use finite means to generate infinite utterances. Language users are creative: they can produce and interpret utterances they have never heard before. So Chomsky sees some of the rules of a language as liberating and positive, where traditional grammars tended to seem negative: for example, 'don't split infinitives; don't have plural nouns with singular verbs; etc. Christine's language shows positive, productive rules of this kind. She could produce an indefinite number of sentences using just a few rules: 'Chilly was a dog with a white and black spot on her ear, and also a black hair on her knee, and . . . .' Michael has productive rules in speech which he does not use in writing. He also has rules which are constraints, which serve to reduce the number of possible forms he can produce. A grammar will have both kinds of rule, because it has to explain which forms are unacceptable as well as which forms are possible.

Chomsky divides the rules of a grammar into base rules which generate the basic forms of the language, and transformational rules which rearrange and re-order the basic structures. So for Chomsky, a sentence has a surface structure — the form it actually has, and a deep structure — the underlying basic forms before they have been transformed. Michael has used basic forms in his writing, but uses transforms in his speech; for instance: 'They read a story before this, talking about someone who lived in London who got a parcel.' Michael has fused together simpler forms: 'They read a story before this/the story talked about someone/someone lived in London/someone got a parcel.' The transformations are minor in their effect here, but they contribute to a more complex organisation of the sentence. Christine has a more complex transformational apparatus. A word like 'also' is the trace left on the surface by a complex transformation. Underlying 'Bam Bam was a dog also' is the pair of sentences 'Chilly was a dog and Bam Bam was a dog.'

Although transformational analyses in textbooks often look very complicated and technical, the essential point is clear; and since the professional linguist is only trying to make explicit the knowledge that the ordinary speaker possesses implicitly anyway, the classroom teacher in any subject can still make use of the basic insights of this grammar. Chomsky is suggesting a typical form for your hypotheses about an individual's grammar. Christine has a grammar with a productive base, and many ways for combining and reordering simple units (i.e. a rich transformational component). Michael has a different set of base rules for his written language, and he hardly uses the transformational component he has available for the spoken language.

Another important linguist is Michael Halliday. Where Chomsky emphasises structure, Halliday emphasises function. He is concerned more with what language can do than with the structures it has, though the two emphases are complementary. In Chapter 6 we gave an outline of Halliday's functional account of language. He is also concerned with systematic choices available to the speaker, so his theory has been called also a systemic grammar. This is essentially a simple idea which anyone can apply. It sees the language user as working with meaning potential, choosing a single form from a network of choices. Take Michael's first sentence: 'This person live in London.' Each word, of course, is chosen from the total set of words of each kind that Michael knows. 'Person' could be replaced by 'bloke', 'man', 'gentleman', etc. The choice of one word rather than another is directed by motives

Michael has, purposes his language is meant to perform, in the context he sees himself in.

As we saw in Chapter 6, Halliday sees three general functions which language serves for adult speakers: ideational (to represent or convey ideas), interpersonal (to interact with others), and textual (to order language itself into a specific kind of text). 'This' (as against 'a' or 'that', or 'Mr. Joe Brown' as against 'this person') serves several functions simultaneously. It indicates that there is just one person being talked of. It suggests a close relationship between writer and reader ('this person who you and I know about'). It is also part of the informational structure of the sentence. Usually the first element in a sentence is the given — what the speaker and hearer take for granted. What follows is usually the new information. By starting with 'this', Michael gives the impression that we know who 'this person' is, and only need to know where he lives. But Michael then goes on to give his name, in the 'new' position of the sentence. This contradicts the structure of the opening. So either Michael is not in control of the textual function, or he is doing something unusual with his narrative technique. From the rest of the narrative it would seem that Michael's writing mainly conveys ideas, with a simple informational structure, making minimal intrusions of himself into the speech situation. In Halliday's terms, his meaning potential in two major functions of language is greatly reduced in written language, though this is not the case with his spoken English.

Christine represents ideas well, and organises the text with a high degree of coherence; but she is not, in this passage, using language to act on the reader. This side of her language seems relatively underdeveloped. Such judgments as these on Michael and Christine are not technical, and they could easily be made by any thoughtful teacher. What I have been trying to bring out in this chapter is precisely that — the ways in which the findings of modern linguists connect with the experience, insights and needs of the average intelligent and concerned teacher.

Metacommunication

A grammar is a formal way of talking about some aspects of language, mainly its structures and the rules that underlie them. Linguistics is one stage further: it is a way of talking about language generally. This book as a whole is trying to help you do that more effectively.

Communication about communication has been called Metacommunication by Gregory Bateson, who worked on communication of schizophrenics but whose basic model is relevant to education as well (1956). (See also Chapters 1 and 6.) Bateson focuses on the relation between the mother and the schizophrenic, seeing the schizophrenic's modes of language and thought as a logical strategy for coping with a particular kind of communication structure and content. Communication occurs through verbal and non-verbal channels. Communication about communication, according to Bateson, most often comes via non-verbal channels. For instance, a hostile remark accompanied by a laugh is a joke. The normal person in society knows how to take such messages. The sort of communication situation Bateson studied, though, is totally ambiguous, because the mother transmits double messages — one message by her words, and its opposite through implication or tone of voice or by other non-verbal signals. One message is positive, the other a rejection. The two add up to what Bateson calls a double-bind. The child is required to be loving, and forbidden to be loving, and is forbidden to leave the conflict situation. The child cannot win. Moreover, neither mother nor victim can understand the situation, since what is essential for both is a metacommunication level, a model for understanding the communication impasse they are both in. There are three strategies that a child is likely to evolve in this situation: paranoiac (seeing hidden meanings everywhere), hebephrenic (staying at the literal level all the time), and catatonic (total withdrawal).

The following extract from some interviews carried out by R.D. Laing and A. Esterson (1962) is relevant:

MOTHER: And why the lack of a feeling of affection?
DAUGHTER: Well I never have had much affection for you.
MOTHER: You haven't? Can you give any reason? — And yet you did when you were quite tiny Claire. I remember when you were a little girl, I remember when you were a year old — it comes back to me now. I was in bed, I was ill for three months. I was in bed and you used to love to sit on my bed and hug me. As a matter of fact sometimes I know I was in such pain I almost couldn't bear it, and you loved — you were just a year old when you began to walk. And I remember after that illness I went to the seaside for six months for a rest, to cure my bad leg — and I just — you just wouldn't let me out of your sight. 'I want my Mummy, I want my Mummy!' You kept on for a long time. I remember one week-end my mother offered to take you home for the week-end. She said, 'Let me take Claire home with me. She'll stay with me, that'll break it.' And mother took you home that week-end. It must have been a horrid week-end, but I had to promise I'd come on Sunday and fetch you. 'Don't you leave me too long!' — Well that's all a sign of affection, isn't it? — all a sign of affection.

INTERVIEWER: The possibility that your daughter may not
               have a great deal of affection for you, Mrs
               Church, seems to make you rather uneasy.
MOTHER: Pardon?
INTERVIEWER: You are uneasy that your daughter says she
               has not much affection for you.
MOTHER: Well I wouldn't say it would make me uneasy. I
               just accept it naturally, but I wonder when she
               says that she never had any affection. I
               wonder when she started on this, because she
               was certainly affectionate enough when she
               was a child. Of course I know youngsters
               grow up and don't like to be hugged and
               kissed and all that. Well, naturally you drop
               that out when they grow up, because it's not
               accepted, and also the same if one offers
               advice, it's not accepted, so after the second
               time, if it isn't accepted, well just drop it, at
               least I do. But we've never made any fuss
               about it. We've just let the children carry on
               their own sweet way, whatever way they
               wanted to go, provided it was the right one.
               We never really interfered an awful lot with
               their activities.
INTERVIEWER: Provided it was the right way ...
MOTHER: Provided it was the right way. Yes I don't think
               we ever had ... Claire's been a good girl really
               compared with what I hear from different
               parents, today especially.

From this we can recreate a situation where the mother accuses Claire
of lack of affection, when she has been communicating lack of affection
herself. She denies that she is uneasy about the charge of lack of affection, but demonstrates that she is. She claims to let Claire go her own
sweet way, as long as it was 'the right one'. She communicates contradictory messages even within what she says, and there is even more
scope for contradictions between verbal and non-verbal components. But
she is not aware of these contradictions. This is where the interviewer
has a role to play. He can draw attention to contradictions within the
verbal message, or to contradictions between verbal and non-verbal
messages. Both contributions are metacommunication: communication
about communication. Neither the mother nor Claire is able to see the
nature of the communication taking place between them, even though
they have experienced it for so many years.

Something similar, though less extreme and pathological, occurs in
many classrooms. In Chapter 8 we saw that many teachers conceal
what for them is the real point of the lesson. Douglas Barnes uses the

term 'the hidden curriculum' for the kind of exchange where the teacher conceals this message from students, who have to guess what it is. This is an example Barnes gives (1973). A class is looking at a photograph of sand-dunes:

T   Sand dunes. They're usually in an unusual...a specific shape...a special shape...Does anybody know what shape they are? Not in straight lines...

P   They are like hills.

T   Yes, they're like low hills.

P   They're all humpy up and down.

T   Yes, they're all humpy up and down.

P   They're like waves.

T   Good, they're like waves.

P   They're like...

T   They're a special shape.

P   They're like boulders...sort of go up and down getting higher and higher.

T   I don't know about getting higher and higher.

P   Something like pyramids.

T   Mm...wouldn't call them pyramids, no.

P   They're in a semi-circle.

T   Ah, that's getting a bit nearer. They're often in a semi-circle and nearly always...we call them...well, it's part of a semi-circle...What do we call part of a semi-circle? You think of the moon...perhaps you'll get the shape.

P   Water.

T   No, not shaped like water...Yes?

P   An arc.

T   An arc...Oh, we're getting ever so much nearer.

P   Crescent.

T   A crescent shape. Have you heard that expression...a crescent shape? I wonder if anybody could draw me a crescent shape on the board. Yes, they're nearly all that shape...

The teacher, here, is after a particular word which the pupils are meant to guess. But Barnes points out that the pupils at first do not even know what kind of game it is they are meant to be playing. For a while they think they are being asked to explore particular shapes (hills, humpy up and down, waves). The teacher's words seem to encourage them along this line ('Good, they're like waves'). One pupil is misled by this into starting off on another comparison ('They're like —') but is cut short. 'They're a special shape' repeats the initial starting point.

This has one important similarity to the kind of communication analysed by Bateson. This teacher is communicating a double message: explore/don't explore; range freely/answer the question; your experience is valuable/irrelevant; you are important/unimportant. It corresponds very closely to Mrs. Church's 'We've just let the children carry on their own sweet way, whatever way they wanted to go, provided it was the right one.' With Bateson's model in mind we are led to wonder how non-verbal communication worked in this exchange. For instance, when the teacher said 'Good, they're like waves', did her voice sound lively and encouraging — totally misleading the children but giving a single (wrong) message at that point? Or did she say it tentatively, half irritatedly, her intonation cancelling out 'good'? If so, this would be a bewildering double-message: good/not good, with no clues as to what really would be good. The appropriate response for a child in this situation would be rational paranoia, a search for hidden meanings. The children who are most vocal are unwisely hebephrenic, taking only the literal meaning of the teacher's question. The children who are silent are rationally catatonic, silently waiting to find out what is really wanted.

This teacher is not producing schizophrenics. The point of the comparison is the relevance of Bateson's general model. This teacher's teaching method is inefficient at best and it can have unfortunate consequences for pupils' strategies for learning. She is ambivalent about her attitude to pupils' experience and individuality, and this becomes a confusing double message of which she is probably unaware. As in the therapeutic context with schizophrenics and their parents, both teacher and pupils need a metalanguage in which the ground rules of their communication can be discussed or communicated. The teacher should be aware of her propensity for double messages, and provide explicit clues for her pupils; and the pupils need to be able to ask, in some effective way, 'what kind of answer do you want?'

Knowledge of this kind is not normally found in grammars, traditional or modern, yet the term 'grammar' can arguably be extended to include it. If a grammar is a total theory about a language, it ought to include the rule systems that are at issue here. The same procedures which linguists use to establish a grammar in the limited sense apply equally well here. First you determine the corpus, that is, a body of examples that you believe obey the same rule system. Then you look for regularities: things which go together, or things which can replace each other. With schizogenic communication, we might initially suggest the rule that every message about the relationship should be accompanied by the negation of it, either in the same channel or in a different channel. Items which can replace each other might include indicators of aversion (such as looking away; pursing the lips; adopting a whining tone), and indicators of positivity (such as statements of goodwill; smiles; movements towards the speaker). This will give a very rudimentary grammar of the rules which underlie schizogenic communication, but this 'grammar' can then be greatly refined. What rules underlie the 'hidden curriculum'? The concept of a grammar is a powerful way of thinking about communication in general. Or you might want to be more positive. What rules would you suggest to *prevent* schizogenic communication, or to avoid perpetuating a hidden curriculum?

Conclusion

'Grammar' can refer to two distinct kinds of thing. It can be the complex set of rules which have been internalised as the basis for effective communication. It can be a textbook which describes some of the rules which have been internalised. Errors in terms of one such set of rules may be systematic in terms of another set. So in understanding errors, a teacher needs to consider which rules they might be obeying, as well as which rules they break. With this kind of understanding a teacher can now judge better when and how to intervene, and what the student most needs at this stage of development. Different kinds of works on grammar provide terms, concepts and perspectives which can help the teacher to understand and talk about language better. As well as looking at grammars, teachers should develop awareness of communication generally, so that they can understand and communicate **about communication itself**.

Suggested activities

1. Take a piece of writing with errors in it, and try to formulate the rules broken, *and* the alternative rule system being used by the student. Work out what you might say or do to help the student to write more effectively.

2. Set out the rules that account for the majority of forms in a particular piece of writing and suggest modifications/extensions of these rules that would lead to greater productivity or diversity of forms.

3. Analyse a classroom exchange, looking for double messages and metacommunication clues given by the teacher or students. Rewrite it, so that both teachers and students have effective metacommunication exchanges.

Bibliography

Bibliography

Albrow, K.	(1972) *The English Writing System: role towards a description*. Schools Council Programme in Linguistics and English Teaching: Papers Series II Vol. 2 Longmans.
Barnes, D.	(1971 (a)) *Language the Learner and the School* Harmondsworth; Penguin.
Barnes, D.	(1971 (b)) Classroom Contexts for Language and Learning *Ed. Review* Vol. 23, No. 3.
Barnes, D.	(1976) *From Communication to Curriculum*, Hammondsworth; Penguin.
Barnes, D. & Todd, F.	(1977) *Communication and Learning in Small groups* London: Routledge and Kegan Paul.
Bateson, G.	(1972) *Steps to an Ecology of Mind* San Francisco: Chandler Publishing Co,
Bennett, B.	(1979 (a)) *The Process of Writing and the Development of Writing Abilities, 15–17*: Australian Research in Progress (Mimeographed)
Bennett, B.	(1979 (b)) *Michael: A Case Study* (Mimeographed)
Berlin, B. & Kay, P.	(1969) *Basic Colour Terms* Berkeley: U Of California
Berristein, B.	(1971) *Class, Codes and Control* London: Routledge & Kegan Paul.
Birdwhistell, R.L.	(1972) 'Kinesics and Context' In Laver J. & Hutcheson, S. *Communication in Face to Face Interaction* Harmondsworth: Penguin.
Birdwhistell, R.L.	(1973) *Kinesics and Context*: Harmondsworth: Penguin Books.
Britton, J.	(1970) *Language and Learning*: Harmondsworth: Penguin.
Brown, R. & Gitman, A.	(1960) 'The Pronouns of Power and Solidarity' In T.A. Sebeok *Style in Language*. Cambridge, Mass: MIT Press.
Brown, R. & Ford, M.	(1961) 'Address in American English' *Journal of Abnormal and Social Psychology*.
Brown, R.	(1964) Three processes in the Child's Acquisition of

& Bellugi — Syntax. *Harvard Ed. Review 34.*

Brown, R.
Cazden, L.
& Bellugi, U. — (1969) 'The Child's Grammar from I to III in Brown, R. *Psycholinguistics* New York: The Free Press, 1970.

Brubaker, D.L.
& Nelson,
Roland H. Jr. — (1974) *Creative Survival in Educational Bureaucracies.* Berkeley; Mc Cutchan.

Burnett, J.H. — (1973) 'Culture of the School: A Construct for Research and Explanation and Education.' In *Anthropology and Language Science in Educational Development* Paris: UNESCO Educational Studies and Documents No. 11.

Chomsky, N. — (1957) *Syntactic Structures*, The Hague; Mouton.

Chomsky, N. — (1965) *Aspects of the Theory of Syntax*, Cambridge, Mass: MIT Press.

Chomsky, N.
& Halle, M. — (1968) *The Sound Pattern of English* New York, Harper & Row.

Clyne, M. — (1977) 'Communicative Competences in Contact: A Progress Report', Paper presented to the 9th Annual Conference of the Linguistic Society of Australia, Melbourne.

Condon, J.C.
and Yousef, F. — (1975) *An Introduction to Intercultural Communication* The Bobbs-Merril Co.

Criddle, R.,
Zett, W.
and Ryan, C. — (1975) *Towards Tomorrow, Book I,* Sydney: McGraw Hill.

Delamont, S. — (1976) *Interaction in the Classroom.* London: Methuen.

De Hoog, J.
& Sherwood, J. — (1979) *Working with Aborigines in Remote Areas* Mt. Lawley CAE Publication.

Deutzch, M.,
Katz I
& Jeusen, A.R. — (1968) *Social Class, Race and Physiological Development.* New York: Holt Rinehart & Winston.

Douglas, W.H. — (1964) *An Introduction to the Western Desert Language*

Doung Thanh Binh — (1975) *A Handbook for Teachers of Vietnamese Students* Center for Applied Linguistics, Arlington, Virginia.

D'Souza, W.L. — (1979) *The Black as a Group Method in the Teaching of English in a Ugandan Secondary School.*

Ervin, Tripp, S. — (1972) 'On Sociolinguistic Rules: Alternation and Co-occurrence'. In Gumperz, J. & Hymes D. *Directions in Sociolinguistics* NY; Holt Rinehart & Winston.

Fast, J. — (1970) *Body Language* Pan Books.

Freud, S. — (1905) 'Fragment of an Analysis of a Case of Hysteria' in *Collector Papers* Vol .3, NY: Basic Books.

Gattogno, C.   (1962) *'Words in Colour* Reading, Educational Explorers.

Goldman-Eisler, F.   (1961) 'Hesitation and Information' in *Information Theory* Ed. Cherry, C. London: Butterworth.

Goodman, K.   (1969) *'Analysis of Oral Reading Miscues'* Reprinted Smith, F. (ed) *Psycholinguistics and Reading* NY: Holt Rinehart and Winston, 1973.

Goodman, P.   (1973) *Speaking and Language* London: Wildwood House.

Goody, J. & Watt, I.   (1963) *'The Consequences of Literacy'* Comparative *Studies in Society and History*, Vol. 5, 1902–3.

Gregory, M. & Carroll, S.   (1978) *Language and Situation* London: Routledge & Kegan Paul.

Hall. E.T.,   (1959) *The Silent Language* NY; Doubleday & Co.

Halliday, M.A.K.   (1963) Foreword to American Edition of Mackay, D., Thompson, B. & Schanf, P. *Breakthrough to Literacy*, California: Glendale.

Halliday, M.A.K.   (1973) *Explorations in the Functions of Language* London: Edward Arnold.

Halliday, M.A.K.   (1975) *Learning How to Mean: Explorations in the Development of Language* London: Edward Arnold.

Halliday, M.A.K.   (1978) *Language as Social Semiotic* London: Edward Arnold.

Hammersley, M.   (1976) 'The mobilization of Pupil Attention' in Hammersley, M. & Woods, P. (Eds) *The Process of Schooling* London: Routledge & Kegan Paul.

Harris, S.   (1977) *Milingimbi Aboriginal Learning Context*. Albuquerque: Ph.D. dissertation, University of New Mexico.

Hart, N., Walker, R., & Grey, B.   (1977) *Mt. Gravatt Reading Series*, Sydney Addison Wesley.

Hymes, D.   (1972) 'On Communications Competence' In Pride, J. & Holmes, J. (Eds) *Soliolinguistics* Harmondsworth: Penguin.

Illich, I.   (1971) *Deschooling Society*. Harmondsworth: Penguin.

Jacobs, C. & Berndt, R.   (1979) *The Aboriginal Child* Perth: YC National Committee for NGOs.

Jakobson, R.   (1960) 'Concluding statement: Linguistics and Poetics,' in Sebeok, T. Ed. *Style in Language*. Cambridge, Mass.' MIT Press.

Jakobson, R.   (1968) *Child Language, Aphasia and Phonological Universals* The Hague: Mouton.

Joyce, J.   (1964) *Finnegans Wake*: London: Faber

Key. M.   (1975) *Male/Female Language* New Jersey: Scarecrow Publications.

Kress, G.   (ed.) (1976) Halliday: *System and Function in Language* London. Oxford University Press.

Kress, G.
& Hodge, R.
(1979) *Language as Ideology*. London: Routledge & Kegan Paul.

Kuhn, T.S.
(1962) *The Structure of Scientific Revolutions* Chicago: Chicago U.P.

Labov, W.
(1966) *Social Stratification of New York Speech*.

Labov, W.
(1970) The Study of Non-Standard English Urbana : NCTE.

Labov, W.
(1972) *Sociolinguistic Patterns* Philadelphia: U. of Pennsylvania Press.

Laing, R.
& Esterson, A.
(1964) *Sanity, Madness and the Family*. London: Tavistock.

McLuhan, M.
(1962) *The Gutenberg Galaxy* — London: Routledge & Kegan Paul

Malcolm, I.
(1979 (a)) 'Speech Use in Aboriginal Communities' Unpublished paper, Perth Mt. Lawley CAE.

Malcolm, I.
(1979 (b)) *Classroom Communication and the Aboriginal Child*. Nedlands: Ph. D. Dissertation, University of Western Australia.

Malcolm, I.
(1979 (c)) 'The West Australian Aboriginal Child and Child and Classroom Interaction: A Sociolinguistic Approach'. *Journal of Pragmatics*, Vol. 3.

Mallery, J.
Garrick
(1972) *Picture Writing of the American Indians* New York: Dover Go.

Mehan, H.
(1978) 'Structuring School Structure' in *Harvard Ed. Review* Vol. 48, No. 1.

Mehan, H.
(1979) *Learning Lessons*. Cambridge, Mass: Harvard V.P.

Oakshott, M.
On Human Conduct

Piaget, J.
(1959) *The Language and Thought of the Child* 3rd. revised Ed. London: Routledge and Kegan Paul.

Piaget, J.
(1968) *Six Psychological Studies* NY: Vintage Books.

Pinter, H.
(1965) *The Birthday Party* London: Methuen.

Philips, S.
(1972) 'Participant Structures and Communication Competence: Warm Springs Children in Community and Classroom' in Cazden, C., John, V. and Hymes, D. (Eds) *Functions of Language in the Classroom*. NY Teachers College Press.

Quick, R.,
Grienbaum,
S., Beech, G.,
& Svartvik, J.
(1972) *A Grammar of Contemporary English*, London: Longmans.

Richardson, E.
(1967) *Group Study for Teachers*, London: Routledge & Kegan Paul.

Robinson, W.
& Rackstrau S.
(1972) *A Question of Answers Vol. 1* London: Routledge & Kegan Paul.

Rosen, H.   (1972) 'The Language of Textbooks' in Cashdau, A.
                    & Grugeon, E., (Eds) *Language in Education*.
                    London: Routledge & Kegan Paul.
Rosenfeld. L.   (1977) 'Setting the Stage for Learning' *Theory into*
                    Practice.

Sacks, H.,   (1974) 'A Simplest Systematics for the Organization
Schegloft, E.   of Turn-Taking for Conversations' in Language
& Jefferson.   Vol. 50, No. 4.
Schegloft, E.   (1974) 'Opening up closings' in Turner, R. (Ed).
& Sacks, H.   *Ethnomethodology*, Harmondsworth: Penguin.
Sinclair, J.   (1975) *Towans and Analysis of Discource* London:
& Coulthard, R.   Oxford University Press.
Smith, F.   (1978 (a)) *Reading* London: Oxford University
                    Press.
Smith, F.   (1978 (b)) *Understanding Reading*, 2nd Edition,
                    NY. Holt Rinehart & Winston.
Sommer, R.   (1969) *Personal Space: the Behavioural Basis of*
                    Design Englewood Cliffs, N.J. Prentice Hall.
Sommer, R.   (1977) 'Classroom Layout' *Theory into Practice*
                    Vol. 16, No.
Sooby, A.   (1979) *Adrian: A Case Study*. Mimeograph,
                    University of Western Australia.

Trager, T.   (1964) 'Paralanguage: A First Approximation' in
                    Language in Culture and Society, Ed. Hymes D.
                    NY: Harper & Row.
Truilyan, G.   1944 *English Social History*, London: Longman.

Venezky, R.   (1976) 'Orthography' in Wardhaugh, R. & Brown,
                    H. (Eds) *A Sunny of Applied Linguistics*. Ann Arbor;
                    University of Michigan Press.
Vygotsky, L.   (1962) *Language and Thought* Cambridge, Mass:
                    MIT Press.

Webber, D.   (1978) 'Interpersonal Behaviour in relation to
                    Aboriginal Programs' *Aust J. of Social Issues*
                    Vol. 13, No. 1.
Wharf, B.   (1956) *Language, Thought and Culture* Ed. J.
                    Carroll, Cambridge, Mass: MIT Press.
Woods, P.   (1976) 'Having a Laugh: An Antidote to Schooling'
                    In Hammersley, M. & Woods, P. (Eds) *The Process*
                    of Schooling, London: Routledge and Kegan Paul.

Index

Contents

The menopause: what happens to your body?

The word 'menopause' strictly means a woman's last menstrual period, which typically occurs around the age of 51, and defines the end of the fertile phase of a woman's life. The 'change of life' or 'climacteric' is the time when your body is adjusting before, during and after the menopause. There are hormonal changes and symptoms in the years leading up to, and beyond, your final menstrual period. It has been estimated that, by the age of 54 years, most women (80 per cent) have had their last menstrual period – they are then termed postmenopausal.

Some women experience a natural menopause before the age of 40. This is considered premature. Menopause can be induced prematurely by radiotherapy or chemotherapy used to treat some cancers, or following surgery to remove the ovaries. In such women, hot flushes and sweats can be particularly severe.

Many women adjust to the changes without problems and some revel in their new-found freedom – free from the monthly 'curse' of periods, particularly if periods were painful or heavy, and free from the fear of unwanted pregnancy. However, not all women find the change of life easy and, although some may benefit from self-help treatments, others need medical support.

HORMONAL CHANGES

From puberty to the menopause, women's bodies follow hormonal cycles – the monthly periods. Each month the levels of the female hormone, oestrogen, rise over the early part of the cycle, stimulating the growth of an egg, which is released from one of the two ovaries at mid-cycle. Following ovulation, another female hormone, progesterone, stimulates the lining of the uterus to thicken, ready for a possible pregnancy. If the egg is not fertilised by sperm, it dies and the egg and uterus lining are shed as a period.

In the years leading up to the menopause, the ovaries become less efficient, resulting in irregular and often heavy periods. Eventually, they stop functioning, no further eggs are released and periods stop. At the same time, the monthly hormonal cycle becomes more erratic. Blood levels of oestrogen fluctuate – low levels give rise to hot flushes, night sweats and many other symptoms.

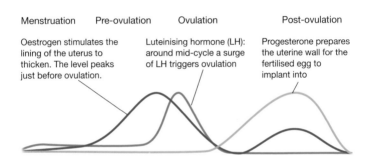

| Menstruation | Pre-ovulation | Ovulation | Post-ovulation |

Oestrogen stimulates the lining of the uterus to thicken. The level peaks just before ovulation.

Luteinising hormone (LH): around mid-cycle a surge of LH triggers ovulation

Progesterone prepares the uterine wall for the fertilised egg to implant into

The principal changes in hormones during the menstrual cycle

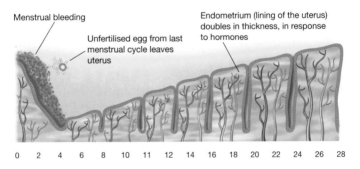

Menstrual bleeding

Unfertilised egg from last menstrual cycle leaves uterus

Endometrium (lining of the uterus) doubles in thickness, in response to hormones

0   2   4   6   8   10   11   12   14   16   18   20   22   24   26   28

Changes in the lining of the uterus during the menstrual cycle

Changes during the menstrual cycle.

If you swim regularly, wear a swimming hat and apply plenty of moisturiser after showering, as chlorine is very drying to both skin and hair.

Dry eyes

Women frequently experience problems with dry eyes as they enter the menopause. Many find relief simply from using artificial tears that can be bought from a pharmacy. There are a variety of different chemicals used, including hypromellose, hydroxyethylcellulose, liquid paraffin or saline solution. Preservative-free tears are the most soothing. Avoid products that whiten the eyes – they do not have adequate lubricating qualities and often make the problem worse. Simple lifestyle changes can significantly improve irritation from dry eyes; for example, drinking eight to ten glasses of water spaced over the course of each day keeps the body hydrated. Make a conscious effort to blink frequently – especially when reading, working at the computer or watching television. Avoid rubbing the eyes as it only worsens the irritation.

If simple remedies are not effective, see a doctor – certain medications, thyroid conditions, vitamin A deficiency and diseases such as Parkinson's disease and Sjögren's syndrome, a condition where the immune system attacks the glands that produce tears and saliva, can also cause dryness.

Weight gain

Increasing evidence suggests that postmenopausal weight gain is nature's way of producing more oestrogen. After the menopause a certain amount of oestrogen is formed in fat, so the fatter you are, the more oestrogen you produce. This may explain why, in general, fat women have stronger bones than thin women. Obviously, a balance is necessary because obesity is linked to heart disease. The simple message is that, in most cases, keeping fit and eating a healthy balanced diet allow weight to settle at its natural level.

Emotional symptoms

Most of us have felt low at some time in our lives. Usually it is the result of a particular event, and these feelings eventually ease with time. Hormonal changes can make it harder to cope. Finding ways to relax and unwind, eating healthily and taking adequate exercise will all improve mood. Limit consumption of alcohol because it can aggravate depression. Seek medical help early – a supportive doctor may be all that is needed, but counselling or drug therapy may be necessary.

PREVENTING HEART DISEASE AND OSTEOPOROSIS

What is heart disease?

The heart is essentially a muscle that pumps blood around the body. Blood vessels, or arteries, supply blood to the heart muscle. When blood flow through the arteries becomes obstructed, the heart muscle can die – this is when a heart attack occurs. The most common way such obstructions develop is through a condition called atherosclerosis, a largely preventable disease. Blood vessels to the brain can also be affected by atherosclerosis, which can result in strokes.

Lifestyle changes to prevent heart disease

Many of the risk factors for heart disease can be reduced by simple lifestyle changes: losing weight, stopping smoking, modifying diet and taking more exercise.

What is osteoporosis?

Osteoporosis is a disease in which bones become fragile and more likely to break. Unfortunately there are no symptoms of osteoporosis until a bone breaks. These broken bones, known as fractures, typically affect the hip, spine, and wrist.

A hip fracture can cause prolonged or permanent disability or even death. Spinal or vertebral fractures also have serious consequences, including loss of height, severe back pain and deformity.

Lifestyle changes to prevent osteoporosis

Adequate exercise and a healthy calcium-rich diet keep bones strong. Effective prevention of osteoporosis starts early, however, preferably in childhood – there is plenty that can be done to protect children. They need exercise and a good diet including calcium-rich foods, and should be warned about the hazards of smoking. Peak adult bone mass is reached around the age of 35. The peak bone mass for men is 25 to 30 per cent greater than for women, placing women at greater risk of osteoporosis. Bone loss starts shortly after the peak, starting earlier in women than in men, and is accelerated by the menopause.

Exercise for a healthy heart and strong bones

The value of exercise cannot be overemphasised. Studies show that being physically fit lowers heart disease risk even in people who have other health problems such as high blood pressure and high cholesterol. To minimise risk, however, you should be physically fit and avoid the other major modifiable risk factors: cigarette smoke, high blood pressure and high blood cholesterol.

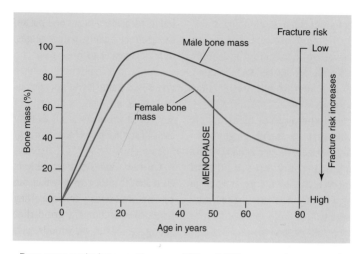

Bone mass peaks between the ages of 25 and 40 in men and women and then starts to fall. In women, accelerated loss of bone mass occurs around the time of the menopause.

It is never too late to start exercising – one study showed that an 80 year old gains the same percentage improvement in muscle strength as a 25 year old. If you are inactive, doing anything is better than nothing! Studies show that people who have a low fitness level are much more likely to die earlier than people who have achieved even a moderate level of fitness. It is not just your heart and bones that benefit from regular exercise; muscle strength and power also improve, making falls less likely and, if you do trip, you have more strength to grab on to something. If you take drugs such as tranquillisers, hypnotics or alcohol, reassess your need for them as they may

affect your judgement, making you more likely to trip or stumble.

Weight-bearing exercise strengthens bone and can also help to prevent fractures. The easiest and most convenient exercise is walking – which strengths your heart and bones. Start gently and gradually increase the distance. Swimming is not weight bearing because the body is supported by the water, but it is excellent if you have joint problems and is also good for the heart.

Although the ideal recommendation for exercise is 20 to 30 minutes of brisk activity, three times a week, this need not be as daunting as it sounds. When done for as little as 30 minutes a day, activities such as climbing stairs, gardening, moderate-to-heavy housework, dancing and home exercise are all beneficial. Again, doing anything is better than nothing.

Middle-aged or older people who are inactive and at high risk for heart disease or who already have a medical condition should seek medical advice before starting or significantly increasing their physical activity.

Exercise as a daily routine

The main reason why people fail to take exercise is simply a lack of time to incorporate exercise into their daily routine. Why not walk or cycle to the shops instead of taking the bus or car; if it is too far, get off the bus one stop earlier, or park your car further away. If you feel up to more formal exercise, such as jogging, go ahead but be careful not to overdo it in the early stages.

Always warm up and cool down gradually to prevent injury to muscles. Avoid vigorous exercise if you are unwell because it can put an undue strain on your heart. Remember, an exercise programme should be maintained for life, not just for a few weeks a year.

Watch your diet

- **Natural oestrogens:** Some studies suggest that natural oestrogens found in many plant foods, particularly beans and pulses, can protect against osteoporosis, heart disease and breast cancer. Certainly, the incidence of these diseases is much lower in countries such as Japan where oestrogen-rich soya bean products, such as tofu, are an essential part of the diet.

- **Calcium:** Bones contain calcium, so a healthy diet with adequate calcium is necessary to ensure that bones develop properly and remain strong. Periods of growth obviously increase the relative demands for calcium, so teenagers and pregnant women need greater amounts. The recommended daily amount for adults is 700 milligrams (mg). Dairy foods such as milk, cheese and yoghurt are the best sources of calcium, which is readily absorbed into the bloodstream. Unfortunately, the current fashion for dieting has meant that many women cut out dairy products because they also contain high levels of fat. The answer is to continue eating dairy products but switch to low-fat alternatives – skimmed milk actually contains slightly more calcium than whole milk. Tinned bony fish such as sardines or salmon are excellent because the softened bones are rich in calcium.

- **Vitamin D:** This vitamin helps the absorption of calcium. Dietary intake of vitamin D has declined over the

The benefits of HRT

HRT can benefit several groups of women. These are considered below.

WOMEN WHO HAVE AN EARLY MENOPAUSE

The average age at menopause is 51, but it can occur in younger women. If you have a menopause under the age of 40, it is recognised as a premature menopause.

Often no cause for a premature menopause is found but it can also be a result of radiotherapy or chemotherapy for cancer, or following surgical removal of the ovaries (oophorectomy). Women who have a hysterectomy but retain their ovaries frequently reach menopause a few years earlier than would otherwise have occurred.

Women who have an untreated premature menopause are at particular risk of developing osteoporosis and heart disease. They are more likely to die at a younger age than women who have the menopause at the usual time.

To reduce these risks, HRT is usually recommended until at least the age of 50. Unlike HRT used beyond the average age at menopause, HRT for a premature menopause is merely replacing hormones that would normally be present. There is no evidence that HRT increases the risk of breast cancer, heart disease or strokes over and above that found in menstruating women with a normally timed menopause. After 50, HRT can be continued if there are reasons to do so and should be reviewed annually.

WOMEN WITH MENOPAUSAL SYMPTOMS

HRT is very effective in relieving the symptoms of the menopause. The lowest dose of oestrogen necessary to control symptoms is recommended. Hot flushes and night sweats usually improve within a few weeks of starting treatment. Vaginal dryness or soreness and urinary urgency and frequency may take longer to respond. Most women using HRT solely for control of menopausal symptoms should not need to take it for more than five years, although longer treatment may be necessary if symptoms recur when HRT is stopped. It is important gradually to reduce HRT over two or three months to assess the return of any symptoms. If HRT is stopped too quickly flushes and sweats will return just because of the sudden drop in hormone levels.

WOMEN AT RISK OF OSTEOPOROSIS

Osteoporosis is a disease in which bones become more fragile and so more likely to break.

Oestrogen plays an important role in building and maintaining bone. Throughout a person's life, old bone breaks down and new bone forms in the skeleton. In childhood and adolescence, new bone is formed faster than old bone is broken down, and the bones become larger, heavier and denser. Women usually have their peak amount of bone around age 35. When oestrogen levels fall following the menopause, the rate of bone loss increases and less new bone is

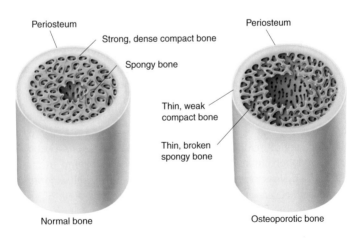

Periosteum

Strong, dense compact bone

Spongy bone

Periosteum

Thin, weak compact bone

Thin, broken spongy bone

Normal bone

Osteoporotic bone

Changes in osteoporotic bone.

formed. In some women, the bone loss can be so great that the bones become osteoporotic and the risk of fractures increases. About one in three women over the age of 50 fracture a bone as a result of osteoporosis. HRT prevents osteoporosis but needs to be continued for life because bone strength starts to fall when treatment is stopped. Within

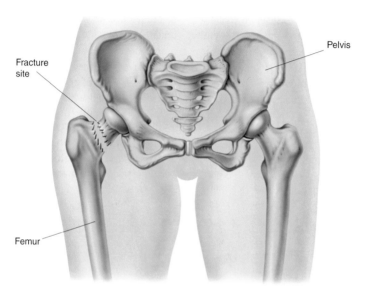

Fracture site

Pelvis

Femur

Hip fracture.

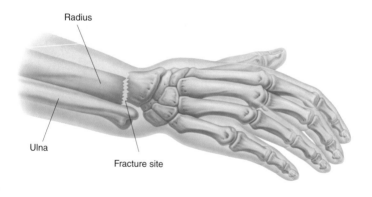

Radius

Ulna

Fracture site

Wrist fracture.

five years of stopping HRT, the benefit of HRT on bone has been lost. This means that, unless a woman is at particular risk of osteoporosis, the risks of long-term HRT may out-weigh the benefits.

Osteoporosis can be confirmed by measuring bone mineral density using dual energy X-ray absorptiometry (DEXA). Recent advice from the regulatory authorities is that HRT should not be used as a first-line treatment for osteoporosis. However, menopause specialists believe that the balance remains in favour of HRT for women who are at particular risk of osteoporosis. HRT is still recommended for women who are unable to take alternative treatments or for whom other treatments have been unsuccessful.

The table on page 37 shows factors associated with increased

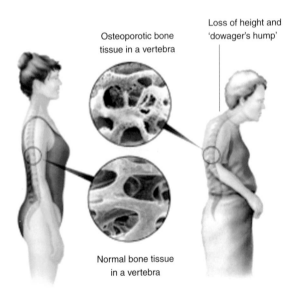

Osteoporotic bone tissue in a vertebra

Loss of height and 'dowager's hump'

Normal bone tissue in a vertebra

Osteoporosis is a common form of bone disease mainly affecting women after the menopause. Hormonal changes lead to a thinning of the interior structure of the bones, making them weaker and more prone to fracture. Weakened vertebrae may become crushed, causing loss of height and severe bending forwards, giving a hunched appearance.

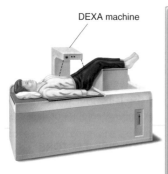
DEXA machine

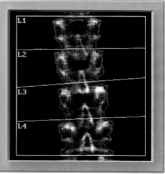
L1
L2
L3
L4

Monitor image
of lumbar spine

Dual energy X-ray absorptiometry (DEXA).

risk of osteoporosis; the more risk factors you have, the higher your personal risk.

Increased age
The older you are, the greater your risk of fractures.

MAJOR RISK FACTORS FOR OSTEOPOROSIS

- Early menopause
- Increased age
- High alcohol consumption
- Smoking
- Low body mass index
- Family history
- Lack of exercise
- Extended bed rest
- Calcium-deficient diet

- History of infrequent or absent periods
- Certain medical conditions
- Lack of exposure to daylight
- Previous fractures
- Certain racial origins
- Prolonged steroid use
- High caffeine intake

FACTORS PROTECTIVE FOR OSTEOPOROSIS

- Oral contraception use
- High number of pregnancies

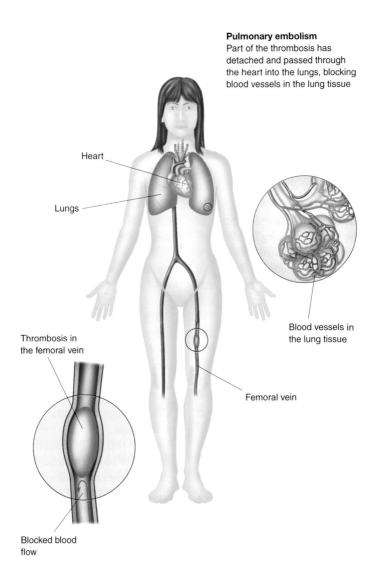

Pulmonary embolism
Part of the thrombosis has detached and passed through the heart into the lungs, blocking blood vessels in the lung tissue

Heart

Lungs

Blood vessels in the lung tissue

Thrombosis in the femoral vein

Femoral vein

Blocked blood flow

Deep vein thrombosis is a condition in which a blood clot forms in a large vein, usually in the leg. There is a risk that the clot may travel through the heart and become lodged in another part of the body, for instance a blood vessel supplying the lungs, which can be fatal.

pessaries, tablets and rings) to help vaginal dryness. For hot flushes and sweats, non-hormonal treatments such as selective serotonin reuptake inhibitors (SSRIs – antidepressants) may help (see page 97).

VENOUS THROMBOSIS

Increasing age is the main risk for venous thrombosis (blood clots in veins). However, research suggests that women using HRT are more likely to develop venous thrombosis than women of a similar age who are not using HRT, especially in the first year of use. About three per 1,000 women in their 50s who do not use HRT are likely to have a venous thrombosis in any five-year period compared with seven per 1,000 women of the same age who take HRT.

By the time they reach their 60s, the risk in non-users increases to eight per 1,000 women in a five-year period compared with 17 per 1,000 women taking HRT. However, published data suggest that non-oral HRT such as patches and gels is less likely to increase the risk of ven-

ous thrombosis than HRT tablets.

If you have multiple risk factors for venous thrombosis (see below), HRT is probably best avoided. If you have major surgery and will be off your feet for a while, you will probably be given drugs to help prevent blood clots. Some doctors advise stopping HRT four to six weeks before major surgery. You can usually start HRT again once you are fully mobile.

If you or a close relative has had an unexplained venous thrombosis under the age of 45, you may need to have a blood test to check your blood clotting before you can take HRT. This can identify those women who have a genetic risk factor for venous thrombosis, the most common of which is known as factor V Leiden. This genetic condition affects around five per cent of the population and causes an increased tendency for blood to clot. People carrying the factor V Leiden gene have a five times greater risk of developing a blood clot than the rest of the population.

NON-HRT RISK FACTORS FOR VENOUS THROMBOSIS

- Severe varicose veins
- Obesity
- Increased age
- Inactivity
- Diabetes
- High blood pressure

THE PROCESS OF ATHEROSCLEROSIS

Atherosclerosis, atheroma and hardening of the arteries are all the same thing – the process leading to the blockage or weakening of arteries.

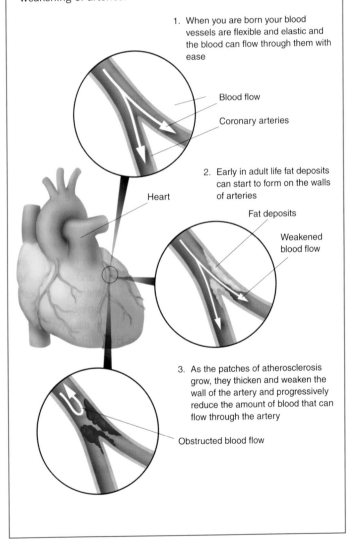

1. When you are born your blood vessels are flexible and elastic and the blood can flow through them with ease

Blood flow

Coronary arteries

Heart

2. Early in adult life fat deposits can start to form on the walls of arteries

Fat deposits

Weakened blood flow

3. As the patches of atherosclerosis grow, they thicken and weaken the wall of the artery and progressively reduce the amount of blood that can flow through the artery

Obstructed blood flow

NON-HRT RISK FACTORS FOR HEART DISEASE

- High blood pressure
- High cholesterol
- Smoking
- Previous heart attack or stroke
- Irregular heart beat (atrial fibrillation)
- Diabetes
- Obesity
- Personality – people who are competitive and easily stressed are more likely to develop heart disease than people who are laid back about life

HRT for you. However, if you are already taking HRT when you have your first heart attack or stroke, there is probably no reason to stop HRT because continuing treatment may reduce your long-term risk of a repeat event.

CANCER OF THE UTERUS

Around 8 per 100,000 women a year over age 50 who are not using HRT develop cancer of the lining of the uterus (endometrial cancer). Women taking 'unopposed' oestrogen-only HRT for five years have a sixfold increased risk. A breakthrough in research showed that 'opposing' the oestrogen by adding progestogen reduced this risk. With combined oestrogen/progestogen HRT, the risk of endometrial cancer is at least the same as for non-HRT users, if not lower.

OVARIAN CANCER

There appears to be a small increase in the risk of ovarian cancer in women using oestrogen-only HRT for more than five years. The background risk in non-users aged 50 to 69 is 9 per 1,000 women, which rises to 10 per 1,000 women after 5 years' use of oestrogen-only HRT and to 12 per 1,000 women after 10 years of HRT. The effect of long-term combined oestrogen/progestogen HRT on ovarian cancer has not yet been studied.

each time as recommended, it is normal for the skin underneath the patch to redden. However, a few women develop a severe skin reaction that prohibits further use. Switching to a different brand of patch can occasionally help.

GEL
Oestrogen, but not progestogen, is available as a gel and is becoming an increasingly popular method of taking HRT. The gel is applied daily to the arms and shoulders, or thighs, and absorbed through the skin into the bloodstream.

Advantages of gel
Many women find a gel convenient and easy to use, with few side effects. Unlike some oestrogen patches, skin irritation is rarely a problem. The dose is easy to change, balanced against symptoms.

Disadvantages of gel
Some women worry that they are not applying the gel to the correct amount of skin. On a practical note, it is easiest just to apply the gel to the upper thighs, like a skin cream, without worrying too much about how much skin is covered. The gel dries quickly and it is only necessary to wait five minutes at most before dressing. Avoid using other skin products or washing the area for an hour after application. Unless the woman has had a hysterectomy, additional progestogen is necessary.

NASAL SPRAY
This relatively new route for oestrogen assimilation works in a different way to other forms of HRT. It is sprayed into the nostrils and is rapidly absorbed through the lining of the nasal passage, delivering a pulse of oestrogen into the bloodstream.

Advantages of nasal spray
Some studies suggest that this method is associated with fewer side effects than other routes of delivery.

Disadvantages of nasal spray
Surges of oestrogen may aggravate conditions such as migraine, which benefit from constant oestrogen levels. Unless the woman has had a hysterectomy, additional progestogen is necessary.

SYSTEMIC VAGINAL RING
A new ring has been developed for insertion into the upper third of the vagina, enabling oestrogen to be absorbed through the lining of the vagina into the bloodstream. This will also effectively treat hot flushes and sweats. It lasts for three months of continuous use before it needs to be replaced.

Advantages of vaginal ring

The main advantages are that it is easy to use with few side effects. It can be removed for intercourse, although this is not necessary. It should be rinsed in lukewarm water before being re-inserted.

Disadvantages of vaginal ring

Some women note initial discomfort, although this usually settles with time. The ring may become dislodged when coughing or straining. Unless the woman has had a hysterectomy, additional progestogen is necessary.

IMPLANTS

Oestrogen

Small pellets of oestrogen, inserted into the fat under the skin of the lower abdomen or buttock, typically last for about six months. The downside is that if the woman decides to stop HRT, they cannot easily be removed. Insertion is a simple procedure that can be done at the local surgery or in the hospital outpatient department. An injection of a local anaesthetic is given to numb the skin before a small cut is made. After the implant is inserted, the wound is closed

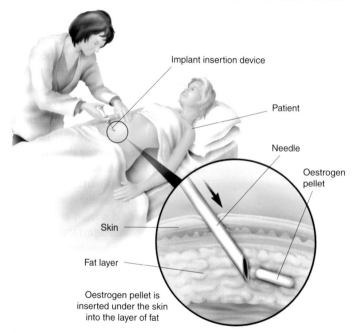

Oestrogen implantation is a simple procedure involving a local anaesthetic, a small cut in the lower abdomen and the insertion of an oestrogen pellet into the layer of fat under the skin. The wound is then closed with a stitch or a piece of tape.

PROGESTOGEN PREPARATIONS

In place of a combined oestrogen/progestogen preparation, the doctor may prescribe one of the oestrogen-only preparations previously listed, together with any of the following progestogen preparations.

Tablets

Duphaston-HRT (Solvay)
- dydrogesterone 10 mg

Micronor-HRT (Janssen-Cilag)
- norethisterone 1 mg

Provera (Pharmacia)
- medroxyprogesterone acetate 2.5 mg, 5 mg or 10 mg

Suppositories/pessaries

Cyclogest (Shire)
- progesterone 200 mg or 400 mg by vagina or rectum

Vaginal gel

Crinone (Serono)
- progesterone 8% (not licensed for HRT)

Intrauterine

Mirena (Schering)
- Levonorgestrel 52 mg (20 mg per 24 hours)

progestogen levonorgestrel, which is slowly released directly into the uterus, keeping the lining of the uterus thin so that there is no build-up of lining to be shed as a 'period'.

Side effects are much lower than with other progestogens and the contraceptive effect can be an advantage for women whose periods have not yet stopped. The main disadvantage is irregular

bleeding but, for most women, periods stop completely.

OTHER PRESCRIPTION TREATMENTS

Tibolone

Tibolone (Livial) is a synthetic preparation of a type known as a selective tissue oestrogenic activity regulator (STEAR). It is derived from plant sources and combines the

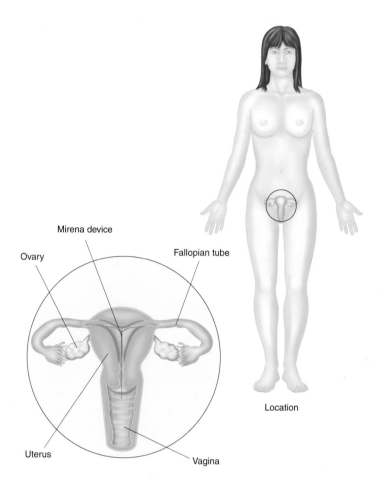

Mirena device

Ovary

Fallopian tube

Uterus

Vagina

Location

The levonorgestrel intrauterine system (IUS) or Mirena is an effective contraceptive.
It has a reservoir of progestogen that is slowly released directly into the uterus.

properties of oestrogen, progesterone and testosterone, in a single tablet. It is suitable for women whose periods have stopped because it is taken continuously. It relieves menopausal symptoms, while protecting the uterus and breast tissues from oestrogen stimulus. There is some evidence to suggest that tibolone is associated with a reduced risk of breast cancer compared with the standard oestrogen/progestogen HRT but further research is necessary to confirm these preliminary findings.

ADVANTAGES AND DISADVANTAGES OF DIFFERENT TYPES OF HRT

Advantages	Disadvantages
Tablets	
• Easy to take • Easily reversible • Cheap • Can combine with progestogen	• Unnatural delivery of hormone via the liver • Must be taken every day
Skin patches	
• Convenient • Easy to use • More natural delivery of hormone into the bloodstream • Easily reversible • Can combine with progestogen	• Can become detached • Can irritate the skin • More expensive than tablets • Must be changed once or twice a week
Gel	
• Easily reversible • Easy to use • More natural delivery of hormone into the bloodstream	• Must cover correct amount of skin • More expensive than tablets • Must use every day • If necessary, progestogen must be taken in a different formulation

Tibolone has the advantage of being period free. It can also be taken to prevent osteoporosis or to improve mood or libido. It is useful for women who are prone to breast tenderness with standard oestrogen therapy.

Unexpected bleeding is an occasional problem affecting around 10 to 15 per cent of users, and bleeding is more likely if the ovaries are still producing even small amounts of hormones. For this reason tibolone is recommended only for women who have not had a natural period for at least 12 months. This reduces the incidence of unnecessary investigations for erratic bleeding.

ADVANTAGES AND DISADVANTAGES OF DIFFERENT TYPES OF HRT (contd)

Advantages	Disadvantages
Nasal spray	
• Easy to use • More natural delivery of hormone into the bloodstream • Possibly fewer side effects than other routes • Easily reversible	• Nasal symptoms can be a problem but are usually mild • Long-term effects unknown • More expensive than tablets • Must use every day • If necessary, progestogen must be taken in a different formulation • Surges of oestrogen can aggravate conditions such as migraine
Implants	
• No missed doses • More natural delivery of hormones into the bloodstream • Prolonged effect: 4–12 months • Cheap	• Needs a small surgical procedure • Can cause unnaturally high levels of hormones • Not rapidly reversible • Progestogen must be continued for some time after the final implant
Vaginal	
• Useful if vaginal symptoms are the only problems • Easily reversible	• Some types of oestrogen are absorbed into the bloodstream • Progestogen may be necessary if used for longer than three months • Creams and pessaries can be messy

Raloxifene

Raloxifene (Evista) is the first of a new class of synthetic compounds known as selective oestrogen receptor modulators (SERMs). They mimic some of the actions of oestrogen but oppose others. Raloxifene has been shown to increase bone density in post-menopausal women, but not as effectively as oestrogen. It does not treat hot flushes or sweats, which may even occur as a side effect of use. Its theoretical advantage is that it does not stimulate the lining of the uterus. At present, it is recommended for the prevention of spinal fractures in postmenopausal women at risk of osteoporosis. Studies also suggest that raloxifene can reduce the risk of breast cancer, particularly oestrogen-dependent tumours. However, the risk of venous thrombosis is doubled in raloxifene users in the first years of use.

SAFETY ISSUES WITH OESTROGEN ± PROGESTERONE, TIBOLONE AND RALOXIFENE

	Oestrogen	Oestrogen + progestogen	Tibolone	Raloxifene
Breast	No change in risk	More risk	Possibly less risk	Possibly less risk
Endometrium (lining of uterus)	More risk	No change in risk	No change in risk	No change in risk
Heart disease and strokes	More risk	More risk	Less risk/no change in risk	More risk/no change in risk
Venous thrombosis	More risk	More risk	Less risk/no change in risk	More risk/no change in risk

EFFECTIVENESS OF OESTROGEN ± PROGESTERONE, TIBOLONE AND RALOXIFENE

	Oestrogen	Oestrogen + progestogen	Tibolone	Raloxifene
Bone density	Improves symptoms	Improves symptoms	Improves symptoms	Improves symptoms
Flushes and sweats	Improves symptoms	Improves symptoms	Improves symptoms	Symptoms may worsen
Vaginal symptoms	Improves symptoms	Improves symptoms	Improves symptoms	No change in symptoms

UNOPPOSED OESTROGEN

If you have had a hysterectomy only oestrogen treatment is necessary.

Brand	Oestrogen	Dose	Formulation
Aerodiol	Oestradiol hemihydrate	150 µg	Nasal spray
Climaval	Oestradiol	1 or 2 mg	Tablets
Elleste Solo	Oestradiol	1 or 2 mg	Tablets
Elleste Solo MX	Oestradiol	40 or 80 µg	Patches
Estraderm MX	Oestradiol	25, 50, 75 or 100 µg	Patches
Estraderm MX	Oestradiol	25, 50 or 100 µg	Patches
Evorel	Oestradiol	25, 50, 75 or 100 µg	Patches
Fematrix	Oestradiol	40 or 80 µg	Patches
FemSeven	Oestradiol	50, 75 or 100 µg	Patches
Femtab	Oestradiol valerate	1 or 2 mg	Tablets
Harmogen	Estropipate	1.5 mg	Tablets
Hormonin	Oestriol, oestrone and oestradiol		Tablets
Menoring	Oestradiol	50 µg	Vaginal ring
Oestrogel	Oestradiol	1.5 mg	Gel
Premarin	Conjugated oestrogens	0.625 or 1.25 mg	Tablets
Progynova	Oestradiol valerate	1 or 2 mg	Tablets
Progynova TS	Oestradiol	50 or 100 µg	Patches
Sandrena	Oestradiol	0.5 or 1 mg	Gel
Zumenon	Oestradiol	1 or 2 mg	Tablets

SIDE EFFECTS OF OESTROGEN AND PROGESTOGEN

Oestrogen and progestogen are associated with a number of side effects. Some of the most frequently occurring side effects that women may experience when they start HRT are listed below. Many resolve within the first two to three months.

Oestrogen	Progestogen
Fluid retention	Fluid retention
Feeling of bloatedness	Breast tenderness
Breast tenderness	Depression
Nausea	Nausea
Stomach upset	Irritability
Leg cramps	Headaches
	Mood swings
	Abdominal pain
	Backache
	Acne

common problem is 'premenstrual' symptoms, which affect up to 20 per cent of women taking cyclical progestogen. These symptoms include fluid retention, breast tenderness, mood swings, depression, acne, lower abdominal pains and backache. They are most apparent when starting HRT and often resolve with continued use.

If they persist, altering the dose or type of progestogen can help. Changing the route of delivery can also help – for example, from tablets to patches.

If symptoms are particularly severe, the progestogen course could be taken every three months rather than monthly. Alternatively, the duration of the progestogen could be shortened, but reducing the course to less than ten days reduces the protective effect against cancer of the lining of the uterus and can provoke irregular bleeding.

Postmenopausal women can change to continuous combined HRT, which requires a lower dose of progestogen than cyclical regimens and has the advantage of being period free.

OTHER EFFECTS OF HRT

Bleeding

Unless you have had a hysterectomy, you will probably need cyclical progestogen, taken as a course, usually as tablets or patches, every month. If you are taking cyclical progestogen, a withdrawal bleed or 'period' usually starts around the end of the progestogen course.

It is useful to keep a record of when you use the progestogen and when your period starts. If your bleeding starts early in the progestogen course or if you get bleeding unexpectedly at other times of the month, you should report this to your doctor. It is quite common in the first few months of taking HRT, but if unusual bleeding starts after taking HRT for six months or longer, the cause needs to be assessed.

You may only need to change the dose, timing, duration or type of progestogen but your doctor may want to check that the progestogen is providing adequate protection against cancerous changes developing in the uterus.

In many gynaecology departments, one of the first steps after a manual internal examination has been done is to arrange for you to have a transvaginal (TVS) ultrasound scan. A small probe is inserted into the vagina and the ultrasound waves create a picture of the uterus and ovaries. A TVS can also be used to measure the thickness of the endometrium and identify common benign causes of bleeding such as fibroids or polyps.

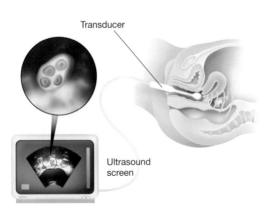

Transducer

Ultrasound screen

During a transvaginal ultrasound scan (TVS) a small probe is inserted into the vagina and the ultrasound waves create a picture of the uterus and ovaries.

HRT: who can and who can't take it

There are very few conditions that prevent women from using HRT. However, there is often some misinformation about who can and who can't take it.

WHO CAN TAKE HRT?

Women with any of the following conditions can use HRT, although some may need specialist supervision:

- Cervical cancer
- Coeliac (non-oral route preferred)
- Crohn's disease (non-oral route preferred)
- Diabetes
- Epilepsy
- High blood pressure (non-oral route preferred)
- High cholesterol (route depends on lipid profile)
- Kidney failure
- Mild liver disease (non-oral route preferred)
- Malignant melanoma
- Migraine (non-oral route preferred)
- Ovarian cancer
- Parkinson's disease
- Rheumatoid arthritis
- Thyroid disease
- Heart valve disease.

WHO SHOULD BE CAUTIOUS ABOUT HRT?

Benign breast lumps

There is no convincing evidence that this condition is associated with a greater than expected risk of breast cancer in women using HRT.

If a woman has breast lumps, they should be checked before starting HRT to make sure that they are not cancerous. Regular checks should be continued once treatment has begun.

Endometriosis

Sometimes the tissue that lines the uterus is found in abnormal sites such as the rectum or navel. In the same way that the lining of the uterus is shed each month during menstruation, these other sites also bleed, causing severe pain and heavy periods. This condition, known as endometriosis, is stimulated by oestrogen and improves with the menopause.

HRT can occasionally reactivate the condition so if you have had endometriosis you should be cautious when taking HRT, monitoring any symptoms particularly of pain on intercourse and heavy or irregular bleeding. Even if you have had a hysterectomy, some doctors will recommend that you take continuous progestogen to prevent the endometriosis recurring. This is because the lining of the uterus cannot grow in the presence of progestogen.

Fibroids

Fibroids (non-cancerous growths in the muscle of the uterus) are very common. They are sensitive to oestrogen so they often grow during pregnancy as the level of oestrogen in the body rises, and shrink after the menopause. As a result of this, fibroids can enlarge with HRT, causing heavy withdrawal bleeding. Continuous progestogen can reduce the likelihood of fibroids increasing in size. The levonorgestrel intrauterine system (see pages 63–64) is sometimes used to help treat fibroids.

Gallstones

If you have gallstones you should discuss HRT use with your doctor because the gallstones may enlarge, particularly with oral therapy. If you have had problems with gallstones in the past, some doctors suggest that you should use patches or implants rather than tablets to reduce the amount of oestrogen passing through the liver. It is safe to use HRT if you have had an operation to remove gallstones.

Otosclerosis

Otosclerosis is an inherited cause of hearing loss caused by the growth of extra bone which prevents the small bones in the ear from working properly. This condition can deteriorate rapidly during pregnancy, suggesting a link with oestrogen. HRT may have the same effect, so specialist advice should be sought before starting treatment.

WHO SHOULD NOT TAKE HRT?

Breast cancer

There are two main types of breast cancers – those that are sensitive to oestrogen and those that are not. If you have been successfully treated for non-oestrogen-dependent breast cancer you may still be able to take HRT, particularly if you have a specific reason to do so – such as relieving severe hot flushes. However, you need to be carefully supervised by a specialist. Even women with oestrogen-dependent cancers can usually take vaginal oestrogen to treat local symptoms.

Endometrial cancer

The majority of women found to have endometrial cancer are likely to be cured by hysterectomy. Following successful surgery, many women subsequently develop debilitating menopausal symptoms, which may not always respond to non-hormonal treatment. If a woman with a history of endometrial cancer develops symptoms that warrant HRT, it can usually be prescribed. However, because endometrial cancer is oestrogen dependent, most doctors prescribe progestogen as well as oestrogen in order to minimise the likelihood of recurrence.

Severe liver disease

You should not take HRT if you have jaundice as a result of severe liver disease. This is because most of the oestrogen, particularly if taken by mouth, is broken down by your liver, increasing its metabolic load. This is not a problem for a healthy liver but a diseased liver may not be able to cope with this extra workload. If your jaundice improves and your liver works normally again, then there is no reason why HRT should not be taken. Non-oral forms – patches or implants – are recommended because lower hormone levels pass through the liver.

Blood clots (venous thrombosis)

Venous thrombosis can result from an underlying genetic condition or a blood clotting disorder (thrombophilia). If you have a close family member who had an unexplained blood clot under the age of 45, investigations to screen for thrombophilia or underlying disease may be necessary before HRT can be considered.

Heart attacks and strokes

It is not recommended that you should start HRT in order to try to prevent heart attacks or strokes if you have already experienced one. However, if you have a history of either of these, you may be given HRT if you have severe menopausal symptoms or are at risk of osteoporosis. If you have had a heart attack or stroke and are already taking HRT, this is not a reason to stop it.

Pregnancy

Despite fertility being low as women approach the menopause, it is still possible to become pregnant. Most HRTs are not contraceptive. Women who have taken HRT and then found that they are pregnant can be reassured that it is unlikely that HRT will adversely affect outcome of pregnancy. However, miscarriage rates are high in older women for other reasons.

Undiagnosed vaginal bleeding

HRT should not be used to control unusual bleeding until the cause of the bleeding has been assessed. This is because HRT itself can cause unexpected bleeding and mask an underlying problem that may need treatment.

KEY POINTS

✓ Few women are unable to take HRT on medical grounds

✓ HRT is not recommended if you have oestrogen-dependent cancers such as cancer of the endometrium or oestrogen-dependent breast cancer

✓ You should not start HRT while you have venous thrombosis, active liver disease or unexplained vaginal bleeding

Controlling symptoms without HRT

Although HRT is the 'gold standard' for controlling menopausal symptoms, relieving up to 80 per cent of hot flushes, not every woman can, needs to or wants to take it. For many women, particularly those with mild symptoms, one or other of the following options can be effective.

CONTROLLING HOT FLUSHES

Many women use non-prescription remedies to treat hot flushes, such as isoflavones. Also popular are dong quai, evening primrose oil, vitamin E, ginseng, liquorice and natural progesterone creams. Most of these are classed as dietary supplements and so are not regulated in the same way as drugs. Hence these treatments can be sold in health shops, supermarkets and pharmacies without evidence that they are either effective or safe. Also, information about how they interact with other therapies and prescription drugs is often limited.

Isoflavones

These plant oestrogens are often called phytoestrogens. Two common sources of isoflavones are soy and red clover. The recommended dose is 40 to 80 mg a day – the same dose used in most of the studies using isoflavones for the treatment of hot flushes, but it can take several weeks before any benefit is seen. The potential for toxic or adverse side effects with these doses is minimal. Soy products or foods fortified with soy are often advertised as alleviating flushes but supplements allow a consistent daily intake.

Black cohosh

Preparations made from the thick underground stems (rhizomes) of the herb black cohosh have been studied, with varying reports of efficacy. Almost all the studies have used different formulations and doses, so the results are difficult to compare. Although a popular remedy, black cohosh is not recommended because there have been reports of toxic effects on the liver with long-term use.

Dong quai

This herb is commonly used in traditional Chinese medicine to treat gynaecological problems. Studies using the herb to control hot flushes have shown little benefit. Women using warfarin should not take dong quai.

Evening primrose oil

Although very effective for treating breast tenderness premenstrually, even high doses of evening primrose oil (two grams daily) have shown little benefit for hot flushes. Side effects include nausea and diarrhoea.

Vitamin E

Studies using vitamin E in doses up to 400 IU twice daily have not shown much effect on hot flushes. Side effects are few and not serious.

Ginseng

Studies with ginseng have not shown benefit on hot flushes. Ginseng can adversely interact with monoamine oxidase inhibitors (MAOIs), which may be prescribed for treatment of depression, and with anticoagulants such as aspirin and warfarin.

Liquorice

The root of the liquorice plant is used in many Chinese preparations for menopausal symptoms. However, there are no studies to show either safety or efficacy. Women taking diuretics should not use liquorice. High doses of liquorice can cause fluid retention and high blood pressure.

Natural progesterone cream

Progesterone is synthesised by a chemical process from plants such as soy beans or wild yam. Some of the products contain progesterone indistinguishable from a woman's own natural progesterone. Others contain only chemical precursors of progesterone found in plants, which are inactive in humans because they cannot be converted to progesterone. As these creams are regulated as dietary supplements, it is not possible to know which products are which.

Although creams containing progesterone, often combined with vitamin E and aloe vera, have shown a positive effect on flushes there are safety concerns about unregulated hormonal treatments. Women using oestrogen replacement therapy should not use progesterone creams in place of prescribed progestogens (synthetic progesterones), because they may not protect the endometrium.

REDUCING HOT FLUSHES WITHOUT HORMONAL TREATMENT

Some women prefer to try non-prescription and non-hormonal remedies to control hot flushes. These include herbal and homoeopathic options. If these do not work, women should ask their GPs to consider which of the non-hormonal prescriptions (in other words not HRT) are suitable for them.

Serotonin inhibitors

Serotonin is a neurotransmitter in the brain and is important in the control of mood and behaviour, feeding and hunger, temperature regulation and sleep. Selective serotonin reuptake inhibitors (SSRIs) are licensed for the treatment of depression. Depression is caused by low serotonin levels and SSRIs increase the serotonin levels. However, research has also shown that lower doses of SSRIs are effective for a wide variety of other conditions, including control of chronic pain conditions, migraine and hot flushes. The three most commonly used for hot flushes are venlafaxine (Efexor), paroxetine (Seroxat) and fluoxetine (Prozac). Trials suggest that there can be up to a 60 per cent reduction in flushes. Although symptoms can improve immediately, it may take up to eight weeks before any benefit is seen. The most common side effects are nausea, weight loss and reduced sex drive.

Gabapentin

This drug is licensed for the control of epilepsy but is also used for chronic pain conditions. and can halve the rate of hot flushes. Side effects include dizziness and feeling light-headed as well as some fluid retention and tiredness. As antacids (indigestion remedies) can reduce the amount of gabapentin that gets into the body, gabapentin should be taken at least two hours after an antacid is used.

Clonidine

This drug, originally developed for the treatment of high blood pressure, can alleviate mild hot flushes but is less effective than SSRIs or gabapentin. Side effects of drowsiness, dizziness, constipation and depression are common.

OTHER NON-HRT TREATMENTS

Combined oral contraceptives (see pages 99–100)

Combined oral contraceptives (COCs), containing synthetic oestrogen (ethinyloestradiol) and synthetic progesterone (progestogen), inhibit ovulation. Healthy, non-smoking women can take low-dose COCs right up to the menopause. They provide contraception and prevent hot flushes but the doses of hormones are much higher than HRT. This means that the risk of blood clots is greater than for HRT but benefits, particularly of lighter menstrual periods, can make COCs a good option for some women.

Progestogen

Although progestogen is usually taken together with oestrogen for HRT, high-dose progestogen can be effective on its own. Medroxyprogesterone acetate or MPA (Depo-Provera) can be given by injection every three months and also provides contraception. The side effects can include weight gain and irregular bleeding. There is also some controversy about the effect of injectable MPA on bone density. MPA tablets, 20 mg a day, are also effective and result in less irregular bleeding. It can take up to six weeks to reach its maximum effect. Another progestogen tablet, megestrol acetate, 20 mg twice a day, is also effective.

KEY POINTS

✓ HRT is the most effective treatment for menopausal symptoms

✓ Non-hormonal remedies such as dietary isoflavones may alleviate mild symptoms in some women

✓ For more severe symptoms, venlafaxine, paroxetine, fluoxetine or gabapentin is available on prescription

Contraception around the menopause

Women approaching the menopause often wrongly assume that they no longer need to use contraception. It is certainly true that a woman in her 40s is about half as fertile as a woman in her 20s. Also, her eggs are of a poorer quality and ovulation is less regular, until she finally stops ovulating and experiences the menopause. Despite this, pregnancy can occur. If you are not protected and your periods suddenly stop, you might assume it is the menopause, but it could be that you are pregnant.

Although many babies born to older mothers are very healthy, genetic abnormalities such as Down's syndrome become more common. The risk of miscarriage and risks to mother and baby are also increased in older women.

Therefore effective contraception can be as important for a woman in her late 40s as it is for a woman in her teens or 20s.

Contraception should be continued for at least 12 months after the last period in women over the age of 50. Women who have an earlier menopause are advised to continue contraception for at least two years after the last period.

HORMONAL CONTRACEPTION

Combined hormonal contraceptives

Combined oral contraceptives (COCs; commonly known as the pill), the contraceptive patch and the contraceptive vaginal ring, contain both synthetic oestrogen and progestogen. They work by inhibiting ovulation. In addition to their contraceptive effects, they will also provide relief from menopausal symptoms. Healthy, non-smoking women can use modern, low-dose, combined hormonal contraceptives until one or two years after the menopause. Although synthetic oestrogens increase the risk of blood clots, this has to be balanced against potential health benefits for perimenopausal women including relief of premenstrual symptoms and regular periods that are less painful and heavy than natural periods. There is also some evidence that combined oral contraceptives have a positive effect on bone density.

Progestogen-only methods
Although postmenopausal use of progestogen is associated with increased risk of breast cancer, there is no evidence of this effect when progestogens are taken before the menopause. The advantage of progestogen-only methods over combined hormonal contraception is that there is no associated increased risk of blood clots with the former. There are several types of contraception that contain just progestogen. Each of them works in a slightly different way. Progestogen-only methods can be prescribed to many women at risk of blood clots who cannot use combined hormonal contraceptives, including smokers.

- **Progestogen-only pill**: The progestogen-only pill (POP), also known as the mini-pill, is taken every day and contains a very low dose of progestogen. Unlike COCs, which inhibit ovulation, standard POPs have minimal effect on ovulation but act by thickening cervical mucus and preventing sperm getting into the uterus. For women over 35, standard POPs are as effective as combined oral contraceptives. A newer POP, called Cerazette, does inhibit ovulation. The main potential problem with POPs is irregular bleeding. This may be resolved by changing to a different type of POP. In contrast, some women find that their periods stop.

- **Injectables**: There are two types of progestogen that can be injected: depot medroxyprogesterone acetate (DMPA; Depo-Provera) and norethisterone acetate (NETA; Noristerat). As with the combined pill, they work by inhibiting the monthly release of the egg from the ovaries. Both types are administered by health-care professionals by deep intramuscular injection into the buttock or upper arm: DMPA every twelve weeks and NETA every eight weeks. Injectables can relieve premenstrual symptoms and heavy, painful periods. They can be associated with weight gain and irregular bleeding, although this usually resolves with continued use.

• **Implant**: Implanon is a single rod, about the size of a hairgrip, which contains progestogen. It works by switching off the normal menstrual cycle, similar to the combined pill and injectables. A trained health-care professional injects the rod just under the skin on the inner side of the upper arm. It is both palpable and visible after insertion but is a highly effective contraceptive, lasting for up to three years.

It is not licensed (see Glossary, page 111) for use in women aged over 40, although you can use it if you and your doctor think it is a suitable method for you. Implants can relieve many period-related problems, particularly heavy, painful periods. The main drawbacks can be weight gain and irregular bleeding, which can be frequent or prolonged in up to 20 per cent of users.

Levonorgestrel intrauterine system

The levonorgestrel intrauterine system (Mirena) is a small T-shaped device containing progestogen inserted into the uterus by trained health-care professionals. Progestogen is released directly into the uterus, keeping the uterine lining or endometrium thin (important for lower risk of endometrial cancer). Side effects are few as the hormonal effect is essentially within the uterus, and only small amounts of hormone reach the bloodstream. The IUS is as effective as sterilisation but is easily reversed by removal of the device. It is also an effective treatment for heavy, painful periods. In addition to its use as a contraceptive, the IUS can also be used together with natural oestrogen supplements as HRT. Occasionally, irregular, frequent or prolonged bleeding can necessitate removal of the device.

NON-HORMONAL CONTRACEPTION
Sterilisation

Both vasectomy and female sterilisation are popular in older couples. However, sterilisation needs to be considered very carefully because this method is essentially irreversible. Many reversible methods such as the IUS and implants are as effective as sterilisation, often with added benefits for period-related problems.

Copper intrauterine device

Modern intrauterine devices (IUDs), often called coils, offer highly effective reversible contraception. They contain copper, which kills sperm before they can reach the uterus. If inserted after your fortieth birthday, an IUD can remain in place until after your menopause. The main disadvantage of this method is

Questions & answers

• My doctor showed me how to examine my breasts for lumps but they feel lumpy all over. How can I tell if a lump is cancer?

Examining your own breasts is the best way to identify any unusual lumps or other changes. It is not unusual for breasts to feel generally lumpy without there being anything wrong. Ask you doctor or nurse to check your breasts first, and then feel them yourself so that you get to know what is normal for you. Then you will notice changes more easily.

Breast tissue is naturally affected by different hormones so your breasts will feel much lumpier during the progestogen phase of seq-

uential combined HRT, just as they did before your period during a natural menstrual cycle. The best time to check your breasts is just after a period has finished. If you are taking continuous combined HRT, you can check your breasts at any time.

If you find anything that worries you, check with your doctor. You should look for changes such as dimpling of the skin, changes in the nipple or any lumps that you can see or feel. In most cases, breast lumps are simple fluid-filled cysts and are not the result of cancer. However, if cancer is present, provided that it is treated early, it can often be cured.

• Since the menopause, I feel tired most of the time, have lost interest in sex and feel generally low. Can HRT help?

Symptoms of depression are common in the years around the menopause, so it is not surprising that hormones are blamed. Hot flushes and night sweats can disrupt your sleep leading to loss of energy and low mood. By treating the flushes and sweats, HRT can certainly help you to get the best out of life again.

However, depressive symptoms can result from many other significant events that occur at much the same time as the menopause – children leaving home, separation or divorce, and illness or death of parents. Depression resulting from events such as these will not respond to HRT.

If you have menopausal symptoms that are a problem, it is certainly worth trying HRT. If your flushes and sweats improve but you are still feeling low, it is unlikely that hormones are the cause and you need to look for other reasons. Some women may need both HRT and antidepressants at this time.

• My doctor has just started me on HRT. I was expecting to have blood tests or something to check my hormone levels but I was just asked lots of questions, given a prescription and told to make an appointment for three months' time. Don't I need any tests?

Hormone levels vary considerably and do not provide as much information as the symptoms you are experiencing. So your doctor is far more likely to ask questions than do tests! You will also be asked about your own and your family's medical history to ensure that it is safe for you to take HRT. If you are up to date with smear tests and mammograms, your doctor will not need to examine your breasts or do an internal examination, unless you have certain symptoms.

Once you have started HRT, you will usually be seen three months later to make sure that the type of HRT is right for you and to sort out any problem or concerns that you may have. When you are settled on HRT, you need only annual checkups. However, if you have any concerns you should make an early appointment for review.

• Most of the studies recently reported have been about one particular type of HRT. Do the results apply to all types of HRT or just this one?

Many of the recent studies about the long-term risk of HRT relate to one type of oestrogen (conjugated equine oestrogen) and one type of progestogen (medroxyprogesterone acetate or MPA). In the UK, products containing these hormones are tablets called Premarin, Premique and Premique Cycle.

It is impossible to know if the long-term risks shown in these studies also apply to HRT using oestradiol and different progestogens. Clinical trials using different hormones and different routes of delivery are under way.

● My mother shrank as she got older and was told that her spine was collapsing because her bones had got thin. What can I do to prevent the same happening to me?

Your natural build, how much exercise you take and your diet will provide some indication of how likely you are to be affected. Thin women, who take little exercise and avoid dairy products, are particularly at risk, especially if they smoke. As oestrogen protects bone, the menopause, with decreasing levels of oestrogen, represents an additional risk factor.

Your doctor may send you for a bone density scan to assess your baseline bone density before considering treatment. If you are experiencing menopausal symptoms and are at risk of osteoporosis, you may be offered HRT. Otherwise, non-hormonal treatments available on prescription such as the bisphosphonates are the first choice to prevent osteoporosis in older women.

● I am 46 and my periods are very erratic but I'm not getting any other symptoms. Could this be the start of the menopause?

The first symptom of the 'change' or menopause is often a change in the pattern of periods, as you describe. Typically, periods will become more frequent and then they come further apart. You may skip one or two periods between otherwise regular cycles.

For some women, their periods cease with very few other symptoms. For others, flushes and sweats at first happen just in the week before a period and gradually become more frequent. Most women have had their last menstrual period by the time they are 54.

● I've heard all about a new type of HRT called Evista (raloxifene). What is it?

Raloxifene is not a natural hormone but is the first of a new class of synthetic compounds know as selective oestrogen receptor modulators (SERMs). These mimic the protective actions of oestrogen on bone without the unwanted effects on the lining of the uterus and breast tissue.

Clinical trials have shown that raloxifene can increase bone density, although not as well as conventional HRT. Raloxifene also seems to reduce the levels of cholesterol in the blood but there is no proof that this means that the risk of heart disease is reduced.